The Asbury Theological Seminary Series in Christian Revitalization Studies

This volume is published in collaboration with the Center for the Study of World Christian Revitalization Movements, a cooperative initiative of Asbury Theological Seminary faculty. Building on the work of the previous Wesleyan/Holiness Studies Center at the Seminary, the Center provides a focus for research in the Wesleyan Holiness and other related Christian renewal movements, including Pietism and Pentecostal movements, which have had a world impact. The research seeks to develop analytical models of these movements, including their biblical and theological assessment. Using an interdisciplinary approach, the Center bridges relevant discourses in several areas in order to gain insights for effective Christian mission globally. It recognizes the need for conducting research that combines insights from the history of evangelical renewal and revival movements with anthropological and religious studies literature on revitalization movements. It also networks with similar or related research and study centers around the world, in addition to sponsoring its own research projects.

Sensing the need to bridge the gap between Wesley's day and ours, Professor Kenneth Kinghorn, distinguished emeritus dean and professor of church history at Asbury Seminary, offers a new edition of twelve of John Wesley's most definitive treatises. Wesley published these tracts in a novel, eighteenth century "chapbook" (paperback) medium, and now Kinghorn introduces contemporary readers to the message and mission of early Methodism, in the voice of its honored founder. Here Wesley's voice presents "vital, practical religion" in plain language for ordinary people in the present day. Kinghorn has rendered Wesley's vocabulary into clear but inspired discourse that embraces and illumines the author's intent. This volume renders Wesley accessible to twenty-first century readers, and so fulfils the intent of this Series to embrace and enhance the movement of Christian revitalization in our time.

J. Steven O'Malley
    Editor, The Asbury Theological Seminary Series in World Christian Revitalization Movements in Pietist/Wesley Studies

John Wesley On Methodism

Edited by
Kenneth Cain Kinghorn

Asbury Theological Seminary Series:
The Study of World Christian Revitalization Movements
in Pietist/Wesleyan Studies

EMETH PRESS
www.emethpress.com

John Wesley on Methodism

Copyright © 2014 Kenneth Cain Kinghorn
Printed in the United States of America on acid-free paper

All rights reserved. No part of this book may be reproduced, or stored in a retrieval system or transmitted in any form or by any means, electronic, mechanical, photocopying, recording, scanning or otherwise, except as permitted by the 1976 United States Copyright Act, or with the prior written permission of Emeth Press. Requests for permission should be addressed to: Emeth Press, P. O. Box 23961, Lexington, KY 40523-3961.   http://www.emethpress.com.

Library of Congress Cataloging-in-Publication Data

Wesley, John, 1703-1791.
  [Works. Selections. 2014]
  John Wesley on Methodism / edited by Kenneth Cain Kinghorn.
     pages cm. -- (Asbury Theological Seminary series: the study of world Christian revitalization movements in Pietist/Wesleyan studies)
   ISBN 978-1-60947-075-3 (alk. paper)
  1. Methodism. 2. Methodist Church--Doctrines. I. Kinghorn, Kenneth C. II. Title.
  BX8217.W54K57 2014
  287--dc23
                              2014002601

The Cover Photograph

The photograph of the painting on the front cover appears with the permission of its artist, Richard Douglas, of Thirsk, England. This painting (36-inches by 24-inches) is titled, "John Wesley Preaching at a Market Cross." This scene and more than two dozen of Douglas's paintings of eighteenth-century Methodists are permanently on display in the B.L. Fisher Library at Asbury Theological Seminary.

Dr. Douglas wrote the editor of this book, "I began to study the masters [of illustration] of the [eighteenth-century] period such as William Hogarth (1687-1764); James Gillray (1756-1815); and Thomas Rowlandson (1756-1827). Gradually I gained the knowledge and confidence to draw accurate pictures of events in the 18th century revival.... I have carefully researched period costume, studied old pictures, observed hairstyles, faces, boots and figures from all sorts of sources, looked at saddlery, poses, hats and gestures and gradually learned how to compose a good picture from this internal information."

John Wesley's itinerant preaching ministry throughout England took him to many cities, towns, and villages, where he often preached in the open air at central locations marked by "market crosses." These carved stone monuments identified the places where people gathered to trade, hear public announcements, listen to speakers, buy and sell, and converse with others.

Market crosses still stand in some English towns and villages as reminders of an earlier time. Douglas is a master of showing the variety of emotions and reactions of those who listened to Wesley preach. In this painting, the artist pictures John Wesley as he probably looked at about the age of eighty.

Contents

Editor's Preface / 9

Editor's Introduction / 13

1. A Plain Account of the People Called Methodists / 21

2. The Character of a Methodist / 73

3. A Letter to a Clergyman / 103

4. Advice to the People Called Methodists / 119

5. The Nature, Design, and General Rules of the United Societies / 139

6. An Estimate of the Manners of the Present Times / 159

7. Four Serious Admonitions / 175

8. Prayers for Family and Children / 209

9. Thoughts Upon Methodism / 223

Editor's Conclusion / 237

Editor's Preface

From the middle of the seventeenth century to the middle of the eighteenth century the intellectual climate in England was rationalistic. Proponents of the "Age of Enlightenment" exuded an almost unbounded confidence in human reason and judgment. Philosophers examined existing beliefs and institutions from the point of view of what they claimed were "the clear and distinct perceptions of the intellect." Rationalists questioned the credibility of the Bible, and they discarded many of the beliefs of historic Christianity—including such doctrines as the Trinity, original sin, the atonement, and miracles. Categorically, many intellectual trendsetters rejected the idea of divine revelation. Philosopher John Locke said, "No man's knowledge here can go beyond his experience." Alexander Pope, often called "the prince of rhyme and the grand poet of reason," articulated this rationalistic outlook:

> Know then thyself, presume not God to scan
> The proper study of Mankind is Man.

Even while rejecting divine revelation, many rationalists retained a belief in the existence of God, although they posited the notion that God is removed from human affairs and personal experience. They wanted stable order in society, and they supported a general morality and decency. The supreme literary achievement of that age was the French *Encyclopédie*, a thirty-five volume set of books that contained a virtually complete review of the arts and sciences of that day. Many of the contributors to these volumes rejected revealed religion in favor of natural religion. The articles were brilliant, especially in the areas of the arts, mechanics, and the natural sciences. These rationalists, however, failed to recognize the Christian origins of many of the ethical and social values they endorsed. They had confidence in humanity, without reference to historical Christianity.

Even within the church some leaders became enticed by rationalism. The theological expression of the Age of Reason was Deism, a philosophy which argued that all we need to know about religion comes through reason and experience. According to Deism, the sum of religion is to live uprightly according to our best thinking. The Deists acknowledged that God made the world, but Deism did not accept the idea that God is active in our daily lives, in human history, or world affairs.

Quite to the contrary, John Wesley and the emerging Methodist movement advocated an experience of one's personal relationship with God, who enables us personally to experience his transforming grace and providential guidance. John Wesley contended that to experience the promises found in Scripture is not fanatical, but rather the privilege of every Christian.

The rationalists strongly objected to such "impertinent" and "outrageous" claims. Opponents of the Methodists charged them with "Enthusiasm"—an eighteenth-century sobriquet that meant religious zealotry or fanaticism. Critics considered it bad form for one to speak of one's personal faith. It is reported that someone asked Lord Henry St. John Bolingbroke, a Tory statesman and would-be philosopher, "What is your religion, my Lord?" Bolingbroke replied, "The religion of all sensible men." The questioner replied, "Yes, but what is that?" Bolingbroke retorted, "Ah, that is what no sensible man ever tells." Voltaire, who visited England, famously remarked, "In France I am looked upon as having too little religion; in England as having too much."

Some Christian thinkers, such as Bishop Joseph Butler, sought to oppose Deism by defending Christianity on the basis of reason. Butler was a masterful logician, and he held orthodox Christian beliefs. However, his laborious academic work, *Analogy of Religion* (1736) contrasted with John Wesley's approach to apologetics, which was to write "plain truth for plain people."

Butler wrote Wesley,

> I will deal plainly with you. I once thought you and Mr. [George] Whitefield well-meaning men: But I cannot think so now; for I have heard more of you.... Sir, the pretending to extraordinary revelations and gifts of the Holy Ghost is a horrid thing, a very horrid thing!"

Wesley replied, "I pretend to no extraordinary revelations or gifts of the Holy Ghost; none but what every Christian may receive, and ought to expect and pray for." Wesley was convinced that finally Christianity stands not on reason, but on God's divinely revealed truth in the Bible. In a letter to William Law, Wesley said that to rely on reason without trusting in supernatural revelation is the "one main hinge on which the controversy between Christianity and Deism turns."

If the Deists neglected the spiritual condition of the common people, John Wesley had a passion for taking the Christian message to the neglected masses. Many eighteenth-century Anglican churches were open only one hour a week, and few people attended the services. Most uneducated and deprived people felt unwelcome in the churches. Those who did venture into a church found little spiritual help. The sermons of many Anglican clergymen failed to mention heaven, hell, repentance, or justification by faith. It has often been joked that the two favorite texts for sermons were, "Let your moderation be known to all men," and "Be not righteous overmuch."

One historian concluded, "The Church was not dead, but it slumbered." Another historian wrote, "The general run of preachers . . . contented themselves with instilling morality on the principles of which all parties agreed, Christians and Rationalists alike." Jonathan Swift (author of Gulliver's Travels), Dean of St. Patrick's Cathedral in Dublin, lamented that the spirit and power of religion were "well-nigh worn out of the country." Some Anglican priests alleged that "the Word of God is a stale unpolished Piece of Antiquity." The French skeptic Voltaire described English sermons as "dry dissertations which [priests] read to the people without gesture and without particular exaltation of the voice." The working classes received little if any pastoral attention from the vicars. Across England it was undeniable that the general state of private and public morals was dismal.

If rationalistic philosophers and pedestrian priests failed to improve the lives of the laity, John Wesley believed that the vilest of sinners could be redeemed, educated, and transformed into virtuous people and productive citizens. The results of Wesley's ministries among the poor and un-churched were impressively far-reaching and fruitful. The *Oxford Dictionary of the Christian Church* states that Wesley "was the central figure in the rise of Methodism and one of the greatest Christians of his age." *The Cambridge Modern History* (volume VI on the eighteenth century) concluded, "In the most intellectual of ages, it is the glory of Methodism to have appealed to the heart, and to have restored emotion . . . to its rightful place in religion. Such an effect as this upon a people may not be measured in the statistical balance or measured with the numerical rod."

Although John Wesley held firm theological views, he was not sectarian separatist. His mainstream, catholic ministry remains relevant to Protestantism, Roman Catholicism, and Eastern Orthodoxy. Wesley insisted that he was "a Church of England man" and that he taught no other doctrines other than what the Scriptures made plain and the church professed. His main mission was to clarify and communicate Christianity's enduring principles, quite different from the pernicious principles so prominent in Wesley's day and in ours. Wesley designed his tracts to guide and renew a culture entangled in the grip of theological drift, moral uncertainty, and institutional decline in both church and state. John Wesley's tracts in this book address practical theological and moral issues that determine the destiny of any nation in any generation. A career of careful study of John Wesley prompted British scholar Maldwyn Edwards to write, "Like all the truly great, [John Wesley] makes a fresh appeal to each new age: still he can stir the mind and still can move the heart."

Introductions to each of the chapters in this volume explain the historical and theological context of Wesley's tracts. Footnotes include scripture references and annotations that provide background information. When deemed necessary, footnotes clarify obsolete English words and phrases.

Kenneth Cain Kinghorn
Asbury Theological Seminary

Editor's Introduction

Prior to John Wesley's time, most religious publishing in England consisted of lengthy volumes intended for educated specialists. Those tomes appeared mostly as quartos (about 12 by 9 inches) and octavos (about 8 to 9-½ by 5 to 6 inches). Publishers released these expensive volumes in stiff, leather-bound covers, often with ribbed spines outside, and engravings within. These works contained weighty subjects and dense prose, often laden with Greek and Latin phrases. Most people could not afford or understand them; only scholars read these works. Affluent people sometimes bought these handsome volumes, if only to add prestige and beauty to their library shelves.

As the eighteenth century unfolded, British publishers, in order to sell publications to the masses, printed small paperbacks called chapbooks. Peddlers (called chapmen) sold these tracts on the streets. These pocket-sized tracts contained stories, folk tales, legends, life-lessons, almanacs, ballads, romances, and poems. Printers produced these low-cost pieces on cheap paper, and they were considered disposable. Their intellectual content was typically shallow, and the moral content was sometimes salacious.

The chapbook vogue prompted John Wesley to publish paperback tracts of his own. They contained sermons, hymns, moral guidelines, and religious advice. Wesley instructed his printers to issue these tracts with improved quality of print and paper. Many of these publications appeared in duodecimo format (about 7-½ by 5 inches). They sold for a pence or two pence. Hence, these publications gained the name, "penny tracts." Of Wesley's more than four hundred published works, about two-hundred were tracts that sold for a pence or two pence. Three fourths of these publications contained less than one-hundred pages and almost half of them had fewer than twenty-five pages. Thousands of Wesley's tracts cost nothing; their covers read, "This book is not to be sold, but given away."

In 1782, John Wesley and Thomas Coke formed England's first tract society—seventeen years before the Anglicans and Nonconformists founded the Religious Tract Society. The sale of Wesley's tracts helped stimulate an appetite among the common people for reading religious material. Wesley did not try particularly to curry favor or distinction among the literary elite, nor did he publish to gain money. Even so, his publications generated handsome profits, almost all of which Wesley gave away. When he died he left only eighteen pence and a half a dozen silver teaspoons.

Vocabulary

When William Shakespeare died in 1616, no English dictionary existed. After Shakespeare's death, English dictionaries began to appear, but they were incomplete and soon outdated. For example, one guilty of murder was *naughty*. To drink water was to *swig* it; to be frightened was to be *freyed*; a piece of bread was a *shive*; to gossip was to *blab*. To be *silly* meant to be innocent or pure. The people to whom Wesley preached used *suffer* to mean permit; *soft* to mean half-witted; *rare* to mean splendid; *kennel* to mean street gutter; *incontinent* to mean immediately; *conversation* to mean conduct; *temper* to mean disposition or attitude. To doubt something often meant *not* to doubt it. Concerning the evolution of the English language, the *Encyclopedia Britannica* notes,

> Changes are constantly taking place in the course of the learned transmission of a language from one generation to another.... Languages change in all their aspects, in their pronunciation, word forms, syntax, and word meanings.... [S]ome areas of vocabulary ... are subject to equally rapid and therefore noticeable changes within a generation or even within a decade."[1]

Modern readers may raise their eyebrows when reading, "Take heed, lest thou be either wavering in thy judgment, or straitened in thy bowels." Today we would say, "*limited in your compassion*. An eighteenth-Century Anglican Bishop, William Warburton, opined, "The English tongue is yet destitute of a test or standard to

---

[1] *The New Encyclopædia Britannica*, 15th ed. Macropædia, 10:660.

apply to in cases of doubt or difficulty. We have nether Grammar or Dictionary, neither Chart nor Compass to guide us through the wide sea of words."[2]

Concerning vocabulary, Wesley said,

> Clearness in particular is necessary for you and me; because we are to instruct people of the lowest understanding. Therefore, we, above all, if we think with the wise, yet must speak with the vulgar [ordinary people]. We should constantly use the most common, little, easy words (so they are pure and proper) which our language affords. What is it that constitutes a good style? Perspicuity, purity, propriety, strength, and easiness, joined together.[3]

Even during Wesley's lifetime, successive editions of his sermons and tracts demonstrate the changing nature of English. Wesley sensed that evolution, and he compiled an English dictionary.[4]

Style

John Wesley made every effort to communicate with ordinary people by using "plain" sentences. In the preface of his sermons, he said,

> I dare no more write in a fine style than wear a fine coat. But were it otherwise, had I time to spare, I should still write just as I do. I should purposely decline, what many admire, an highly ornamental style. I cannot admire French oratory: I despise it from my heart. . . . Let who will admire the French frippery, I am still for plain, sound English. As for me, I never think of my style at all; but just set down the words that come first. Only when I transcribe anything for the press, then I think it my duty to see every phrase be clear, pure, and proper. Conciseness (which is now, as it were, natural to me) brings . . . strength [to writing]. If, after

---

[2] Whitley, J. H., *Wesley's England: A Survey of XVIII*th *Century Social And Cultural Conditions*, London: The Epworth Press, 1954, 239.

[3] Letter to Mr. Furley, The Works of John Wesley, 15 July, 1764, Jackson ed., XIII, 417.

[4] *The Complete English Dictionary, Explaining Most of those Hard Words, which are found in the Best English Writers, By a Lover of Good English and Common Sense* (London: Printed by R. Hawes, 1777). Wesley added to the title page, "The Author assures you, he thinks this is the Best English Dictionary in the World."

all, I observe any stiff expression, I throw it out, neck and shoulders.[5]

In the eighteenth century, Wesley succeeded admirably in communicating clearly.

However, the English language of his day has changed in several particulars. For that reason, twenty-first-century readers often stumble or bog down in attempts fully to grasp eighteenth-century prose.

In 1755, Wesley's famed contemporary, Samuel Johnson, published his celebrated *Dictionary of the English Language*, in the preface of which he said,

> When I took the first survey of my undertaking, I found our speech copious without order, and energetick without rules: wherever I turned my view, there was perplexity to be disentangled, and confusion to be regulated; choice was to be made out of boundless variety, without any established principle of selection; adulterations were to be detected, without a settled test of purity; and modes of expression to be rejected or received, without the suffrages of any writers of classical reputation or acknowledged authority."

Dr. Johnson admitted that he had "flattered himself for a while with the prospect of fixing [the English] language." He added that he had "indulged [this] expectation which neither reason nor experience could justify." Language is too fluid to establish permanently. Since John Wesley began publishing more than two-hundred and seventy-five years ago, alterations in the English language have continued.

Language scholars and those accustomed to reading John Wesley's writings have become familiar with eighteenth-century English. They understand such phrases as "He quitted the door" to mean, "He left the room, or house." Today, even educated people who are unfamiliar with eighteenth-century prose often find Wesley's language difficult to comprehend fully. International students, even those with TOEFL scores above 600, report that Wesley's prose seems mysterious and murky to them.

This book, *John Wesley on Methodism*, contains my transcription of twelve of Wesley's tracts. I have supplied today's meanings to eighteenth-century words that now have different connotations. This transcription also modernizes such

---

[5] Sermons on Several Occasions, Second Series, Preface, The Works of John Wesley, Bicentennial ed. II, 356–57.

words as *thou art, believeth, hast, hath, knoweth, thinketh, thy, lieth, standeth,* and *worketh.* In most instances, gender inclusive language conforms to modern usage.

John Wesley habitually used such demonstrative pronouns as *this, these,* and *that* as the subject of a sentence. Sometimes one must backtrack one or several sentences to find the antecedent to which these pronouns refer. In these cases, for clarity, this transcription of Wesley's selected tracts supplies the proper subject, usually a noun or a name. Eighteenth-century grammarians were not able to settle the propriety of such constructions as, "Between you and I," "You better leave," "How things goes there," "He and me was a-going," "I had rather not," "It is me," "He do not know how," and "The river was froze over." Wesley and others often used the past tense for a passive participle, leading to such constructions as, "She hath rose up from the chair," or "I had a thought, which I writ down as follows."

John Byrom (1692–1763), a contemporary of John Wesley, wrote a good-humored poem about the inconsistent used of English grammar. Byrom's poem, *Passive Participle's Petition,* contains a stanza that says playfully,

> Till just of late, good English has thought fit
> to call me written, or to call me writ;
> But what is writ or written, by the vote
> of writers, now hereafter, must be wrote;
> And what is spoken, too, hereafter spoke,
> and measures never to be broken, broke.

Samuel Johnson moaned, "In a language subjected so little and so lately to grammar, such anomalies, even in good writers must frequently occur."

If vocabulary has evolved, so have syntax and style. Wesley often uses long sentences, sometimes stretching several lines, and occasionally lacking an antecedent. This practice requires one to scan such lengthy constructions more than once to ascertain their meaning. The transcriptions in this book frequently recast long constructions into two or more sentences. As was the case with other eighteenth-century writers, Wesley often used a comma in place of conjunctions such as, *and, however, that, but, if, nor,* and *for.* This transcription supplies missing conjunctions to make the sentences clearer, smoother, and more in agreement with today's English.

Wesley habitually used the passive voice. Of course, the passive voice is not grammatically incorrect, and occasionally it works well. Ordinarily, though, the passive voice lengthens a sentence and leaves the reader with an uncertain subject.

This transcription often changes the passive voice to the active voice, in order to shorten, clarify, and quicken sentences.

Between 1749 and 1755, John Wesley compiled *A Christian Library containing Extracts and Abridgments of the Choicest Pieces of Practical Divinity*. In those volumes, Wesley included works of the early Christian fathers, Roman Catholic divines, and Protestant writers. That collection came to fifty duodecimo volumes, and later the collection appeared in a thirty-volume octavo edition.[6] Considering that Wesley edited the words of others, one may fairly assume that he would not object to this present book's editing of twelve of his tracts. Assiduously, I have kept to Wesley's meaning, altering sentences only to clarify them.

A couple of generations ago, in 1964, Methodist theologian Philip S. Watson said,

> One need not read very far [in the writings of John and Charles Wesley] to discover how dim and distorted their message has become for the greater part . . . of their Methodist successors. . . . In particular, their quality of mind, the range and depth of their thought, the true nature of the ideas and ideals that inspired their work—these are all too often either wholly unknown or represented by garbled fragments that only misrepresent them.[7]

Ours is a time when many could benefit from a better acquaintance with John Wesley's biblical fidelity, keen mind, seasoned wisdom, and spiritual genius.

William Ralph Inge (1860–1954), former Dean of London's St. Paul's Cathedral, reminds us, "The future is safe only in the hands of those to whom her past is dear." America's declining old-line denominations can recover their roots, and once more become forces for God and good. To recover an institutional heritage, however, it is necessary to know it. Albert Outler, a leading twentieth-century Wesley scholar, said, "No summary review of Wesley's life and work can convey an adequate sense of constant vitality and cumulative force that comes with a . . . reading of Wesley himself."[8]

John Wesley's introduction to his sermons contains the following declaration:

---

[6] In 1752, Wesley said about this massive project, "I cost me £200; perhaps the next generation may know its worth."

[7] Philip S. Watson, *The Message of the Wesleys* (London & New York: The Macmillan Company, 1964) xi.

[8] *John Wesley* (New York: Oxford University Press, 1964), 33.

I design plain truth for plain people. Therefore, of set purpose, I abstain from all nice and philosophical speculations; from all perplexed and intricate reasonings; and, as far as possible, from even the show of learning, unless in sometimes citing the original Scripture. I labour to avoid all words which are not easy to be understood, all which are not used in common life; and, in particular, those kinds of technical terms that so frequently occur in Bodies of Divinity; those modes of speaking which men of reading are intimately acquainted with, but which to common people are an unknown tongue.

John Wesley asserted, "I have one point in view—to promote, so far as I am able, vital, practical religion; and by the grace of God to beget, preserve, and increase the life of God in the souls of [all]. On this single principle I have hitherto proceeded, and taken no step but in subservience to it."[9] The aim of this book is to bring Wesley's voice to those who want to learn from this eighteenth-century evangelical reformer.

Kenneth Cain Kinghorn
Asbury Theological Seminary

---

[9] Letter to Samuel Walker, 3 September 1756, *The Letters of the Rev. John Wesley, A.M.*, John Telford ed. (London: The Epworth Press, 1931) 3:192

Selection 1

*A Plain Account of the
People Called Methodists*

Editor's Introduction

A Plain Account of the People Called Methodists

The word *Methodist* arose around as 1729 as a pejorative term. John Wesley, a Fellow at Oxford's Lincoln College, had begun meeting certain evenings of the week with three others (Charles Wesley, Robert Morgan, and Robert Kirkham) "to read and observe upon the Classicks, and on Sunday upon some Book of Devotion" and to read the Greek New Testament. In contrast to many students and faculty members at the university, Wesley's band of sincere young men strictly observed the standards of the school, including chapel attendance and academic expectations. The members of the group went so far as to go hungry so they could give money to desperately needy townspeople. This small group read Christian devotional writers, discussed religious duty, fasted twice weekly, and developed a means of regular self-examination. They did their best to keep the following rules: (i) To visit and relieve prisoners and the sick, giving away Bibles, Common-Prayer Books, and devotional books; (ii) To observe spiritual disciplines, including attending weeks communion services; (iii) To observe the fasts of the church.

Although these young men did not press their practices on others, critics ridiculed them for their zeal and severely disciplined manner of Christian practice.

In an article in *Fog's Weekly Journal* (9 December 1732) said, "They avoid as much as possible every Object that may affect them with any pleasant and grateful Sensation." Faultfinders called them "Sacramentarians," 'Supererogation men," "Bible Moths," "The Godly Club," and "The Holy Club." Due to the methodical methods of the group, critics called them *Methodists*. One bit of exaggerated doggerel about Wesley's band appeared in the following sarcastic verse:

> *By rule they eat, by rule they drink,*
> *Do all things else by rule, but think—*
> *Method alone must guide 'em all,*
> *Whence Methodists themselves they call.*

Although John Wesley had not chosen the word *Methodist*, that name became permanently attached to him and to those who joined his quest for authentic Christianity.

Catholic Christianity. When asked to define Methodism, John Wesley explained that Methodism stands within the stream of historical Christianity, as expressed in Scripture, Christianity's early creeds, Protestantism's confessions of faith, and the beliefs of faithful Christians through the centuries. For him, if a theological doctrine was new it was not true, and if it was true it was not new. American Methodism's Book of Discipline states that Methodism shares "a common heritage with Christians of every age and nation. This heritage is grounded in the apostolic witness to Jesus Christ as Savior and Lord, which is the source and measure of all valid Christian teaching."

Although certain non-essential differences exist among denominations and non-denominational Christian movements, a solid core of Christian orthodoxy runs through the Church from the first century to the present. To be sure, heresies and theologically misguided people have always existed, even as weeds sprout in grain fields. However, a fundamental core of Christian truth has continued through the centuries. Methodism's stated doctrines agree with those of the universal Church through the centuries. These body biblical truths found expression in the early ecumenical creeds and in the stated articles of religion of most denominations.

With many other branches of Christianity, Methodism holds that the Bible is the chief written authority of Christianity. For instance, British Methodism declares,

> The Doctrines of the Evangelical Faith, which Methodism has
> held from the beginning and still hold, are based upon the Divine

revelation recorded in the Holy Scriptures. [Methodism] acknowledges this revelation as the supreme rule of faith and practice.

In the United States, United American Methodism's Book of Discipline states,

> We believe the Holy Bible . . . reveals the Word of God so far as it is necessary for our salvation. It is to be received through the Holy Spirit as the true rule and guide for faith and practice. Whatever is not revealed in or established by the Holy Scriptures is not to be made an article of faith nor is it to be taught as essential to salvation.

Christian experience. From the beginning, Methodism has emphasized a personal encounter with God by grace through faith. In 1765, Wesley wrote an acquaintance, "Do you now see that true religion is not a negative or an external thing; but the life of God in the soul of man; the image of God stamped upon the heart?" It is often said that Methodism teaches that all can be saved, all can know they are saved, and all can be saved to the uttermost.

Methodism teaches that God relates to us individually, engages himself in the details our daily lives, and he guides each Christian disciple. John Wesley's sermons and tracts speak much of an individual relationship with God. Charles Wesley's hymns are rich in personal pronouns. The inward testimony of the Holy Spirit in the lives of believers became a part of the message of Methodism. The Methodists make use of the scriptural phrase, "the witness of the Spirit" (Rom. 8:16). The Methodists speak of the personal certainty of one's reconciliation with God. The development of this doctrine of assurance became an important contribution of Methodism to the worldwide Christian community.

Holiness. The theme of holiness of heart and life stands prominent in the Methodist tradition. John Wesley fully agreed with the sixteenth-century Protestant reformers that salvation comes by grace through faith, not by human merit or good deeds. The Protestant reformers championed the doctrines of justification and adoption. Wesley fully embraced these doctrines. He also taught the importance of the doctrines of regeneration and sanctification. Justification and adoption are works of grace that God does *for* us. Wesley believed that regeneration and sanctification are works that God does *in* us. Wesley agreed with the doctrine of *imputed* righteousness, but pressed further to embrace the biblical teaching on *imparted* righteousness. An anatomy of Methodism reveals the belief that God can do more for the problem of sin than forgive it. God can both save from wrath and make us pure. In a word, God can save us both from sin's guilt and sin's grip.

Entire sanctification, as taught by Methodism, does not mean freedom from ignorance, infirmities, mistakes, imperfect performance, or the possibility of spiritual apostasy. The Methodist understanding of pure religion is loving God with all of one's heart, soul, and mind; and so loving one's neighbor (Matt. 22:37). Wesley said that sanctification leads to having the mind that was in Christ Jesus (Phil. 2:5). The Apostle Peter articulated God's call to holiness as involving the total self: "As he who called you is holy, be holy yourselves in all your conduct (1 Pet. 1:15). St. Paul prayed, "May the God of peace himself sanctify you entirely; and may your spirit and soul and body be kept sound and blameless at the coming of our Lord Jesus Christ" (1 Thess. 5:23). Wesley said that the doctrine of sanctification is "the grand depositum which God has lodged with the people called Methodists; and for the sake of propagating this chiefly he appeared to have raised us up."

Social responsibility. From the start, Methodism sought to minister to both the souls and bodies of others. Methodism has preached the gospel and also worked to feed, clothe, and heal the needy. If John Wesley taught social responsibility, he also demonstrated it. In a letter to a detractor, John Wesley wrote, "You exhorted us to 'strive to enter in at the strait gate.' I am willing so to do. But I find one chief part of my striving must be, to feed the hungry, to clothe the naked, to instruct the ignorant, to visit the sick and such as are in prison, bound in misery and iron." American Methodism's Book of Discipline reminds us that personal salvation always involves Christian mission and service to the world: "By joining heart and hand, we assert that personal religion, evangelical witness, and Christian social action are reciprocal and mutually reinforcing."

John Wesley established a lending society for those who needed small sums of money and who had no places from which to obtain assistance. Some of Wesley's helpers, called stewards, administered the fund. They loaned money for workers to purchase the tools they needed ply their trades. This plan enabled hundreds of honest workers to earn a living for their families.

Wesley also ministered to those incarcerated in the foul prisons of his day. In 1778, the British Methodist conference of preachers formally established the policy that it was a duty of Methodist preachers to visit prisoners. Wesley's journal contains many instances of visiting prisons. When Wesley was past the age of eighty he visited Newgate Prison, where he preached to more than one-hundred inmates, five of whom were awaiting execution. Some who had never heard the gospel were converted to Christ, and went to their deaths "in peace." Wesley was a pioneer in caring for prisoners of war. John Howard, the "Father of Prison Reform," admired John Wesley, who encouraged him in his monumental work to reform England's penal system.

John Wesley's final letter before he died was to William Wilberforce to encourage him in his campaign to end the slave trade. Wesley deemed human bondage "that execrable villainy which is the scandal of religion in England, and of human nature." Wesley wrote a book titled *Primitive Physic* that went into twenty-three editions during his lifetime. Wesley also opened free medical dispensaries at Bristol and London. He founded homes for aged widows. In 1777, the Methodists in London opened The United Society for Visiting and Relieving the Sick, and Methodism has built hospitals. A Charles Wesley hymn contains the following prayer:

> To serve the present age,
> my calling to fulfill;
> O may it all my powers engage
> to do my Master's will!

Theological Method. Methodism embraces a conjunctive theology that connects what on the surface may seem unconnected or contradictory. For example, Methodism balances such parallel themes as personal religion and social religion; heart and head; reason and experience; the church's priestly role and its prophetic role. In this conjunctive approach to theology, Methodism seeks to conform to biblical teaching. For instance, in balancing divine sovereignty and human freedom, Wesley affirms that God initiates our relationship with him. Yet, Wesley also underscored our need to respond to and cooperate with God. God does not force us to cooperate with his gracious working in our lives. St. Augustine (354–430) had said, "God who made us without ourselves, will not save us without ourselves."

A twentieth-century Methodist Bishop William R. Cannon summarized, "Faith as the one condition of justification is offered unto [us] as a free gift by a gracious God, but then [we] must actively respond to that offer and reach out with the arms of true repentance to receive the gift." Methodism's Book of Discipline states, "God's grace calls forth human response and discipline. . . . Salvation evidences itself in good works. . . . Both faith and good works belong within an all-encompassing theology of grace, since they stem from God's gracious love 'shed abroad in our hearts by the Holy Spirit.'"

The priesthood of believers. A fundamental Protestant principle is that God calls Christians to be "priests" who have direct access to God and to whom he assigns various ministries. Some ministries are ordained, and many are non-ordained. The Apostle Peter described all believers as "a holy priesthood," summoned "to offer spiritual sacrifices acceptable to God through Jesus Christ." That apostle writes his readers that they are "a chosen race, a royal priesthood, a holy nation, God's own people, in order that [they] may proclaim the mighty acts of him who called [them] out of darkness into his marvelous light."[1] The Christian mission to the world is too important to restrict ministry to ordained members of the clergy.

John Wesley invited lay people to share in the first Methodist conference held in London in June, 1744. The ten who met at that gathering consisted of six ordained clergymen and four lay preachers. Early Methodism multiplied rapidly, and the number of clergymen who assisted Wesley was too small for the expanding movement. Lay workers emerged from the ranks of the growing number of converts. Indeed, most of early Methodism's workers were lay men and women. Methodist scholar Frank Baker emphasized, "It is impossible in a few sentences to give any adequate idea of the part played by these [lay people] who formed the backbone, as Wesley was the directing intelligence, of early Methodism."[2] Lay people served as preachers, teachers, helpers, stewards, exhorters, and leaders of class meetings and bands.

Methodism's lay people preached, taught, witnessed to their faith, accounted for contributions and subscriptions, dispensed funds, and apprised the preachers and congregations of the needs and opportunities in the local communities. They sometimes conversed with the preachers if they noticed anything amiss in their preaching or "deportment." Now throughout the World Methodist Council, representing more than eighty million people, lay people support, serve, and spread Methodism in an ever-widening circle.

At first, only a few Anglican priests befriended John and Charles Wesley and their followers. One of those who supported Methodism was Vincent Perronet, an Anglican priest. Both John and Charles Wesley preached in Perronet's church. Perronet encouraged John Wesley in his important ministries and counseled him in matters pertaining to Methodism's relationship with the Church of England. Years later, Perronet wrote Wesley, "It has been always a leading principle with me . . . to love all those labourers of Christ, who give proof by their diligence,

---

[1] 1 Pet. 2:5, 9.
[2] Frank Baker, *A Charge to Keep: An Introduction to the People Called Methodists*, (London: The Epworth Press, 1947), 132.

their holy and heavenly behaviour, that they love our Lord Jesus Christ in sincerity. . . . To 'keep the unity of the Spirit in the bond of peace,' is the indispensable duty of all Christians." Wesley and Perronet remained warm friends until death.[3]

In 1748, Perronet asked John Wesley for a description of Methodism. Wesley wrote the tract below, *A Plain Account of the People Called Methodists*. Wesley sent this tract to Perronet with these introductory words:

> I send you this account, that you may know, not only [our] practice on every head, but likewise the reasons whereon [Methodism] is grounded, the occasion of every step [the Methodists] have taken, and the advantages reaped thereby.

First written with a quill pen, the following account of Methodism's genesis and development gives us the most accurate historical account of how the movement began. That religious awakening significantly influenced England and the American colonies. Indeed, Methodism became one of the most significant religious movements after the sixteenth-century Protestant Reformation.

John Wesley has two chief aims in *A Plain Account of the People Called Methodists*. First, he affirms that Methodism was not seeking to divide the church, but rather to contribute to its spiritual renewal. Second, he contends that Methodism upholds the message and mission of scriptural Christianity. This tract contrasts the difference between the religion of form and the religion of power. "We [have] no view," Wesley states, "but, so far as we are able, to convince those who would hear what true Christianity is, and to persuade them to embrace it."

---

[3] Perronet died in 1785 at the age of ninety-one. On learning of his friend's death, Wesley recorded in his journal, "Oh that I may follow him in holiness, and that my last end may be like his!"

A Plain Account of the People Called Methodists in a Letter to the Reverend Mr. Vincent Perronet, Vicar of Shoreham, in Kent

(Written in 1748)

1. Reverend and dear sir, some time ago, you asked me for an account of the whole structure and arrangement of the people commonly called Methodists. As far as it went, I sent you a true explanation, but not a full one. To supply what I think was lacking in my description, I am sending you this account. I want you to understand Methodist practice on every point—its foundations, the stages of its development, and the advantages that have resulted.

2. First, however, I must state that the Methodists did not have the least expectation of anything like what developed after I wrote to you earlier. The Methodists had no prior intentions or plans; everything developed as circumstances unfolded. Methodism progressed as the people saw or sensed some approaching or pressing evil, or else they saw some good purpose they should pursue. At many times, the Methodists unexpectedly discovered the very thing that gained the good or eliminated the bad. At other times, only by following common sense and Scripture, they deliberated on the most plausible course of action. Even so, by looking back, they generally found something in Christian antiquity that almost paralleled the matter at hand.[1]

---

[1] Next after Scripture, John Wesley was most influenced by the "ancient fathers." By this term, Wesley meant the early second- and third-century Christian writers who wrote in the decades before the Council of Nicea, which convened in 325 shortly after the end of the empire-wide persecutions of Christians and Christianity's gaining state recognition as

I.

1. About ten years ago,[2] throughout many parts of London, many people asked us to preach to them. In our sermons, we had no other purpose than, as far as we were able, to preach to those who were willing to hear about the nature of true Christianity.[3] We wanted to persuade them to embrace it, and we knew that God could work through whomever he pleased.

2. Mainly, we emphasized four points. First, we preached that at best orthodoxy and right opinions constitute only very small part of religion, if we can allow them to be any part of it at all.[4] We said that religion does not consist of negatives or of being merely harmless people. We said that true religion does not lie merely in externals, only doing good deeds, just using the means of grace, or loyally doing works of piety or works of charity.[5] We preached that true Christianity is nothing short of, or different from, the mind that was in Jesus,[6] the image of God stamped

---

a legal religion. Wesley advised that these early Christian writers were "the most authentic commentators on Scripture, as being both nearest the fountain, and eminently endued with that Spirit by whom all Scripture was given." He added, "Who would not . . . desire to have some acquaintance with those that followed them?"

[2] 1738, soon after John Wesley's heart-warming experience of Christian assurance.

[3] Wesley assiduously avoided theological innovation. He aimed strictly to convey "the faith that was once for all entrusted to the saints." He insisted, "Whatever doctrine is new must be wrong; for the old religion is the only true one; and no doctrine can be right, unless it is the very same which was from the beginning."

[4] If eighteenth-century rationalism had produced philosophical skeptics, it also influenced the tone of Christian apologetics. Many of those attempted to defend Christianity on the same ground occupied by the rationalists—reason and "natural religion." Natural religion, without divine revelation, fell short because it lacked spiritual nourishment for the soul. Reason could be twisted to prove to the contrary the theses of the well-meaning defenders of orthodoxy. A popular quip was, "The learned bishop is *dead* right." When Wesley said that orthodoxy and right opinions at best constitute only very small part of religion, he was seeking to avoid the approach to Christian apologetics that was so cerebral that it lacked luster and life.

[5] Works of piety focus on Christian devotion, and works of mercy pertained to Christian action in the world. Works of piety, called "arts of holy living," focused on one's relationship with God. These works include using the means of grace, such as Holy Communion, prayer, singing hymns, listening to sermons, class meetings, studying Scripture, devotional reading, and meditation. Works of mercy pertain to our relationships with others. These works include helping the poor, feeding the hungry, clothing the needy, visiting prisoners, ministering to the sick, practicing hospitality, teaching others, and working to end slavery, child labor, immorality, and graft.

[6] Phil. 2:5.

upon the heart;[7] inward righteousness,[8] attended with the peace of God[9] and joy in the Holy Spirit.[10]

Second, we preached that the only way under heaven to biblical religion is, to repent and believe the gospel.[11] As St. Luke states in the Book of Acts, "repentance toward God,[12] and faith toward our Lord Jesus Christ."[13]

Third, by this faith the one who does not work but trusts God, who justifies the wicked, is justified freely by his grace through the redemption that came by Christ Jesus.[14]

Fourth, being justified by faith,[15] we taste of the heaven to which we are going.[16] We are holy and happy; we tread down sin and fear, and we sit with him in the heavenly realms in Christ Jesus.[17]

3. Many of those who heard this message began to exclaim that we brought "strange ideas to their ears." They alleged that this was doctrine that they had never heard (or at least they had never heeded it). They examined the Scriptures every day to see if what we said was true,[18] and they acknowledged that it accorded with the truth that is in Jesus.[19] The gospel influenced their hearts and minds, and they determined to follow Jesus Christ and him crucified.[20]

4. Immediately, difficulties surrounded these people. The entire world rose up against them. Neighbors, strangers, acquaintances, relatives, and friends, began to cry out forcibly, "Do not be over righteous, neither be over wise—why destroy yourself?"[21] They said, "Your religion is driving you insane."[22]

5. Because they were stressed on every side, one after another came to us to ask what they should do. Opponents worked to weaken their hold on God, and

---

[7] Ezek. 11:19.
[8] 2 Cor. 4:16.
[9] Rom. 15:13.
[10] Rom. 14:17.
[11] Matt. 4:17; Mark 1:15; 6:12; Luke 13:3, 5; Acts 2:38; 3:19; 17:30; 26:20.
[12] Luke 5:22; 24:47; Acts 20:21; Rom. 2:4; 2 Cor. 7:10; 2 Tim. 2:25; 2 Pet. 3:9.
[13] Acts 20:21.
[14] Rom. 3:4; Eph.1:7; Col. 1:14.
[15] Rom. 3:28; 5:1; Gal. 2:16; 3:11, 24.
[16] Phil. 3:20.
[17] Eph. 2:6.
[18] Acts 17:11.
[19] Eph. 4:21.
[20] 1 Cor. 2:2.
[21] Eccl. 7:16.
[22] Acts 26:24.

no one tried to strengthen their hands in God.[23] We advised these new Christians, "Strengthen one another. Talk together as often as you can. Pray earnestly with and for one another that you may endure to the end, and be saved.[24] We assumed that there would be no objection to this advice. It is grounded in the clearest reason and in so many Old and New Testament Scriptures as to be tedious to recite them.

6. These new Christians said to me, "We want you to talk with us often. We want you to direct and hasten us in our way, to give us the advice that you well know we need, and to pray with us and for us." I asked these converts, "Who among you want my help? Give me your names and addresses." They did so, and I soon found that there were too many for me to talk with individually as often as they wished. Therefore, I told them, "If all of you will gather every Thursday evening, I will gladly spend some time with you in prayer, and I will give you the best advice I can."

7. Consequently, without any previous intention on my part or theirs, there arose what later became a Society.[25] *Society* is a very innocent term, and various

---

[23] Here, Wesley overstates the strength of opposition against him and the early Methodists. A few Anglican priests supported Wesley and his work. This list included John Fletcher, William Grimshaw, John Berridge, William Romaine, Thomas Coke, and the recipient of this letter, Vincent Perronet. Nonetheless, it is true that the majority of the Anglican clergy worked to dissuade new converts from joining the Methodists.

For example, the Bishop of London, George Lavington, asked all his clergy to join together to stamp out the Methodists. Wesley wrote him, "My Lord, the time is short. I am past the noon of life, and my remaining years flee away as a shadow. Your Lordship is old and full of days, having past the usual age of man. It cannot, therefore, be long before we shall both drop this house of earth, and stand naked before God. . . . On his left hand shall be those who are shortly to dwell in everlasting fire, prepared for the devil and his angels. In that number will be all who died in their sins; and, among the rest, those whom you preserved from repentance. Will you then rejoice in your success? The Lord God grant it may not be said in that hour, 'These have perished in their iniquity; but their blood I require at your hands!'"

[24] Matt. 24:13; Mark 13:13.

[25] This reference is to the founding of the first Methodist Society in London in late 1739.

societies have been quite common in London.[26] A number of people had associated themselves with these societies.[27] The aims of those who joined the with the Methodist societies was obvious to everyone. They wanted to flee from God's wrath to come, and to assist each other in doing so. Therefore, they united themselves to pray together,[28] to receive words of exhortation,[29] and to watch over one another in love,[30] to help each other to work out their salvation.[31]

8. There is only one condition for those who seek admission into a Methodist Society—a desire to flee from God's future wrath and to be saved from their sins. The Methodist Societies had three rules for working out their salvation. They agreed that as many of them as could to meet together every Friday, and spend the dinner hour in calling upon God for each other, and for all people everywhere. Now, wherever this desire lodges in one's soul, its fruits will show it.[32] We expect those want to continue in the society to evidence their desire by following three rules.[33]

---

[26] Prior to the Methodist Societies, other religious societies emerged in England. About 1668, in England Anthony Horneck founded religious societies among young Anglican laymen who agreed to "resolve upon a holy and serious life." In 1691, the Society for the Reformation of Manners emerged in London to suppress public indecency and immorality. This society particularly worked to end public profanity, alcoholism, and prostitution. In 1698, Thomas Bray founded The Society for Promoting Christian Knowledge (S.P.C.K.). This Anglican society promoted and encouraged the erection of charity schools for the poor, the dispersion of Bibles and religious tracts in England and abroad. In 1701, Bray also founded The Society for the Propagation of the Gospel in Foreign Parts (S.P.G.). This Anglican society assisted missionary work begun by the S.P.C.K. The aims of the S.P.G. were to provide the ministrations of the Church for British people overseas, and to evangelize non-Christian people who were subject to the British monarchy. Thus, in England there was a precedent for founding religious societies within the Anglican Church.

[27] Josiah Woodward's *Account of the Rise and Progress of the Religious Societies in the City of London* (4th ed., 1712) tells that the chief aim of these religious societies was "to resolve upon a holy and serious life."

[28] Matt. 18:20.

[29] 2 Tim. 4:2; Heb. 3:13.

[30] Rom. 12:10; Eph. 4:2; 1 Thess. 3:12; 1 Pet. 1:22; 1 Jn. 4:12.

[31] Phil. 2:12.

[32] Matt. 12:33.

[33] John and Charles Wesley drew up Methodism's General Rules in 1743, with the title, *The Nature, Design, and General Rules of our United Societies*. The three rules stated that all who are to continue in their salvation by "doing no harm, doing good, and attending upon all the ordinances of God." These three rules appeared in the first Book of Discipline of America's Methodist Episcopal Church, founded in 1784. American Methodism's 1808 General conference Restrictive Rule No. 5 forbade revoking or changing the General Rules. The General Rules have continued to appear in every edition of American Methodism's Book of Discipline.

First, by doing no harm, by avoiding every kind of evil—especially that which many commonly practice. These evils include taking the name of God in vain, profaning the day of the Lord, drunkenness, fighting, quarrelling, brawling; the buying or selling goods that do not pass import customs, doing to others as we would not want them to do to us, uncharitable or unprofitable conversation, particularly speaking evil of judicial officers and ministers.

Second, by doing good, being as merciful and kind as we can, as far as it is possible to everyone, by all diligence and frugality to bring no reproach on the gospel. They should be willing to bear the reproach of Christ[34] and to be as the dregs of the earth, the rubbish of the world,[35] accepting that others will falsely say all kinds of evil against us because of Christ.[36]

Third, by using the ordinances of God, such as public worship, Holy Communion, private prayer, studying the Scriptures, and fasting or abstinence.[37]

These Methodists also agreed that as many as were able would meet each Friday to spend the dinner hour calling out to God for each other and all humankind.

9. It quickly appeared that uniting in this way fulfilled its purpose. People found the salvation they sought.[38] Within a few months, most of them began to revere God and do what is right and acceptable to him.[39] However, those who had not joined together in a society grew weary.[40] They lost heart and fell back into what they were before.[41] Meanwhile, the far greater part of those who united together continued striving to enter in at the strait gate,[42] and to take hold of eternal life.[43]

---

[34] Heb. 11:26.
[35] 1 Cor. 4:19.
[36] Matt. 5:11.
[37] These exercises are called "the means of grace," a term found in the Anglican Book of Common Prayer. The means of grace are certain exercises, words, or actions that are ways by which God mediates his grace to us. John Wesley defined two categories of these means: the Instituted Means of Grace and the Prudential Means of Grace. The instituted means of grace include Holy Communion, prayer, searching the scriptures, and Christian conversation. The prudential means of grace include good works, avoiding evil, attending worship services, visiting the sick, denying oneself, taking up one's cross, and cultivating the presence of God.
[38] Deut. 4:29.
[39] Acts 10:35; Eph. 5:10.
[40] Gal. 6:9; 2 Thess. 3:13.
[41] Luke 8:13; 2 Pet. 3:17.
[42] Luke 13:24.
[43] 1 Tim. 6:12.

10. On reflection, I clearly observed that this pattern is the same one found in original Christianity. In the earliest times, those whom God had sent forth preached the gospel to everyone. The οἱ ἀκροαται⁴⁴ [the hearers, or body of hearers] were mostly unbelieving Jews or pagan Gentiles. However, as soon as any of these people were convinced of the truth, so as to forsake sin and seek the gospel of salvation, the apostles immediately joined them together. They recorded their names and counseled them to watch over each other. The leaders met these κατηχούμενοι⁴⁵ [catechumens], as others called them. They set them apart from the great congregation in order to instruct, correct, exhort, and pray with them and for them according to their different needs.

11. However, it was not long before some people objected to our practice of gathering new Christians together. The reason for of their complaints had not once entered into my thoughts. The issue was whether this practice of gathering serious Christians together was creating a schism in the church. Was joining these people together in effect creating little churches out of the established churches?⁴⁶ We easily answer the question. If you mean just gathering people out of buildings called churches, it is. However, if you mean, dividing Christians from Christians, and thereby destroying Christian fellowship, it is not.

Consider the following:

(i) These people were not Christians before they joined together to seek God. Most of them were outright pagans.
(ii) Those from whom they separated were not Christians. You will not look me in the face and say they are. What! Drunken Christians! Cursing and swearing Christians! Lying Christians! Cheating

---

⁴⁴ Rom. 2:13.
⁴⁵ Rom. 2:18.
⁴⁶ Earlier, separating from the Anglican Church had been the practice of the dissenting Puritans. Robert Browne (c. 1550–1633) had established independent churches in Norwich and other places in England. These congregations formed the basis for Congregationalism. The congregational form of church government is based on the view that Christ alone is the head of the church, and all Christians are priests of God. When two or more Christians meet together, Christ is among them guiding their thoughts and directing their actions. In 1582, Browne wrote a book with the length title, *A Treatise of Reformation without Tarrying for any and of the Wickedness of those Preachers which will not reform till the Magistrate command or compel them.*

Christians! If these are Christians at all, they are devil Christians, as the poor Malabarians call them.⁴⁷

(iii) Those that joined a Methodist Society are no more divided than they were before, even from the wretched "devil Christians."⁴⁸ They are as ready as ever to assist them, and to perform every act of real kindness toward them.

(iv) If it be said, "There are some true Christians in the parish, and you destroy the Christian fellowship between these Methodists and them." I answer that what never existed cannot be destroyed. The fellowship you speak of never existed, so it cannot be shattered. Which of those Christians ever had any fellowship with these Methodist converts? Who watched over them in love? Who tracked their growth in grace? Who from time to time advised and exhorted them? When they needed prayer, who prayed with them and for them?

A kind of true fellowship, and this alone, is Christian fellowship. Regrettably, where do we find it? Look east, west, north, or south. Name whatever parish you please: Do we find this kind of Christian fellowship there? Instead, are not most of the parishioners a mere rope of sand? What Christian connection exists between them? What interaction in spiritual matters do we see? Is there watching over each other's souls?⁴⁹ Are they bearing one another's burdens?⁵⁰ What a mere jest it is to talk so grimly about destroying what never existed! The truth is just the opposite. We introduce Christian fellowship where it did not exist. The fruits of the Methodist societies have been peace, joy, love,⁵¹ and zeal⁵² for every good word and work.⁵³

---

⁴⁷ Malabar is located in the southern part of India, where the Apostle Thomas may have taken the gospel. A number of the Malabarians became Christians, and they were shocked at the faulty morals and ethics among Western Christians.

⁴⁸ When John Wesley was in Georgia, a Native American Chief Tomochihi said to him, "Christian much drunk; Christian beat men; Christian tell lies; devil Christian! Me no Christian."

⁴⁹ Heb. 13:17.

⁵⁰ Gal. 6:2.

⁵¹ Rom. 14:17; Gal. 5:22.

⁵² 2 Cor. 9:2.

⁵³ 2 Thess. 2:17.

II.

1. Nonetheless, as much as we endeavored to watch over each other, we soon found some among us who did not live the gospel. I do not know that any hypocrites had crept into the Society, because there was no enticement to do so. Still, several people grew cold, and they yielded to the sins that had long before entangled them.[54] We soon perceived that there were many harmful consequences of allowing these people to remain among us. It was dangerous to others, because all sin is infectious. Their sinful lives brought such a scandal on their brothers and sisters that it exposed them to something other than the reproach of Christ.[55] The presence of these people in the Society became an obstacle to others, and they brought the way of truth into disrepute.[56]

2. For a long time, and before we found a remedy, we groaned under these aggravations. From Wapping to Westminster,[57] the Methodists were scattered so widely in all parts of London that I could not easily know the behavior of each person in his or her own neighborhood. Consequently, several disorderly ramblers[58] did much harm before I became aware of it.

3. After some time, while we were thinking of something else altogether, we contemplated a method for which ever since we have reason to bless God. I was talking with several members of the society in Bristol about how to pay the debts there. Someone[59] stood up and said, "Let every member of the society give a penny a week until all debts are paid." Another answered, "But many of them are poor, and cannot afford to do it." The first speaker said, "Put eleven of the poorest with me; and if they can give anything, it is well. I will call on them weekly. If they cannot give anything, I will give for them as well as for myself. Each of you call on eleven of your neighbors weekly, receive what they give, and make up what is lacking." We adopted this plan.

Over time, some of the leaders informed me they found that a particular member did not live as he or she should. It struck me immediately, "This is the answer,

---

[54] Heb. 12:1.
[55] Heb. 11:26.
[56] 2 Pet. 2:2.
[57] Two distant parts of London.
[58] Samuel Johnson's eighteenth-century dictionary defines the verb *ramble* as to rove loosely and irregularly. The OED cites an eighteenth-century definition a ramble-headed person as one who is "of a wandering, giddy disposition." A rambler is one who moves aimlessly from place to place, exploring idly and without purpose. Here, Wesley speaks of *disorderly* ramblers who were harming the Methodist societies.
[59] This person was Captain Foy a British sea captain. In Bristol, on 15 February 1742, Foy suggested the plan that Wesley here describes. Out of this plan came the office of Class Leader.

the exact plan we have needed so long." I called together all the class leaders (this is what we used to call them, and their groups we called classes). I asked them to make specific inquiries into the behavior of those whom they saw each week. They did so, and they discovered many disorderly members. Some turned from the evil of their ways. Others, we dismissed from the society. Many regarded the plan with fear, yet we reverently rejoiced in God.

4. As soon as possible, we adopted the same method in London and at all other places. When we detected sinful members, we reproved them. If they forsook their sins for a season, we readmitted them to the class meetings and received them gladly. If they obstinately persisted in their sins, we openly pronounced that they were no longer with us. The others grieved and prayed for them, and yet we rejoiced that, as far as possible, we removed scandal from the Methodist Societies.

5. Here are the responsibilities of the class leaders:

(i) To meet with the individual members in the class, at least once a week to inquire how their souls prospered; to advise, reprove, comfort, or encourage as occasion may require, and to receive what they are willing to give toward the relief of the poor.[60]

(ii) To meet the minister and the stewards of the society to inform the minister of any who are sick, of any that are disorderly and do not accept reproof, and to give the stewards what donations they have received from their several classes during the preceding week.

6. At first, the class leaders visited each person at his or her own house, but we soon discovered that this arrangement was not expedient. There were several problems with that plan:

(i) These visits took more time than most of the leaders had to spare.

(ii) Many people lived with masters, mistresses, or relatives, who would not allow us to visit them in this way.

(iii) At the houses of those who were not so averse to the visits, they often had no opportunity of speaking to them except in the company of others. This inconvenience did not accomplish the purpose of the visits, which was to encourage, comfort, or reprove.

(iv) It frequently happened that the class member and the class leader did not agree on the conversation that passed between them. We could not clear this up without meeting them together.

---

[60] Eph. 5:11; 2 Tim. 4:2.

(v) Little misunderstandings and squabbles of various kinds often arose among relatives or neighbors. To clear up any disagreements effectively, we needed to see the parties face to face.

In consideration of these matters, we agreed that the members of each class should meet together. By this means, we made a fuller inquiry into the behavior of every member. Those whom we could not visit at home or only in the company of others had the same advantage as every other member of the class. We gave advice or reproof as needed, and we mended quarrels and cleared up misunderstandings. After an hour or two spent in this labor of love, the class meetings concluded with prayer and thanksgiving.

7. It can scarcely be conceived what advantages we have reaped from this little prudential regulation—the class meeting. Many Methodists now happily experienced that Christian fellowship of which previously they had not so much as an idea. They began to bear one another's burdens, and genuinely to care for each other.[61] Daily, the class members had a more intimate acquaintance with one another, and they developed a more endearing mutual affection. Speaking the truth in love, they grew up into him who is the head, that is, Christ. From him the whole body, joined and held together[62] by every supporting ligament, grew and built itself up in love.[63]

8. Despite all these advantages, many at first were extremely averse to meeting together in this way. These people viewed the class meetings in in the wrong light. They saw it not as a privilege (indeed an invaluable one), but rather as a restriction. They disliked the meetings because they did not like any kind of restraint. Some were embarrassed to speak in the company of others. Some honestly said, "I do not know why; but I do not like it."

9. Some objected, "There were no such meetings when I first joined the society. Why should we begin them now? I do not understand these developments and continually changing one thing after another." It was easy to answer their objection—it is a pity we did not have class meetings at first. At that time, we did not understand their need or benefit. If you read the rules of the society, you will quickly understand why we now use class meetings. Regarding these little prudential helps for Christian growth, it is not a weakness or fault (as you imagine) that we continually adjust one thing after another. Rather, we enjoy a particular advantage. We declare all these means of grace to be prudential[64]–not essential or

---

[61] Gal. 6:2.
[62] 1 Cor. 1:10.
[63] Eph. 4:15–16.
[64] Prudential = marked by good judgment, good sense, and circumspection.

divinely instituted, but soundly practical. As far as it lies within us, we prevent these means of grace from growing formal or dead. We are always open to instruction, willing to be wiser every day than we were before. We will alter anything we can change for the better.

10. Another objection was, "There is no scripture for classes, and I know of none." I answer with the following points:

(i) There is no scripture *opposed* to class meetings. You cannot show one text that forbids them.

(ii) There is much scripture to support them. I refer to all those texts that urge the substance of those various duties whereof reason and experience infer support for the class meeting.

(iii) You seem not to have noted that in most points the Scripture gives only general rules. Scripture leaves it to our common sense to adjust its teaching to our particular circumstances.

The Scripture, for instance, gives that general rule, "Let all things be done in a fitting and orderly way."[65] On particular occasions, our common sense determines what is proper and orderly. In another instance, the Bible lays down a general and permanent direction: "Whether you eat or drink or whatever you do, do it all for the glory of God."[66] Common good sense applies this principle in a thousand particular instances.

11. Another person said, "But class meetings are human inventions." That allegation is only the same objection in another form. For any reasonable person, the same answer will suffice. These are human inventions—that is, by reason and common sense, they are methods that we have found more effectively to utilize several Scripture rules. We apply general terms to particular situations.

12. Others, speaking far more plausibly, said, "The class meeting is well enough in itself, but the leaders are inadequate for the work. They lack the gifts or graces for such service." I answer as follows:

(i) Nevertheless, such leaders as they are, it is plain that God has blessed their work.

(ii) If any of these leaders are unusually lacking in gifts or graces, we soon notice them and remove them.

(iii) If you know any such class leaders, tell me, not other people. I will undertake to replace them with better leaders.

---

[65] 1 Cor. 14:40.
[66] 1 Cor. 10:31.

(v) We hope all the leaders will become better by experience, observation, the advice the ministers give them every Tuesday night, and our special prayers for them.

III.

1. About this time, I learned that several people in Kingswood[67] frequently met together at the school.[68] When they could spare the time, they spent most of the evening in prayer, praise, and thanksgiving.[69] Some advised me to stop this practice. However, after weighing the matter thoroughly, and comparing it with the practice of the ancient Christians, I saw no reason to forbid it. Rather, I believed that this exercise might be of a more general use. Therefore, so that we might have light back and forth, I sent them word that I planned to meet with them on the Friday nearest the full moon.[70] The previous Sunday I gave public notice of this plan. I also said that I intended to preach, asking the attendance of only those who could meet with me without compromising their business or families. On Friday, many people came. I began preaching between eight and nine; and we continued to a little beyond midnight, singing, praying, and praising God.[71]

---

[67] Kingswood was a small coal mining village that bordered the City of Bristol.
[68] A schoolhouse in Kingswood.
[69] Psa. 100:4.
[70] A full moon was beneficial, if not essential, for night travel. Public lights were almost non-existent. Road conditions were poor. Historian J. H. Whiteley reported, "In the whole of England there [were] but four good roads." Whiteley reported on a typical road: "All travelling should Avoid this Terrible County as they would the Divell [sic], for a Thousand to One they break their Necks or Limbs by Overthrowings [falling from a horse] or Breakings-down." (*Wesley's England: A Survey of XVIIIth Social and Cultural Conditions*, London: The Epworth Press, 1954, p. 56).
[71] Here, Wesley's description is probably that of the first Methodist Watch Night Service. These meetings began in Kingswood. Coalminers, prior to their conversions to Christ, formerly spent evenings at an ale house, drinking and singing bawdy songs. After they became Christians, they spent the evening in prayer and in singing hymns by Charles Wesley, some of which he wrote expressly for these occasions. The opening stanzas of one of these hymns was,

> Gracious Redeemer, shake
> This slumber from my soul!
> Say to me now, Awake, awake,
> And Christ shall make you whole.
> Lay to your mighty hand!
> Alarm me in this hour,
> And make me understand
> The thunder of your power!
> Give me on you to call,

2. In Bristol, London, and Newcastle, as well as Kingswood, we have continued monthly vigils.[72] Exceeding great are the blessings we have found therein. These gatherings are usually suprisingly solemn seasons. The word of God sinks deep into the heart, even of those who until then did not know God. If someone should say, "The good attendance is due only to the novelty of the thing, (the circumstance that still draws such multitudes together at certain times), or perhaps it is due to the awesome silence of the night." I am not concerned enough to respond regarding the matter. So be it. Yet it remains that the watch-night impressions made on many souls have never faded away. Now, if we acknowledge that God did make use of the novelty or any other unimportant circumstance to bring sinners to repentance, nonetheless these services still attract the people. Because this is so, together let us rejoice.

3. May I press the case still further? Suppose, either by the novelty of this ancient custom of vigils, or by any other incidental circumstance, I can turn a sinner from the error of his way and save him from death and cover a multitude of sins.[73] Am I clear before God if I do not do so, if I do not snatch that burning stick out of the fire?[74]

IV.

1. As the Methodist Society increased, I found that it required more and more attention in order to separate the valuable from the vile. To do so, I determined

---

>Always to watch and pray,
>Lest I into temptation fall,
>And cast my shield away.
>For each assault prepared
>And ready may I be,
>
>Forever standing on my guard,
>And looking up to thee.

[72] At times, the Methodists held vigils, which Wesley called the Watch-night Services. Sometimes these services of prayer, praise and preaching lasted several hours. Wesley held them monthly. When Wesley began these services, he received criticism. In June of 1750, to John Bailey, a critic, Wesley wrote, "You charge me . . . with holding 'midnight assemblies.' Sir, did you never see the word Vigil in your Common-Prayer Book? Do you know what it means? If not, permit me to tell you, that it was customary with the ancient Christians to spend whole nights in prayer; and that these nights were termed *Vigiliæ*, or Vigils. Therefore for spending a part of some nights in this manner, in public and solemn prayer, we have not only the authority of our own national Church, but of the universal Church, in the earliest ages." Charles Wesley wrote hymns for these vigils. Today, a form of this service is a yearly watch night for the arrival of a new year.

[73] James 5:20.

[74] Amos 4:11.

that least every three months I would talk with every member. I would determine from their own testimonies and that of their leaders and neighbors whether they grew in grace and in the knowledge of our Lord Jesus Christ.[75] At these times, I also inquired specifically whether any misunderstandings or differences existed among them. I wanted to remove every obstacle to peace and brotherly love.

2. To each of those of whom I found no reason to doubt their seriousness and good conduct I gave a testimony under my own signature, by writing their name on a ticket prepared for that purpose. Every ticket implied a strong recommendation as if I had written, "I believe the bearer of this ticket to be one that fears God and works righteousness."[76]

3. Those who possessed these συμβολα[77] or *tesserae*[78] as the ancients termed them, having the same force as the συστατικαι.[79] The Methodist ticket holders, wherever they went, received acknowledgment from their brothers and sisters, who received them with utter cheerfulness. These tickets also had other advantages. By using them, it was easy to distinguish who were class members, and who were not. The tickets also gave us a quiet and inoffensive way to remove any disorderly member. Such a person receives no new ticket at the quarterly visitation (that is how often we renew the tickets); we know immediately that he or she is no longer in the society.

V.

All this time, I greatly dreaded sectarianism,[80] and I resolved to use every possible method of preventing a narrowness of spirit, a party zeal, or restrictions in our compassion.[81] I feared the appearance of despicable bigotry that makes many people reluctant to believe that there is any work of God other than that among themselves. I thought it might help to avoid this if I frequently read to all who were willing to hear the accounts I received from time to time reports of the work God is doing in our own country and in others. This work of God is not among us alone, but it takes place among people of various opinions and denominations.

---

[75] 2 Pet. 3:18.
[76] Acts 10:35.
[77] Greek, "symbols."
[78] Latin, "tokens."
[79] Greek, "letters of recommendation," 2 Cor. 3:1.
[80] Wesley had no intention to separate from the Anglican Church, but rather to help renew its spirit and mission.
[81] 2 Cor. 6:12.

To this end, I allotted one evening every month; and I find no cause to regret my labor.[82]

Reading these accounts is generally a time of strong consolation to those who love God and all fellow beings for his sake. This practice also breaks down the dividing walls that the devil or the follies of people cunningly erect. The reports of the work of God encourage every one of his children to say, "Whoever does the will of my Father in heaven are my brothers and sisters and mothers."[83]

VI.

1. By God's blessing upon the efforts of the Methodists to help one another, many people found the pearl of great price.[84] Being justified by faith, they found peace with God through our Lord Jesus Christ.[85] More than ever before, these new Christians felt a more tender affection toward those who received a faith as precious as ours.[86] There arose among them such a confidence in each other that they poured out their souls toward one another. Indeed, they greatly needed to do so because the spiritual war was not over, as they had supposed. Rather, they still had to struggle against flesh and blood, and against the rulers, against the authorities, against the powers of this dark world.[87] Temptations came on every side. Often these temptations were such that in a class meeting the members did not know how to speak of them, because people of every sort met together—young and old, men and women.

2. Therefore, these Christians needed the means to form a closer union. They wanted to pour out their hearts without reserve, particularly with regard to the sin that so easily entangled them and the temptations that were most likely to prevail over them.[88] They were even more desirous of these close associations when they observed it was the express advice of an inspired writer, St. James: "Confess your sins to each other and pray for each other so that you may be healed."[89]

---

[82] Many publications of early American Methodism contained reports of God's work across "the connection," that is, the church.
[83] Matt. 12:50.
[84] Matt. 13:44–46.
[85] Rom. 5:1.
[86] 2 Pet. 1:1.
[87] Eph. 6:12.
[88] Heb. 12:1.
[89] James 5:16.

3. According to their desire, I divided them into smaller companies, putting the married or single men, and married or single women, together.[90] The chief rules of these bands—that is, "little companies," as the old English word signifies—are as follows:

In order to confess our faults one to another and to pray for each other that we may be healed,[91] we intend,

(i) To meet together, at least once a week.

(ii) To arrive punctually at the appointed hour.

(iii) To begin with singing or prayer.

(iv) One after another, to speak freely and plainly to each other about the true state of our soul. We share the faults we have committed in thought, word, or deed, and the temptations we have felt since our last meeting.

(v) To ask someone, thereafter called a "Leader," to tell his own state first. Then, in turn, to ask the rest as many and as searching questions as indicated, concerning their spiritual state, sins, and temptations.[92]

4. So that we might more easily realize the purpose of the bands, I asked the bands of men to meet me together every Wednesday evening, and the women's bands to meet on Sunday. The objective was for them to receive such specific instructions and exhortations as from time to time might appear to be most needful for them. We wanted to offer prayers for the needs or requirements of the members. We purposed to give praise to the Giver of every good gift and for whatever mercies the members had received.[93]

---

[90] Here, Wesley describes the Methodist bands. The class meetings (comprised of up to twelve members of both genders and different ages) were for seekers and new Christians. By contrast, Wesley designed the band meetings (not more than five or six members of the same gender, approximate age, and circumstances) for Christians pressing on to a fuller maturity in Christ and entire sanctification. The conversations in the band meetings were more "minute and particular" than would be appropriate for a larger and more diverse group. Band members examined each other very pointedly and strictly, with a view to encouraging and helping one another.

[91] James 5:16.

[92] Some of the stipulations for joining a band included affirmative answers to such questions as: "Do you desire to be told of your faults? Do you desire to be told of all your faults, and that plain and home? Do you desire that every one of us should tell you, from time to time, whatsoever is in his heart concerning you? Do you desire we should tell you whatsoever we think, whatsoever we fear, whatsoever we hear, concerning you? Do you desire that, in doing this, we should come as close as possible, that we should cut to the quick, and search your heart to the bottom? Is it your desire and design to be on this, and all other occasions, entirely open, so as to speak everything that is in your heart without exception, without disguise, and without reserve?"

[93] James 1:17.

5. In order to increase in the people a grateful sense of all God's mercies, I wanted all the men in bands to meet on the second evening every quarter. On the third evening, all the women would meet, and on another evening both men and women would meet together. As the ancient Christians did, we would break bread together with glad and sincere hearts.[94]

At these love feasts (so we called them, retaining the name, as well as the service that was in use from the time of the early church),[95] our food is only a little plain cake and water. We seldom return from these love feasts without receiving natural food and the food that endures to eternal life.[96]

6. Many and great are the advantages that have ever since flowed from this closer union of the believers with each other. They prayed for one another, that they would be healed of the faults they had confessed.[97] Healings came. The chains shattered and the bonds broke into pieces.[98] Sin had no more dominion over them.[99] God delivered many from the temptations out of which, until then, they had found no way to escape. They increased in strength in our most holy faith.[100] They rejoiced in the Lord more abundantly.[101] They were strengthened in love, and became more successfully motivated to abound in every good work.[102]

7. Soon, some people objected to the bands (as others had previously protested the classes). They said, "There were no bands in the beginning; there is no Scripture to support them. The bands are human works, of human making, just human inventions." As before, I replied that the bands are prudential helps, grounded on

---

[94] Acts 2:46.

[95] The Love Feast, called the Agape Meal was observed by the churches in the New Testament. These were common meals, often held in conjunction with the observance of the Lord's Supper (1 Cor. 11:17–34; 2 Pet. 2:13; Jude 1:12). Ignatius (c. 35–c. 107), Bishop of Antioch, referred to Love Feasts in his letter to the Church in Smyrna. Tertullian (c, 160–c. 225) refers to the Love Feast in his *Apology*, connecting it with offerings taken for the poor. Augustine (354–430) refers to the Love Feast as a charity meal for the poor. In 692, the Trullan Synod of Eastern bishops excommunicated those who held Love Feasts in their churches. The Pope rejected the decrees of that synod, but even so, the Love Feast (Agape Meal) fell into disuse during the Middle Ages. The Moravians and John Wesley revived the Love Feasts. In recent years, this service has been revived among some Methodists. The 1992 United Methodist *Book of Worship* discusses the Love Feast and gives a suggested order for observing this ceremony. (pp. 581–84).

[96] John 4:36; 6:27.
[97] James 5:16.
[98] Nahum 1:13.
[99] Rom. 6:9.
[100] Jude 1:20.
[101] Phil. 3:1; 4:4.
[102] 2 Cor. 9:8.

reason and experience. In practice, the bands apply the general rules of Scripture to particular circumstances.

8. A much bolder and more frequent objection was, "All these bands are mere Popery."[103] I hope that I need not pass a harder censure on those people (at least, most of them) who charge the Methodists with popery, other than that they talk about what they do not know. They betray their most gross and shameful ignorance. Do they not know that the only popish confession in the Methodist band meetings is the confession made by a single person? In itself, this practice is in not in any way condemned by our national church. Indeed, in some cases the Church of England recommends confession to another person. What Methodists practice is the confession of several people conjointly, not to a priest, but to each other. Consequently, it has no relationship to Roman Catholic confession. Many people use the worn-out objection of "popery" against whatever they do not like. Impulsively, they label it "popery."

VII.

1. Most of these who were intimately joined in a band, daily moved onward from faith to faith.[104] However, some did fall away from the faith.[105] There were those who fell all at once, by knowingly plunging into willful sin. Others drifted away gradually. They did so almost unconsciously, by succumbing to what they called "little things," such as sins of omission, sins of the heart, or by not maintaining a prayerful life. The pleadings and prayers of believers failed to profit those who had fallen away or drifted away. They needed advice and instructions suited to their case, and as soon as I saw this, I separated them from the rest, and asked them to meet me separately on Saturday evenings.

2. At that hour, I fit the hymns, counsel, and prayers to their circumstances. That is, I ministered appropriately to those who had known God, but who had

---

[103] *Popery* was a disparaging term used in reference to those who wanted to reestablish Roman Catholicism as the state religion of England and Ireland, as in the days of Queen Mary I. She gained the epithet "Bloody Mary," because during her five-year reign (1553–58) she ordered more than 280 Protestants burned at the stake. After her death, her younger half-sister and successor Elizabeth I returned England to the Protestant faith. As well, Protestants rejected the concept of the papacy and certain theological tenants that had come out of the Roman Catholic Council of Trent in the sixteenth century.

[104] Rom. 1:17.

[105] Gal. 5:4; Rev. 2:5.

now lost sight of the light of his countenance.[106] They mourned after God, and they refused to be comforted until knowing that he had healed their backsliding.[107]

3. By applying both the threats and promises of God to these genuinely sincere penitents, and by praying to God in their behalf, we worked to bring them back to the great Shepherd and Bishop of their souls.[108] We did not use any of the follies of the Roman Church, even if in a measure the ancient church practiced some of them.[109] In prescribing hair shirts, and physical austerities, we dared not follow ancient traditions. However, we did divide οι πιστοί[110] from the rest of the society. We separated the penitents from the rest, and arranged a distinct service for them.

VIII.

1. Many of these penitents soon recovered the ground they had lost. Indeed, they rose higher than before.[111] They were more vigilant, gentle, and humble, and stronger in faith that expresses itself through love.[112] They now grew faster than most of their brothers and sisters, walking in the light of God,[113] and having fellowship with the Father and with his Son, Jesus Christ.[114]

2. I saw that it would be useful to advise all those who continued in the light of God's countenance. The rest of their brothers and sisters did not desire this light, and probably could not receive it. Therefore, I invited a small number of those who appeared to be walking in God's light to spend an hour with me every Monday morning. My plan was to show them how to press toward perfection, to exercise their graces, and to develop every gift that God had given them.[115] I also

---

[106] Psa. 4:6; 44:3; 89:15; 90:8.

[107] Jer. 3:22; Hos. 14:4.

[108] 1 Pet. 2:25.

[109] Some of these practices were assuming the unmarried state was superior to marriage. Jerome, for example, said, "Marriage populates the earth; celibacy populates heaven." Seeking holiness, some became hermits in the wilderness. Some monks burned off their fingers at a candle to avoid sinning with their hands; some put ashes on their food in an effort to become holy; some slept without blankets so as not to enjoy sleep at night. Some priests advised sinners to wear an iron girdle. Wesley's point is that even though some practices are ancient, they are not necessarily useful or biblical. He insisted that the scriptures, not traditions, are the standard for faith and practice.

[110] οι πιστοί = the faithful [believers].

[111] The earlier editions of *A Plain Account of the People Called Methodists* contain the words, *rose the higher for their fall.*

[112] Gal. 5:6.

[113] John 12:35; Eph. 5:8; 1 Jn. 1:7.

[114] 1 Jn. 1:3.

[115] 1 Pet. 4:10.

encouraged them to love one another more and more watchfully, and to care for each other. I also formed them into a select company, to which I might confide myself on all occasions, without reserve. Also, I could hold them up to their brothers and sisters as patterns of love, holiness, and good works.[116]

3. The [select] band members did not need to come under the burden of many rules. The members had the best rule of all in their hearts [even Christ]. Therefore, we gave them no other specific directions, except the following three:

(i) Let nothing spoken in this society be spoken again. By this assurance, we had a fuller confidence in each other.

(ii) Each member agreed to submit to the minister in all minor matters.

(iii). Weekly, all the members will bring all the coinage they can spare toward a common reserve.

4. Everyone in a select company of sanctified believers has equal liberty to speak—no one is higher or lower than another. When they met together, I could say freely to them, "Each prophesy in turn, so that all may learn and all be encouraged.[117] (I use the word prophesy to mean speaking God's word, not predicting future events.)[118] I often found the advantage of such an open conversation was that in the abundance of counselors there is safety.[119] Likewise, anyone who is inclined so to do is encouraged to pour out his or her soul in prayer. In this setting, especially, we have found that the prayer of a righteous person is powerful and effective.[120]

IX.

1. This explanation is the plainest and clearest account I can give of the people commonly called Methodists. It remains only for me to give you a short account

---

[116] As noted above, the Class Meetings were for those seeking salvation, and the Bands were for Christians seeking entire sanctification. The Select Bands consisted of sanctified Christians of superior maturity and good judgment. The Select Band was an interesting innovation that Wesley formed of those who longed to walk "in the light of God's countenance." He wanted a select company with which to share in confidence his hopes, cautions, defeats, and victories. He was willing to accept the Select Band's counsel because he considered the members as equal to him in wisdom and judgment. The Select band did not take root in America, and it had a short life in Great Britain.

[117] 1 Cor. 14:31.

[118] To prophesy is not always to foresee the future. The term can also mean to declare and apply truth. For example, such prophets as Isaiah, Jeremiah, and Ezekiel spoke of future events and also of current realities close at hand.

[119] Prov. 24:6.

[120] James 5:16.

of those who through love became servants to one another.[121] In addition to the Class Leaders and Band Leaders (of which I spoke above), there are Assistants, Stewards, Visitors of the sick, and Schoolmasters.

2. In the third part of the *Appeal*,[122] I mentioned how we came to accept Lay Assistants.[123] Their office is to minister in the absence of the minister, and their duties are as follows:

(i) To preach every morning and evening.

(ii) To meet weekly with the united society, the bands, the select society, and the penitents.

(iii). To visit each of the classes once a quarter.

(iv). To hear and mediate all disagreements.

(v) To put the disorderly back on trial, and to receive on trial members for the Methodist societies or bands.

(vi). To see that the Stewards, the Readers, and the Schoolmasters faithfully discharge their different offices.

(vii). To meet weekly with the leaders of the bands and classes and the stewards. In addition, the lay assistants are to examine their financial accounts.[124]

---

[121] Gal. 5:13.

[122] In the 1740s, John Wesley wrote two important apologetic works defending Methodism and its doctrines. In 1743, he published *An Earnest Appeal to Men of Reason and Religion* (about fifty-six pages). In 1747, he published a much longer apologetic, *A Farther Appeal to Men of Reason and Religion*. This work contains three major divisions, totaling more than 220 pages. The reference which Wesley cites here is from Part Three of *A Farther Appeal to Men of Reason and Religion*, where he discusses the state of religion in England.

[123] In 1739, John Wesley allowed qualified laymen to expound the Scriptures. In 1744, Wesley held his first conference of preachers. That first conference consisted of ten people—John and Charles Wesley, four Anglican clergymen, and four lay "Assistants." The second conference of Methodists defined the tests of those called to preach: (i) grace, (ii) gifts, and (iii) success (fruits of their ministries). In 1747, the Methodist Conference distinguished between those "Helpers" who assisted in one place and those who went from place to place ("Traveling Preachers"). After a period of probation, a traveling preacher could enter into "full connexion" as a preacher. These preachers received a modest allowance for their families, and the rules forbade them from engaging in a trade or business.

[124] Later, these rules expanded to "Twelve Rules of a Helper," which were well known by early Methodist preachers:

(1) Be diligent. Never be unemployed a moment. Never be triflingly employed. Never while away time; neither spend any more time at any place than is strictly necessary.

(2) Be serious. Let your motto be, "Holiness to the Lord." Avoid all lightness, jesting, and foolish talking.

(3) Converse sparingly and cautiously with women; particularly, with young women.

(4) Take no step toward marriage, without first consulting with your brethren.

3. I think one is not be a fool who has gifts equal to these duties. Neither can one void God's grace that is able to observe the following rules for Assistants.[125]

(1) Be diligent. Never be unemployed for a moment. Never be triflingly employed. Never while away time. Neither spend any more time at any place than is strictly necessary.

(2) Be serious. Let your motto be "Holiness to the Lord." Avoid all lightness,[126] as you would avoid hell fire.

(3). Believe evil of no one. If you *see* an evil action, that is enough. Yet take caution how you judge it. Put the best construction on everything. You know that a judge is supposed to be on the side of the prisoner.

(4). Speak evil of no one, lest your word would eat like an ulcer. Keep your thoughts to yourself, until you speak to the person of concern.

---

[125] (5) Believe evil of no one; unless you see it done, take heed how you credit it. Put the best construction on everything. You know the Judge is always supposed to be on the prisoner's side.

(6) Speak evil of no one; else your word especially would eat as doth a canker. Keep your thoughts within your own breast, till you come to the person concerned.

(7) Tell everyone what you think wrong in him, and that plainly, as soon as may be; else it will fester in your heart. Make all haste to cast the fire out of your bosom.

(8) Do not affect the gentleman. You have no more to do with this character than with that of a dancing-master. A Preacher of the gospel is the servant of all.

(9) Be ashamed of nothing but sin: Not of fetching wood (if time permit) or drawing water; not of cleaning your own shoes, or your neighbour's.

(10) Be punctual. Do everything exactly at the time. And in general, do not mend our Rules, but keep them; not for wrath, but for conscience' sake.

(11) You have nothing to do but to save souls. Therefore spend and be spent in this work. And go always, not only to those that want you, but to those that want you most.

Observe: It is not your business to preach so many times, and to take care of this or that society; but to save as many souls as you can; to bring as many sinners as you possibly can to repentance, and with all your power to build them up in that holiness without which they cannot see the Lord. And remember! A Methodist Preacher is to mind every point, great and small, in the Methodist discipline! Therefore you will need all the sense you have, and to have all your wits about you!

(12) Act in all things, not according to your own will, but as a son in the Gospel. As such, it is your part to employ your time in the manner which we direct; partly, in preaching and visiting from house to house; partly, in reading, meditation, and prayer. Above all, if you labour with us in our Lord's vineyard, it is needful that you should do that part of the work which we advise, at those times and places which we judge most for his glory.

[125] These ten rules for Assistants are a slight abridgment of John Wesley's Twelve Rules for a Helper (1744).

[126] One eighteenth-century meaning of *lightness* was levity in behavior, fickleness, unsteadiness, frivolity, thoughtlessness, or unconcern.

(5). Tell others what you think is wrong in them, and do so clearly and as soon as you can.[127] Otherwise, your concern will fester in your heart. As quickly as you can, cast the fire from you.

(6). Do nothing as does a gentleman.[128] You have no more to do with his character than with that of a dancing master. You are the servant of all.

(7). Be ashamed of nothing but sin—not of such chores as hewing wood or drawing water, if time permits it.[129]

(8). Take no money from anyone. If others give you food when you are hungry or clothes when you need them, it is good. But do not accept silver or gold. Let there be no occasion for others to say that we grow rich by the gospel.

(9). Be punctual. Do everything exactly at the appointed time.

(10). Act in everything, not according to your own will, but as a son in the gospel.[130]

4. In order to examine these preachers, before we accept them as Assistants, we ask them the following questions.

First: Do they know in whom they have believed?[131] Do they have the love of God in their hearts?[132] Are they holy in all their conduct?[133]

Second, Do they have both gifts and grace for preaching?[134] Do they have, at least in an acceptable degree, a clear, sound understanding of the gospel? Do they have good judgment in the things of God? Do they have a clear conception of

---

[127] In 1788, John Wesley published a sermon titled, "The Duty of Reproving our Neighbour." His text was Lev. 19:17, "Thou shalt not hate thy brother in thine heart: thou shalt in any wise rebuke thy neighbour, and not suffer sin upon him." ["Do not hate your brother in your heart. Rebuke your neighbor frankly so you will not share in his guilt"] (Lev. 19:17, NIV). Wesley believed, as did the Puritans before him, that Christians should engage both in self-examination and as consciences for each other. In that sermon, he said, "Love indeed requires us to warn him, not only of sin, (although of this chiefly,) but likewise of any error which, if it were persisted in, would naturally lead to sin. If we do not 'hate him in our heart,' if we love our neighbour as ourselves, this will be our constant endeavour; to warn him of every evil way, and of every mistake which tends to evil."

[128] Here, Wesley cautions against acting as if one of a high social rank whose chief concerns are affecting elegance in attire and manner. In Wesley's class conscious society, the term *gentleman* referred to a man of independent means who did not work gainfully. To "act the gentlemen" was to focus on outward appearance and frivolous social standards, to the neglect of serious matters, such as integrity, honor, and spiritual concerns.

[129] In Joshua 9:21, the phrase "hewers of wood and drawers of water" was a conventional phrase for servants used among the Hebrews.

[130] Phil. 2:22.
[131] 2 Tim. 1:12.
[132] Rom. 5:5.
[133] 1 Pet. 1:15.
[134] Rom. 12:6.

salvation by faith? Has God given them a measure of speaking ability? Can they express themselves correctly, unhesitatingly, and clearly?

Third, Are they successful in their preaching? When they preach, do they speak so as to affect and convince their hearers? Have any people received remission of their sins by their preaching? Do their hearers experience a clear and lasting sense of God's love?

5. Those preachers in whom these three marks are undeniably evident, we gladly receive into the work of our Preaching Assistants. Here is the advice we give them:

(i) Always arise at 4:00 a.m.

(ii) From 4:00 to 5:00 in the morning, and from 5:00 to 6:00 in the evening, engage in meditation, prayer, reading Scripture and a practical book of divinity.

Good books are,

- The Life of God in the Soul of Man[135]
- The Christian's Pattern[136]

---

[135] *The Life of God in the Soul of Man*, was written by Henry Scougal (1650-1678), a Scottish theologian, clergyman, and author. While a pastor and professor of divinity at King's College at the University of Aberdeen, Scougal wrote a number of well-circulated books on theology. In addition to his published works, Scougal was also known for his piety, understanding of Scripture, and expertise in Latin, Hebrew, Greek, and several of the cognate oriental languages. In addition to English, he spoke Hebrew, Latin, and several Asian languages. Originally, Scougal wrote *The Life Of God In The Soul Of Man* for a friend who had lost his faith. Scougal's book dispels several incorrect ideas about the nature of God, extols the present and eternal benefits of true religion, and explains the challenges that face the followers of Jesus Christ. He encourages our dependence upon God's assistance, and he stresses the importance of studying the Bible in shaping one's life. Susanna Wesley pronounced this volume "an excellent good book," and she recommended it to her son, John Wesley. Both John and Charles Wesley studied *The Life of God in the Soul of Man*, and John published six editions of it—placing it first in his list of recommended books. A number of leaders in the eighteenth-century religious awakening, including John and Charles Wesley. George Whitefield praised this book and he said that he learned from it that "true religion is a union of the soul with God, or Christ formed within us, a ray of divine light instantaneously darted in upon [the] soul."

[136] *The Christian's Pattern* is an alternate title for *A Treatise of The Imitation of Jesus Christ*, in Latin by Thomas à Kempis (c. 1380–1471). Thomas à Kempis was a Dutch Roman Catholic priest and a member of the famed Brothers and Sisters of the Common Life, organized by Geert Groote in 1374 in the Netherlands and later in Germany. The aim of that group was to emulate the life and virtues of the first Christians, including loving God and serving others with simplicity, humility, devotion, and love. Thomas à Kempis's *Imitation of Jesus Christ* emphasizes denying self and bringing one's entire life to conform to the pattern exemplified in the life of Jesus. Wesley published an English edition of this work in 1735.

- Bishop Beveridge's Private Thoughts upon a Christian Life[137]
- Mr. Law's practical *Works*.[138]
- Dr. Heylin's Devotional Tracts[139]

[137] William Beveridge (1637–1708), an Anglican bishop, is noted for his eminence in Oriental scholarship and ecclesiastical learning. Beveridge also wrote theological works and *Exposition of The Thirty-Nine Articles* of the Church of England. John Wesley later edited these Anglican XXXIX Articles, and prepared Twenty-Four Articles of Religion for the newly-formed Methodist Episcopal Church in America. These articles comprise part of the stated doctrinal standards of the United Methodist Church. Beveridge's major work was his collection of the Apostolic Cannons (works attributed to the original apostles) and the records of eleven early church councils—*Pandectae Cononum Conciliorum*, a large two-volume folio of ancient Eastern liturgical texts. Reviewing this work, John Wesley wrote in his journal, "Nothing so effectively have convinced us that . . . Councils may err, and have erred. . . . [T]hings ordained by Councils as necessary to salvation have neither strength nor authority unless they be taken out of Holy Scripture" (Journal, 13 September 1736).

Beveridge with Anthony Horneck and William Smythies, was chiefly responsible for the spread of Anglican voluntary religious societies in London in the 1680s. These were religious associations in the Church of England. In Beveridge's *Private Thoughts upon a Christian Life* (1709) he expressed deep concern that in England "[Scripture's] doctrine and precepts are so generally slighted and neglected" and that "so little of Christianity is now to be found among Christians themselves." Canon J. H. Overton declared, "For plain, homely piety, and practical usefulness in his generation, no name stands higher on the role of English churchmen than that of William Beveridge." [*Life in the English Church, 1660–1714* (London: Longmans, Green and Company, 1885), 76].

[138] William Law (1686–1761), an Anglican clergyman, theologian, and writer, wrote several books on the Christian life, including *On Christian Perfection* (1726) and *A Serious Call to a Devout and Holy Life* (1728). The latter volume's simplicity of message and energetic style established it as a devotional classic. In the eighteenth-century "age of reason" Law contended that, while reason is a noble faculty, it has limitations. Law argued compellingly that Christians need faith to carry them to the fullness of truth and reality. John Wesley wrote, "[In the late 1720s] Mr. Laws 'Christian Perfection' and 'Serious Call' were put into my hands. These convinced me, more than ever, of the absolute impossibility of being half a Christian; and I determined, through [God's] grace . . . to be all-devoted to God, to give him all my soul, my body, and my substance. Will any considerate man say that . . . anything less is due to Him who has given himself for us, than to give him ourselves, all we have, and all we are?" Similarly, George Whitfield was influenced by reading William Law's books. Whitefield recalled, "Before I went to the University [of Oxford], I met with Mr. Law's 'Serious Call to a Devout Life' . . . . God worked powerfully upon my soul, as He has since upon many others, by that and his other excellent treatise upon 'Christian Perfection.'"

[139] John Heylyn (c. 1685–1759) was an Anglican clergyman who influenced the religious atmosphere in eighteenth century England. At a crucial time in John Wesley's life (10 May 1738, two weeks prior to his Aldersgate heartwarming experience), he heard Heylyn preach a "truly Christian sermon" on "They were all filled with the Holy Ghost." In that sermon Heylyn declared "And so may all of you be [filled with the Holy Spirit] if it is not your own fault." Wesley also heard Heylyn preach a sermon on "feigned and hypocritical repentance." Wesley concluded that he (Wesley) had been a hypocrite for twenty years. Heylyn's mystical bent led others to label him "the Mystic Doctor." Heylyn wrote *Theological lectures at Westminster Abbey, with an interpretation of the four gospels, to which are*

- The Life of Mr. Halyburton[140] and of Mr. de Renty[141]

(iii) From six in the morning until twelve, to read, in order, slowly, and with prayer,

- Bishop Pearson on the Creed[142]

---

added some select discourses upon the principal points of revealed religion (1749 John Wesley consulted that work as he wrote his *Explanatory Notes upon the New Testament*. Heylyn was buried in Westminster Abbey.

[140] Thomas Halyburton (1674–1712) wrote a famous autobiography, *Memoirs*, which Wesley edited and published in 1739. Halyburton was a Scottish Presbyterian theologian, pastor and apologist. He pastored a church for ten years, after which he became Professor of Theology at St. Leonard's College in St. Andrews, Scotland. Halyburton's theological and apologetic writings are marked by meticulous care. His published sermons reveal that he was richly theological, "experimental" [experiential], and practical. Halyburton was a master of the classic Puritan style of preaching. He was indebted to the English Puritan, John Owen (1616-1683), yet Halyburton's sermons were more direct and popular in style. In 1715, Halyburton's widow published his spiritual memoirs with an account of his dying discourse. In 1739, John Wesley and George Whitefield added their own foreword to an abridged edition of this volume. In a 1771 letter to a member of the Methodist Society, John Wesley wrote, "It is desirable to glorify God, like Mr. de Renty or Halyburton, in death, as well as in life."

[141] Gaston Jean Baptiste de Renty (1611–1649) was a French Roman Catholic aristocrat and philanthropist. In 1638, after reading of Thomas à Kempis's *Imitation of Christ*, de Renty abandoned public life and devoted himself to the service of the needy and suffering. John Wesley recommended reading de Renty for his disciplined pattern of a devotional life. John Wesley wrote a tract titled, *A Disavowal of Persecuting Papists*, in which he said, "I agree not only that many of these [Roman Catholics] in former ages were good men, (as Thomas à Kempis, Francis Sales, and the Marquis de Renty,) but that many of them are so at this day. I believe, I know some Roman Catholics who sincerely love both God and their neighbour, and who steadily endeavour to do unto every one as they wish him to do unto them." De Renty wrote, "All work is prayer when it is done for God and this work prays of itself and honours God." In 1658, John Baptiste Saint-Jure wrote *The Holy Life of M. de Renty, a Late Nobleman of France*. This work was translated into English by E. S. Gent. In 1741, Wesley published an abridged edition of this biography, which Wesley included in his *Christian Library* collection.

[142] John Pearson (1613–86) was a king's scholar at Eton from 1623 to 1631. One story tells that he lit a candle after the rest of the dormitory was asleep, and into the night he read most of the Greek and Latin Church Fathers before leaving school and matriculating at Cambridge. Pearson became Bishop of Chester in England in 1673. *The Oxford Dictionary of the Christian Church* states, "He was perhaps the most erudite and profound divine of a learned and theological age." Pearson's *Exposition of the [Apostles] Creed* (1659) began as a series of lectures extending over several years. Pearson explained that he wrote this word for both unlearned and learned readers, and that 'the body of it containeth fully what can be delivered and made intelligible in the English tongue', and in the margin is contained whatsoever is necessary for the illustration of any part of the Creed, as to them which have any knowledge of the Latin, Greek, and Oriental languages, of the writings of the ancient Fathers, the doctrines of the Jews, and the history of the Church. (J. Pearson, "To the reader', An Exposition of the Creed," 1659). In its final form, this study of the Apostles' Creed is characterized by clarity, precision, and remarkable insight. As soon as Pearson's book on the Apostles Creed appeared, others recognized it as a work conveying the

- Bishop Fell on the Epistles[143]
- Mr. Boehm's[144] and Mr. Nalson's Sermons[145]
- Mr. Pascal's *Thoughts*[146]

---

theological and liturgical fundamentals of the Church of England. Albert Outler deemed Pearson's work as "a landmark in Anglican theology." John Wesley said that Bishop Pearson was "a man no ways inferior to Bishop Chrysostom."

[143] John Fell (1625–86) was Bishop of Oxford and concurrently the Dean of Christ Church, Oxford. He was a writer who took a keen interest in the intellectual and spiritual development of young scholars at Oxford. Dr. Fell edited and published many works, including editions of the classics and of the early church fathers. Yearly, he published a new book, usually an annotated edition of a classical author, which he distributed to the students of Christ Church College at Oxford. After Oliver Cromwell's time as Lord Protector of England, Fell re-established the Oxford University Press. Wesley's reference to "Bishop Fell on the Epistles," could refer to one or both of Fell's works on St. Paul's epistles: (1) A critical edition of the epistles of St. Cyprian (Oxford University Press, 1682) or (2) *A Paraphrase and Annotations upon the Epistles of St.* Paul (1675), in which Fell had an editorial part.

[144] John Wesley was influenced by the German Pietists, members of a renewal movement in German Lutheranism, one of which was Johann Arndt, who in 1606 wrote the widely influential book, *Vier Bücher vom Wahres Christenthum (True Christianity)*. This book takes the reader beyond a formal understanding of Christ's atonement in forensic terms, and applies Christ's atonement to the personal and experiential work of God in our hearts. Anthony William Boehm (1673–1722) translated this widely read book into English, and John Wesley included it the first volume of his *Christian Library*. Boehm's translations of the works of German Pietists into Latin and English express his desire to spread a classic, non-sectarian Christianity that would transcend denominational differences. Boehm's own published works included sermons, catechisms, and his major treatise *Enchiridion Precum (Manual of Prayer*, 1715), which consisted of prayers and extracts in more than fifty categories. Most of his published sermons were collected in *Several Discourses and Tracts for Promoting the Common Interest of True Christianity* (1717). Boehm's literary output influenced many Anglicans, Puritan nonconformists, and evangelicals. He ranks as a respected non-Anglican writer who promoted neglected Reformation truths during the era between Puritanism and the eighteenth-century evangelical revival led by John Wesley.

[145] Valentine Nalson (1683–1723) was the Anglican vicar of St. Martin's Church in York. He authored *Twenty Sermons Preached in the Cathedral of York* (published in 1724; second edition in 1737).

[146] Blaise Paschal (1623–62) was a French Roman Catholic mathematician, scientist, and philosopher. In 1654, he had a life-changing experience of God, which redirected his interests to spiritual concerns. He began to sketch a defense of the Christian faith, but at age thirty-nine he died prematurely. The fragments of his work were published under the title, *Pensées (Thoughts)*. He sought to persuade non-Christians that human being cannot be truly happy apart from God. For those who had no confidence in God, he formulated his famous "Paschal's Wager," which contends that there is nothing to lose and much to gain in believing in God. Paschal contended that we know the truth about God not only through reason, but also through the heart.

- Cave's[147] and Fleury's[148] *Primitive Christianity*
- Echard's *Ecclesiastical History*[149]

We believe that those who thoroughly digest only these few books will know enough to save both their own souls and those that hear them.

X.

1. Long before approving lay preachers, however, I felt the weight of a far different concern—the care of temporal things. By a rough calculation, the quarterly subscriptions in our Methodist society came to more than three hundred pounds a year. This money paid for repairs on buildings, as well as other necessary expenses and debts. The contributions were a little less than eight pounds weekly, and this money went to those who had temporal needs.[150]

---

[147] William Cave (1637–1713) was a Patristic scholar who gained recognition for the thoroughness of his research, comprehensiveness of his style, and the clear arrangement of his work. Cave is known for his written works of patristic scholarship and church history. In 1673 he published his first book *Primitive Christianity, or the Religion of the Ancient Christians in the First Ages of the Gospel*. This work features ecclesiastical writers up to the fourteenth century. The two-volume work is of high quality, and it went through many editions. Cave's writings provide valuable support for the study of patristic writers, the study of which John Wesley held a lifetime interest.

[148] Claude Fleury (1640–1723) was f French Roman Catholic priest who was Prior of Notre-Dame-d'Argenteuil and tutor to the young Louis XV. Wesley's reference is to the first two volumes of Fleury's twenty volume *Histoire Ecclésiastique* (Paris: 1691). Subsequent editions were larger. To prepare for this history, for thirty years Fleury collected materials. Fleury's historical work was the first large-scale history of the Christian Church to gain scholarly recognition for its scholarship and balance. Wesley admired Fleury, whom others recognized as a person of vast learning, modest simplicity, upright conduct, and respected integrity.

[149] Laurence Echard (c.1670–1730 graduated from Christ's College, Cambridge, was ordained an Anglican priest, and he served in that capacity in a parish and at Lincoln Cathedral. As a writer, his chief work was *The History of England: From the First Entrance of Julius Caesar and the Romans to the end of the Reign of King James the first containing the space of 1678 years*. (1707–1718). Wesley's reference here is to Echard's *A General Ecclesiastical History from the Nativity of Our Blessed Saviour to the First Establishment of Christianity by Human Laws Under the Emperor Constantine the Great*. Echard deserves to be remembered as a path-breaking work in two fields: the history of the Roman republic and the history of England. He represents the scholarly activity of the Anglican clergy before the transfer of the historical profession from private scholars to the universities.

[150] In the eighteenth century, indifference toward the sufferings of the poor was palpable. Neither the church, the state, nor employers demonstrated concern for the needs of those "beneath" them. John Wesley and the early Methodists focused on the needs of these neglected people. Wesley's chief constituency consisted mostly of "Christ's poor." He devised arrangements for work for the poor, and established loan offices, and medical dispensaries to help people rise from poverty. One of Wesley's early biographers estimates that Wesley distributed more than £30,000 of his personal money during his lifetime, mostly, from the proceeds derived from his books.

The society expected me to supervise these matters. However, this responsibility was a burden I was not able to bear.[151] Therefore, at first I chose one, then four, and after a time, seven men who were as prudent as any men I knew. I asked them to take charge of these temporal matters so that I might have no encumbrances pertaining to financial concerns. We called these men *Stewards*.

2. The business of the Stewards is as follows:

    (i) To manage the temporal concerns of the society.

    (ii) To receive the subscriptions and contributions.

    (iii) From time to time to spend what is necessary.

    (iv) To send relief to the poor.

    (v) To keep an exact account of all receipts and expenses.

    (vi) To inform the minister if any of the rules of the society were not punctually observed.

    (vii) In a loving spirit, to speak to the preachers, if they believe anything is amiss in their doctrine or life.

3. Here are the rules of the Stewards:

    (i) To be frugal. To save everything they honestly can.

    (ii) To spend no more than they receive. Never contract any debts.

    (iii) To have no overdue accounts. Pay everything within the week.

    (iv) To give no unkind word or unpleasant look to anyone who asks for financial help. If you cannot help them, do not hurt them.

    (v) To expect no thanks from anyone.

4. Every Thursday, the stewards are to meet at six in the morning. Their duty is to consult about the business that comes before them and to send relief to the sick and those in need. The stewards are to give the remainder of the weekly contributions to those who appear to have the most pressing needs. This way, all business concludes within the week. For instance, what the people give on Tuesday, the stewards are regularly to expend by Thursday.

I soon had the pleasure of finding that the stewards did all these temporal things with the utmost faithfulness and accuracy. Thus, my concerns of these

---

In Wesley's sermon "The Use of Money," he set forth three dictums: Gain all you can; Save all you can; Give all you can. He closed that sermon by saying, "Give all ye have, as well as all ye are, a spiritual sacrifice to Him who withheld not from you his Son, his only Son: So laying up in store for yourselves a good foundation against the time to come, that ye may attain eternal life!'" Wesley's advice "save all you can" did not mean that one should build up a large bank account. Rather, the advice was to spend only what is necessary in order to have funds to help others in need.

[151] Due to his almost constant travel, his voluminous writing, sermon preparation, and general oversight of the Methodist movement.

kinds ended. I needed only to revise the accounts, tell the lay assistants if I thought anything needed change, and to discuss how from time to time we might correct any financial deficiencies. We were very far from abundance, so financial shortages were frequent and large. Our income was by no means adequate for the expenses.

We did not faint,[152] because sometimes in the periods of our greatest perplexity we received unforeseen help. At other times, we borrowed larger or smaller amounts, of which the greatest part we have since repaid. To this day, I owe some hundred pounds—so much have I gained by preaching the gospel![153]

XI.

1. It was not long before the stewards found a great problem with regard to the sick. Some were about to die before the stewards knew about their illnesses. Even when they did know about them, the stewards, being people generally employed in a trade, could not visit the sick as often as they wished.

2. When I learned about this problem, I laid the matter before the whole society. I explained how impossible it was for the stewards to visit all that were sick in every part of the town. I asked the leaders of the classes to inquire more carefully and more persistently to inform the stewards of the sick. I asked the members of the society, "Who among you is willing and able to supply this lack of service to the sick?"

3. The next morning many willingly offered themselves. I chose forty-six of those who I judged to have of the most tender and loving spirits. I divided London into twenty-three parts, and I asked groups of two to visit the sick in each area.

4. These are the duties of those who visit the sick:

(i) To see every sick person within his district three times weekly.

(ii) To inquire into the state of their souls, and to counsel them as circumstances require.

(iii) To inquire into their physical disorders, and procure advice for them.

(iv) To relieve them, if they were financially in need.

(v) To do anything for them that they can.

(vi) Weekly, to bring in their financial accounts to the other stewards.

---

[152] Gal. 6:9.

[153] 1 Cor. 9:14. Some critics accused Wesley of becoming wealthy from the donations of poor people. Elsewhere in this book, Wesley shows how preposterous was that allegation. See pp. 67-68 where Wesley discusses his income.

On reflection, I saw that we had emulated the primitive church in the matter of visiting the sick.[154] What were the ancient Deacons?[155] What was Phoebe the Deaconess, but such a visitor of the sick?[156]

5. I did not think it was necessary to give the deacons any particular rules other than the following:

(i) Be clear and open in dealing with souls.

(ii) Be gentle, tender, and patient.

(iii) Be clean in everything you do for the sick.[157]

(iv) Do not be fastidious, over-sensitive, or squeamish.[158]

6. Since we had already established rules for Stewards, we have had good reason to praise God for his continued blessing on their ministry to the sick. Many lives have been saved, many sicknesses healed, much pain and need prevented or removed. Many heavy hearts have become glad, and many who grieve were comforted. Those who visited the sick receive from God, whom they serve, a present reward for all their labor.

XII.

1. Nonetheless, I remained distressed that many of the poor were sick. Our efforts help them were costly, yet with such small results. First, I was determined

---

[154] Matt, 25:36; James 5:14. In Sermon #13 of Wesley's series of sermons on Christ's Sermon on the Mount, Wesley said, "Are you zealous of good works? Do you, as you have time, do good to all men? Do you feed the hungry, and clothe the naked, and visit the fatherless and widow in their affliction? Do you visit those that are sick? Relieve them that are in prison? Is any a stranger, and you take him in? Friend, come up higher!"

[155] 1 Tim. 3:8–12.

[156] Rom. 16:1. Commenting on the ministry of deaconesses, Wesley said in his *Notes upon the New Testament*, "It was their office . . . to visit the sick, the women in particular, and to minister to them both in their temporal and spiritual necessities."

[157] So far as can be determined, John Wesley first used in print the phrase, "Cleanliness is next to godliness." In 1786, Wesley published in the *Arminian Magazine* a sermon titled, "On Visiting the Sick," in which he said, "Together with the more important lessons, which you endeavour to teach all the poor whom you visit, it would be a deed of charity to teach them two things more, which they are generally little acquainted with, — industry and cleanliness. It was said by a pious man, 'Cleanliness is next to godliness.' Indeed the want of it is a scandal to all religion; causing the way of truth to be evil spoken of."

[158] Wesley's eighteenth-century wording for this directive is, "Be not nice." The OED has seventeen categories of meanings for the word *nice*. Before attempting to define *nice*, that dictionary says, "The precise development of the very divergent senses which this word has acquired in English is not altogether clear. In many examples from the 16th and 17th centuries it is difficult to say in what particular sense the writer intended it to be taken." Wesley obviously used the word in a negative sense. This transcription supplies Here, Wesley's probable meaning of *nice*, in this case is to be *fastidious, over-sensitive*, or *squeamish*.

to seek more help for the sick from the hospitals. On trying this plan, we found that it was indeed less costly, but there was no more good done for the sick than before I asked for assistance. Next, I asked the advice of several physicians concerning the sick, but this effort still did not help those who were ill. I saw the poor people languishing away, and several families were ruined. There was no remedy.[159]

2. Finally, I thought of a desperate measure: I myself would prepare and give medicine to the sick. For twenty-six or twenty-seven years, I had used my leisure hours to study sickness and medicine. I never formally studied the healing arts, except for a few months when I was preparing to go to America. I concluded that I might be of some service to those who had no regular physician among them. Therefore, I applied myself again to the study of medicine, and I engaged an apothecary and an experienced surgeon to assist me.[160] At the same time, I resolved not to go out of my depth. I would leave all difficult and complicated cases to those physicians that the patients would choose.

3. After I started the Methodist Society in London, I notified the people of my decision to help the sick. I also informed all who were ill of a chronic disorder that I did not care to attempt to treat acute ailments. I said that, if they wished to come to me at a certain time, I would give them the best advice I could, and the best medicines I had.

4. Many came to me, and they continued every Friday thereafter. Among them was William Kirkman, a weaver, near Old Nichol street. I asked him, "What

---

[159] In eighteenth-century England, many hospitals were less curative places than as locations where apprenticed doctors could experiment with medicines and cures. Hospitals tended to be hotbeds of disease. Frequent medical practices included bleedings, and cold water baths. Tar water was the panacea for many human ills. On entering these hospitals, patients were required to pay a refundable "burial fee" in case of their death. Hospital janitors, porters, and other workers demanded shillings for their services and clerks required money for required paperwork.

[160] In 1747, John Wesley published his *Primitive Physic*, which he revised and expanded in twenty-two editions. He did not claim to know how remedies worked, but rather he only reported what he observed that did work. He wrote, "I undertake barely to set down what appears in nature; not the cause of the appearances." Two of his cures for a bruise were to "apply treacle (molasses) spread on brown paper" or use "a plaster of chopped parsley mixt with butter." To relieve a cough he suggested that one "make a hole through a lemon and fill it with honey. Roast it and catch the juice. Take a tea-spoon of this frequently." For hoarseness and loss of voice, Wesley recommended applying "pounded garlic to the soles of the feet." Some of Wesley's recommended cures are now mocked. Other suggested cures are in line with proven treatments, such as applying honey to a wound. Wesley's approval of fresh air, cold water, exercise, prayer, and tranquility often worked effectively. In any case, Wesley did not recommend the sometimes lethal remedies that doctors attempted in that day.

medical complaint do you have?" "O, Sir," he said, "a cough, a very sore cough. I can get no rest day or night."

I asked, "How long have you had it?" He replied, "About thirty years: It began when I was eleven years old." I was not happy that this man came to me first, because I feared others would be discouraged if I could not cure him. However, I looked up to God, and then said to Kirkman, "Take this three or four times a day. If it does you no good, it will not harm you." He took the medicine two or three days. His cough healed, and it has not returned to this day.

5. Now, let candid people judge. Does humility require me to deny a notorious fact? If not, which of these is prideful: To say that I by my own skill restored this man to health, or to say that God did it by his almighty power? I do not know in what way this is boasting. I will give no name to such a fact as this. I leave that to the Rev. Dr. Middleton.[161]

6. In five months, I gave medicines to more than five-hundred people. Several of these I had never seen before they came to me. I did not consider whether they belonged to the Methodist Society. At that time, seventy-one of these people who regularly took their medicines and following the prescribed regimen were completely cured of maladies long thought to be incurable. (Three out of four would not take the medicine I offered.) During this time, the total cost of medicines was almost £40. We have continued this ministry ever since, and, by the blessing of God, with more and more success.

XIII.

1. For some years, I had observed that many people who, although not sick, were not able to support themselves. They had no one who cared to provide for them. Most were feeble and aged widows. I consulted with the stewards about how to relieve these elderly people. The stewards agreed that if we could keep

---

[161] This sentence is a satirical reference to the arrogant Conyers Middleton (1683–1750), who denied the possibility of divine healing. Middleton was a gifted writer, but irascible and condescending. He wrote a 373-page treatise titled, *A Free Inquiry Into the Miraculous Powers, Which Are Supposed to Have Subsisted in the Christian Church*. This book denied the miracles in the Bible and denounced the early Apostolic Fathers and Apologists as guilty of superstitious errors. John Wesley wrote Middleton a letter saying, "In your late 'Inquiry, you endeavour to prove, First, that there were no miracles wrought in the primitive Church: Secondly, that all the primitive Fathers were fools or knaves, and most of them both one and the other. And it is easy to observe, the whole tenor of your argument tends to prove, Thirdly, that no miracles were wrought by Christ or his Apostles; and, Fourthly, that these too were fools or knaves, or both. I am not agreed with you on any of these heads. My reasons I shall lay before you, in as free a manner, though not in so smooth or laboured language, as you have laid yours before the world."

them in one house, it would be much less expensive for us and much more comfortable for them. Certainly, we had no money with which to begin. However, we believed that God who defends the "cause of the widow" would provide for them.[162] So we leased two small houses nearby, and we made them warm and clean. We took in as many widows as we had room for, providing for them what is necessary for the body. Toward the cost, I first set aside the weekly contributions of the bands. I also set aside all that was collected at the Lord's Supper. Certainly, this amount did not suffice, and we became considerably in debt on this account. Nonetheless, we are certain that it will not always be so, because the earth is the Lord's and all that is in it.[163]

2. In this arranged community (commonly called The Poor House)[164] we now have nine widows, a blind woman, two poor children, two upper-servants,[165] a maid, and a man. I might add that there are four or five preachers. I, as well as the other preachers who are in town, eat with the poor—the same food at the same table. We rejoice in this, as a pleasant foretaste of our eating bread together in our Father's kingdom.[166]

---

[162] Psa. 68:5.

[163] Psa. 24:1; 1 Cor. 10:26.

[164] On 7 May 1741, Wesley wrote in his journal" I reminded the United Society, that many of our brethren and sisters had not needful food; many were destitute of convenient clothing; many were out of business, and that without their own fault; and many sick and ready to perish: That I had done what in me lay to feed the hungry, to clothe the naked, to employ the poor, and to visit the sick; but was not, alone, sufficient for these things; and therefore desired all whose hearts were as my heart" He asked the Methodists to bring what clothes they could spare and to give a penny a week, or what they could afford, to relieve the poor and sick. His journal for 15–17 February 1744 records, "We observed Friday, 17, as a day of solemn fasting and prayer. In the afternoon, many being met together, I exhorted them, now, while they had opportunity, to make to themselves . . . to deal their bread to the hungry, to clothe the naked. . . . And God opened their hearts, so that they contributed near fifty pounds, which I began laying out the very next hour, in linen, woollen, and shoes for them whom I knew to be diligent and yet in want." In 1747, Wesley fitted two houses for needy and deserving widows. Financial support came from collections given by the bands and by voluntary offerings.

[165] In eighteenth-century England, position and status were prevalent throughout society, even in the ranks of servants. Domestics were divided into classes of Upper Servants and Lower Servants. The supervising Upper Servants were entitled to respect and deference from the Lower Servants. Upper Servants included the housekeeper, the governess, the lady's maid, the butler, the valet, and the house steward. Lower Servants included cooks, housemaids, kitchen maids, and the footmen, who cared for the fireplaces, cleared tables, and washed dishes.

[166] Matt. 26:29; Luke 22:30.

3. I have blessed God for this house ever since it began, recently even more than ever. I honor these widows, for they are "widows indeed."[167] So that it is not in vain, that, without any plan to do so, we have copied another of the institutions of the Apostolic Age. I can now say to all the world, "Come and see how these Christians love one another!"[168]

XIV.

1. Another thing that gave me frequent concern was the abundance of needy children. Their parents could not afford to place them in school, and these children remained like a wild donkey's colt.[169] Some went to school, and learned how to read and write. However, at the same time they learned all kinds of vice. It would have been better for them to be without their knowledge, than to have bought it at so costly a price.[170]

---

[167] 1 Tim. 5:3. The term τας όντως χήρας means *really widows; widows indeed;* or *widows in the full sense.* These widows were constant in their religious duties and had no one to support them. St. Paul teaches that the church has a special obligation to them. The apostle says of them, "Let a widow be put on the list if she is not less than sixty years old and has been married only once; she must be well attested for her good works, as one who has brought up children, shown hospitality, washed the saints' feet, helped the afflicted, and devoted herself to doing good in every way" (1 Tim. 5:1–10). Wesley, in his *Notes upon the New Testament*, commented on the stipulation *married only once*: "That is, having lived in lawful marriage, whether with one or more persons successively."

[168] This sentence based on 1 Tim. 5:3 does not appear in the later editions of *A Plain Account of the Methodists.*

[169] Job 11:12.

[170] Matt. 26:29; Luke 22:30.

[170] 1 Tim. 5:3. The term τας όντως χήρας means *really widows; widows indeed;* or *widows in the full sense.* These widows were constant in their religious duties and had no one to support them. St. Paul teaches that the church has a special obligation to them. The apostle says of them, "Let a widow be put on the list if she is not less than sixty years old and has been married only once; she must be well attested for her good works, as one who has brought up children, shown hospitality, washed the saints' feet, helped the afflicted, and devoted herself to doing good in every way" (1 Tim. 5:1–10). Wesley in his *Notes upon the New Testament*, commented on the stipulation *married only once*: "That is, having lived in lawful marriage, whether with one or more persons successively."

[170] This sentence based on 1 Tim. 5:3 does not appear in the later editions of *A Plain Account of the Methodists.*

[170] Job 11:12.

[170] In eighteenth-century England, the "grammar schools" had sprung from the rubble of the monasteries that, from 1536–40, King Henry VIII had ordered destroyed. In Wesley's day, those in charge of these schools for boys brazenly abused the endowments of these schools. Late in the century England's Lord Chief Justice judged that the schools with large endowments "are empty [and] everything is neglected by the so-called schoolmasters but the receipt of salaries and endowments." Schools for girls focused on devotional books, embroidery, French, "deportment," and household management. John Wesley's assessment

2. Eventually, I determined to have the children taught in my own house so that they might have an opportunity of learning to read, write, and add (if no more) without being under almost a necessity of learning heathenism at the same time. After several unsuccessful trials, I found two schoolmasters that I needed. They were honest men of adequate knowledge, who had talents for the work, and their hearts were in it.

3. They now have nearly sixty children under their care: The parents of some pay for their schooling; but most of them, being very poor, do not. Voluntary contributions defray the expense. Recently, we have clothed as many of them as needed help.

Here are the rules of the school:

(i) We admit no child under the age of six.

(ii) All the children are to be present at the morning sermon.

(iii) They are at school from six to twelve, and from one to five.

(iv) They have no play days.[171]

(v) No child is to speak while in school, except to the schoolmasters.

---

of these schools for girls was negative. On one occasion he wrote, "In the afternoon I drank tea at Am. O. [Adam Oldham's]. But how was I shocked! The children that used to cling about me, and drink in every word, had been at a boarding-school. There they had unlearned all religion, and even seriousness; and had learned pride, vanity, affectation, and whatever could guard them against the knowledge and love of God. Methodist parents, who would send your girls headlong to hell, send them to a fashionable boarding-school!" (Journal, 6 April 1772).

[171]Today, most people concur that John Wesley and the first generation Methodists did not adequately understand child development. Wesley did not differ from his contemporaries. A marred understanding of children was common in the eighteenth century. On the other hand, Wesley's reaction to children was customarily sympathetic, loving, and warm. His close contacts with children revealed a loving tenderness that seems to go contrary to the stiff rule at the Methodist school for poor children that forbad "play days." Numerous chronicled accounts tell of adults who remembered the warm impressions of Wesley's love and kindness they formed when they encountered him when they were children. Leslie F. Church recorded several of these telling incidences of Wesley's interaction with children. Dr. Church wrote, "On 3rd June 1780 [Wesley] preached at Northallerton in a yard . . . A little girl six years of age, sat on her mother's knee and listened. Eighty years after she said she could still remember the sun shining on his face, nor did she ever forget his text: 'If the salt have lost its savor, wherewith shall be salted?' Afterwards she remembered walking by his side, clinging to the hem of his clerical gown. Children do not walk so intimately with those who do not care." [*The Early Methodist* People (London: The Epworth Press, 1948), 236.] One of Wesley's biographers, Thomas Jackson, wrote, "For nothing was [Wesley] so remarkable than his love to children. Often did he lay his hands upon them and bless them in the name of his great master." Despite Wesley's (and the eighteenth-century's) tendency to treat children as small adults, John Wesley's love and care for children was palpable.

(vi) The child who misses two days in one week, without an excuse, is excluded from the school.

4. We also appointed two stewards for the school. Their business is to receive the school's subscriptions, to spend what is necessary, to talk with each of the teachers weekly, twice weekly to pray with and encourage the children, diligently to ask whether the children are growing in grace and in learning,[172] and to know whether they promptly observe the rules. Each Tuesday morning, the stewards, in conjunction with the teachers, are to dismiss those children that do not observe the rules. Every Wednesday morning the stewards and teachers are to meet with and encourage the parents to nurture children at home in the ways of God.[173]

5. We soon observed a favorable change in the children with regard to their attitudes and behavior. They quickly learned reading, writing, and arithmetic. At the same time, they received diligent instruction in the principles of sound religion and an earnest encouragement to fear God, and work out their own salvation.[174]

XV.

1. A year or two ago, I observed among many society members another kind of anguish. Frequently, they lacked the money to carry on their business. On grounds of conscience, they did not want to go to a pawnbroker.[175] Yet, they did not know where to borrow the money they needed. I resolved to find a way to remedy this problem. In a few days, I went from one end of the town to the other to urge those who had this world's goods to assist their needy brothers. We received contributions totaling fifty pounds. Immediately, we placed this money in the hands of two stewards. Every Tuesday morning they met to lend to those who

---

[172] 2 Pet. 3:18.

[173] Deut. 6:7; 11:19; Prov. 22:6; Eph. 6:4.

[174] Phil. 2:12.

[175] Wesley's chief objection to pawn brokers was that in his day they misled, defrauded, and oppressed the poor. In Wesley's sermon, "The Use of Money," he wrote, "We are . . . to gain all we can, without hurting our neighbour. But this we may not, cannot do, if we love our neighbour as ourselves. We cannot, if we love every one as ourselves, hurt anyone *in his substance*. We cannot devour the increase of his lands, and perhaps the lands and houses themselves, by gaming, by over-grown bills, (whether on account of physic, or law, or anything else,) or by requiring or taking such interest as even the laws of our country forbid. Hereby all *pawn broking* is excluded: Seeing, whatever good we might do thereby, all unprejudiced men see with grief to be abundantly over-balanced by the evil. And if it were otherwise, yet we are not allowed to 'do evil that good may come.' [Rom. 3:8] We cannot, consistent with brotherly love, sell our goods below the market price; we cannot study to ruin our neighbour's trade, in order to advance our own, Much less can we entice away, or receive, any of his servants or workmen whom he has need of. None can gain by swallowing up his neighbour's substance, without gaining the damnation of hell!"

needed any small sum, not exceeding twenty shillings,[176] with repayment due in three months.[177]

2. It is almost inconceivable that the stewards' accounts accurately show that within the space of one year this small sum assisted two-hundred and fifty people. Will God not put it into the heart of some lover of humankind to increase this little stock of funds? If this is not "lending to the Lord," what is?[178] O, do not confer with anyone,[179] but help us immediately.

Join hands with God, to make a poor man live![180]

3. Now I now think you know all that I know about the Methodists. You see the nature, occasion, and aim of whatever the Methodists practiced. Further, I trust, you may be satisfactorily able to answer any questions that others may ask about them—particularly by those who inquire concerning my income, and what I do with all of it.

4. Some have supposed my income was no greater than that of the Bishop of London. Others calculated that I received £800 a year just from Yorkshire. Now, if that were so, out of all England I would receive not less than £10,000 a year!derar[181]

---

[176] It takes twenty shillings to equal one pound (20s=£1).

[177] No interest was charged, of course.

[178] Prov. 19:17.

[179] Gal. 1:16.

[180] Wesley adapted this line from a poem, *The Church Porch*, by George Herbert (1593–1633), an English poet and priest in the Church of England. Stanza 63 of this poem reads,
In Almes regard your means, and others merit.
Think heav'n a better bargain, then to give
Onely your single market-money for it.
Joyn hands with God to make a man to live.
Give to all something; to a good poore man,
Till thou change names, and be where he began.

[181] During the eighteenth century, wages were as low as two or three pounds per year for a domestic servant, plus food, lodging and clothing. A well paid servant earned about £8 a year, and a coachman's wages averaged about £18. Skilled artisans could earn about £40 yearly. The wealthy enjoyed a yearly benefit of about £500. The First Lord of the Treasury enjoyed a colossal income of £4,000. The rumor that Wesley received £10,000 yearly was preposterous. In fact, he was usually in debt because he gave money to construct Methodist chapels and to assist the needy.

Wesley's counsel to Sir James Lowther, a man of considerable financial means, reflected his own attitude toward money: "Upon the whole, I must once more earnestly entreat you to consider yourself, and God, and eternity. As to yourself, you are not the proprietor of anything; no, not of one shilling in the world. You are only a steward of what another entrusts you with, to be laid out, not according to your will, but his. And what would you think of your steward, if he laid out what is called your money, according to his own will and pleasure? Is not God the sole proprietor of all things? And are not you to give an account to him for every part of his goods? And O how dreadful an account, if you have expended any part of them not according to his will, but your own? Is not death at hand?

5. Accordingly, a man in Cornwall[182] extends the calculation of my income quite considerably. "Let me see," he said, "Two millions of Methodists; and each of these paying two-pence a week." If that were so, yearly I must receive £860,000, and some odd shillings and pence a-year.

6. A reasonable recompense![183] Whether my income is great or small, it means nothing at all to me. Everything contributed or collected in every place is received and expended by other people. Neither have I so much as feasted my eyes on the offerings. It will be this way unless I turn Turk or Pagan.[184] For I look on all this revenue (be it what it may) as sacred to God and to the poor. If I need anything, others relieve me, as they do for any other poor person. Originally, this was the case with all ecclesiastical revenues, as every person of learning knows.[185] Bishops and Priests used the people's offerings only in this way. If now any ministers use offerings otherwise, God help them![186]

7. I do not doubt that if I err in this or any other point, you will ask God to show me his truth. I strive always to keep my conscience clear before God and people,

Reverend and dear Sir,

Your affectionate brother and servant,

John Wesley

And are not you and I just stepping into eternity? Are we not just going to appear in the presence of God; and that naked of all worldly goods? Will you then rejoice in the money you have left behind you?"

[182] This person was John Collins, the Rector of Redruth in Cornwall, England. Collins was at Queen's College at Oxford at the same time that John Wesley was at Christ's Church College.

[183] Wesley, of course, was speaking sarcastically.

[184] Sarcasm again. By "Turks," Wesley meant followers of Mohamed; by "pagans," Wesley meant those who follow either no God or have a false God or Gods.

[185] Prior to Emperor Constantine and the Council of Nicea, early church bishops received no salary. Christian congregations provided the bare necessities for the clergy and for needy widows. Only in the fourth century did the clergy begin to receive any salary. Wesley received some income from his writings. However, he gave most of this income away, except what he needed to exist.

[186] As the case with many prominent religious leaders, some accused Wesley of plying religion for financial gain. In fact, he incurred debts from his charitable projects. He made a handsome income from his books and tracts, but as soon as he received money, he gave it away—in his later years up to £1,000 a year. The earliest biography of John Wesley states that Wesley gave away more than £30,000 in his lifetime. [Thomas Coke and Henry Moore, *The life of the Rev. John Wesley, A.M.: Including an account of the great revival of religion in Europe and America, of which he was the first and chief instrument*, 2 vols. (London: Printed by G. Paramore, 1792), 2:434.]

Selection 2

The Character of a Methodist

Editor's Introduction

The Character of a Methodist

John Wesley published *The Character of a Methodist* in 1742 when he was thirty-nine years old. Twenty-five years later (1767) he wrote a letter to *Lloyds Evening Post* explaining why he wrote this tract. In that letter, Wesley stated,

> Sir, Many times the publisher of *The Christian Magazine*[1] has attacked me without fear or wit; and hereby he has convinced his impartial readers of one thing at least, — that (as the vulgar say) his fingers itch to be at me; that he has a passionate desire to measure swords with me. But I have other work upon my hands: I can employ the short remainder of my life to better purpose. The occasion of his late attack is this: — Five or six and thirty years ago, I much admired the character of a perfect Christian drawn by Clemens Alexandrinus.[2] Five or six and twenty years

---

[1] This letter to the editor of *Lloyd's Evening Post* was in response to an attack against Wesley written by William Dodd and published in *The Christian Magazine*. Dodd was a flamboyant Anglican preacher whose extravagant sermons and writings attracted many followers. His criticism of Wesley was on the subject of entire sanctification. Dodd later forged the name of the Earl of Chesterfield, a benefactor, on a £4,000 bond, a crime for which he was executed by hanging. Before Dodd's death, Wesley visited him in prison.

[2] Clement of Alexandria (c.150–c. 215) was one of the first Christian theologians to use philosophy to defend Christianity. He claimed that Christianity was the "true philosophy" and that Jesus was the perfect model of reason and justice. On this basis, Clement urged the Greeks to leave corrupt pagan practices and turn to the virtuous Christian life.

ago, a thought came into my mind, of drawing such a character myself, only in a more scriptural manner, and mostly in the very words of Scripture: This I entitled, *The Character of a Methodist*, believing that curiosity would incite more persons to read it, and also that some prejudice might thereby be removed from candid men. But that none might imagine I intended a panegyric either on myself or my friends, I guarded against this in the very title-page, saying, both in the name of myself and them, "Not as though I had already attained, either were already perfect."[3] To the same effect I speak in the conclusion, "These are the principles and practices of our sect; these are the marks of a true Methodist;" i. e., a true Christian, as I immediately after explain myself: "By these alone do those who are in derision so called desire to be distinguished from other men. By these marks do we labour to distinguish ourselves from those whose minds or lives are not according to the Gospel of Christ."

This tract went through nineteen editions during Wesley's lifetime, and after his death uncounted printings continue to appear.

Wesley explained that when he was a young man he became deeply interested in religion. During that time, his reading of Clement of Alexandria's[4] description of Christian character convinced him that true wisdom is a heart-knowledge of God, which we receive by faith, apart from human merit or good deeds. For ten years, Wesley pondered Clement's description of a true Christian, and then wrote *The Character of a Methodist*. This publication details what he thought was a clear and biblical description of Christian character.

Wesley's publishers in Bristol and in London printed the tract and sold copies for two pence each. This tract was the first that Wesley wrote on the subject of entire sanctification. Later, he published *A Plain Account of Christian Perfection*, in

---

He contended that the Christian life is the pursuit of a perfection that unites moral discipline, intellectual training and the works that grow out of divine love for God and neighbor.

[3] Phil. 3:12. "Not that I have already obtained this or am already perfect; but I press on to make it my own, because Christ Jesus has made me his own." Here, the word τετελείωμαι = to fulfill; to complete; to mature; to accomplish; to make perfect . The verb is indicative perfect passive.

[4] Clement of Alexandra (c. 150–c. 215) was a Christian theologian in Egypt who attempted to answer the charge of pagan critics that Christianity it is a religion for ignorant people. He was the first to attempt a synthesis of the Bible and Greek philosophy. Clement stressed that all truth is part of a single whole. He believed that the Christian life is a quest for perfection. The way to perfection, he contended, is through religious discipline, training of the mind, and the reflection of divine love.

which he traced through several decades his development of the biblical theme of holiness. Wesley published the final edition of that work in 1777. Until Wesley's death in 1791, he promoted the ideal of entire sanctification with impressive vigor and lasting success. John S. Simon (1843–1933), a British Methodist historian stated, "The light of far-off days shone around [Wesley] as he wrote his pamphlet. But the light of the days in which he lived also guided him, and the experiences through which he had passed instructed him."[5]

The Character of a Methodist has four aims. First, Wesley points out that the term *Methodist* was not one he invented, but rather it was a term of derision thrust upon the Methodists by detractors. In a letter to the Bishop of Gloucester, Wesley explained the origin of *Methodist*: "Let it be well observed, that this is not a name which they [the Methodists] take upon themselves, but one fixed on them by way of reproach, without their approbation or consent." Charles Wesley wrote in his diary, "Diligence led me into serious thinking. I went to the weekly Sacrament, and persuaded two or three young scholars to accompany me, and to observe the method of study prescribed by the Statues of the University. This gained me the harmless name of Methodist."

Second, John Wesley shows that Methodism is not an innovative new religion recently sprung up in England. He insists that Methodism holds no new doctrines. He did not design a speculative system of esoteric thought. Wesley explains that the rise of Methodism was merely the result of sincere efforts to recover and propagate the central themes of the Scriptures and of the teachings and liturgies of the church, which many in his generation ignored or rejected. He declared, "Whatever doctrine is new must be wrong; for the old religion is the only true one; and no doctrine can be right, unless it is the very same which was from the beginning." Wesley's aim was the same as that of the Apostle Jude—"to contend for the faith that was once for all entrusted to the saints. For certain intruders have stolen in . . . who pervert the grace of our God.[6]

Third, *The Character of a Methodist* shows that Methodism seeks the biblical ideal of a radical transformation of one's entire life, not merely part of it. Wesley explains that Methodism is concerned with the entirely of one's being—one's thoughts, words, and deeds. He states that true religion does not consist of "observing any guidelines, or perhaps a fragment of one of them—such as one who imagines herself a virtuous woman only because she is not a prostitute, or one who imagines he is an honest man only because he does not rob or steal." In short,

---

[5] John S. Simon, *John Wesley and the Methodist Societies* (London: The Epworth Press, 1923), 91.

[6] Jude. 1:3–4.

Methodism teaches that God is concerned with the whole of one's life, from birth to death.

Fourth, Wesley describes the characteristics of the "perfect Christian," which characteristics he believed should be the aim of every disciple of Jesus Christ. These qualities include loving God with all one's heart, soul, and mind.[7] This sanctification includes having the same mind in us that was in Christ Jesus,[8] enabling us to walk as he walked.[9] A true Christian is clothed with a new self, which is being renewed in knowledge according to the image of its creator.[10]

Certainly, the character of a Methodist, as described by John Wesley, is a lofty ideal. Some might object, "You cannot aim at such a high goal; it is unrealistic." We can paraphrase a Wesleyan reply: "Aiming too high? Indeed! You should aim no lower than this plain biblical standard. God has promised it, and God will enable it."

---

[7] Matt. 22:37.
[8] Phil. 2:5.
[9] 1 Jn. 2:6.
[10] Col. 3:10.

The Character of a Methodist

Not as though I had already attained.[1]

To The Reader

1. Since the name "Methodist" first came into wide circulation, many people have been at a loss to know what a Methodist is. They want to understand the principles and the practices of those commonly called by that name. They desire to comprehend the distinguishing marks of this group that people everywhere are speaking against.[2]

---

[1] Phil. 3:12.

[2] Acts 28:22, where St. Luke echoes a prevailing view of Christianity: "with regard to this sect we know that everywhere it is spoken against." Commenting on that statement, Wesley wrote in his *Notes upon the New Testament*, "This is no proof at all of a bad cause, but a very probable mark of a good one."

In Wesley' series of sermons on Christ's Sermon on the Mount, Discourse 3, he addressed the subject of persecution: "Who are they that are persecuted? And this we may easily learn from St. Paul. 'As of old, he that was born after the flesh persecuted him that was born after the Spirit, even so it is now.' (Gal. iv. 29.) Yea,' saith the Apostle, 'and all

2. Most people commonly believed that I was able to give the clearest account of these matters. (I was one of the first that others called *Methodist*, and many assumed I was the group's leader.) In all kinds of ways and with the utmost sincerity, others have asked me to explain Methodism. At last, I yield to these continued entreaties of friends and enemies. In the presence of the Lord and Judge of heaven and earth, as best as I can I will now give the clearest account of the principles and practices by which those called Methodists are distinguished from others.

3. When I say, "those called Methodists," let others understand that it is not a name the Methodists have chosen. Rather, without their approval or consent, others gave them the name *Methodist* as a reproach. John Bingham, a student of Oxford's Christ Church College, gave the name to three or four young men at Oxford.[3] Bingham did so possibly for one of two reasons. (i) The name might allude to the ancient sect of physicians called *Methodists* because they taught that a specific method of diet and exercise would cure almost all diseases.[4] (ii) Possibly, the term *Methodist* came from observations that the Oxford Holy Club observed

---

that will live godly in Christ Jesus, shall suffer persecution.' (2 Tim. iii. 12.) The same we are taught by St. John: 'Marvel not, my brethren, if the world hate you. We know that we have passed from death unto life, because we love the brethren.' (1 John iii. 13, 14.) As if he had said, The brethren, the Christians, cannot be loved, but by them who have passed from death unto life. And most expressly by our Lord: 'If the world hate you, ye know that it hated me before it hated you. If ye were of the world, the world would love his own; but because ye are not of the world, therefore the world hateth you. Remember the word that I said unto you, The servant is not greater than his lord. If they have persecuted me, they will also persecute you.'"

[3] John Bingham ((1709–35) came from a distinguished English family. Bingham was a student at Oxford's Christ Church College, where he received the B.A. degree in 1729 and the M.A. degree in 1732. In the early months of the Holy Club at Oxford, first gathered in early 1729 by Charles Wesley, Bingham attended some of the meetings. When John Wesley returned to Oxford in November of that year, he assumed leadership of the group. The term *Methodist* came into use when, in 1732, John Bingham wrote, "A new set of Methodists . . . has sprung up amongst us."

[4] The Methodic School of medicine seems to have emerged in Greece and Rome in the first century B.C. This theory of medicine held that the treatment of diseases is the awareness of general, recurring features of diseases that show themselves in tangible ways. The Methodic School of medicine believed that doctors need only to know the disease itself, and from that knowledge the doctor can methodically proceed to a treatment and a cure. The physician and philosopher Sextus Empiricus (c. 160-210 AD) said that just as hunger leads a person naturally to food, and thirst leads a person naturally to water, so also when a dog is pricked by a thorn, it naturally removes the foreign object ailing its body. In like way, a disease naturally indicates its cure. Such was the philosophy of the Methodic School of ancient medicine, after which some eighteenth-century people may have coined the term *Methodists*.

a more regular method of study and conduct than was usual with those of their age and station.

4. I would rejoice (I have so little ambition to be at the head of any sect or party) if the very name might never again be mentioned, but rather be buried in eternal oblivion. If that is not so, at least let those who use the term *Methodist* know the meaning of the word. Let us not always be fighting in the dark.[5] Come; let us look at one another face to face. Perhaps if some of you that hate what others call me (a Methodist), may they love what I am by the grace of God.[6] Rather, what I follow after—I press on to take hold of that for which Christ Jesus took hold of me.[7]

1. The distinguishing marks of a Methodist do not consist of opinions of any sort.[8] One's assenting to this or that scheme of religion, any particular set of notions, or the judgment of one person or another, are all quite wide of the point. Therefore, whoever, imagines that a Methodist is a person of such and such an opinion is grossly ignorant of the whole affair. They completely miss the truth. We believe, indeed, that God gave all Scripture by divine inspiration.[9] Here is how Methodists are distinguished from Jews, Turks (Muslims), and Infidels.[10] We believe the written word of God to be the only and sufficient rule of both

---

[5] Psa. 11:2.

[6] 1 Cor. 15:10.

[7] Phil. 3:12.

[8] Wesley distinguished clearly between opinions and doctrines. Opinions are non-essential; doctrines are essential. In Wesley's Sermon #39, "Catholic Spirit," he summarily rejected what he called speculative latitudinarianism. He said that true Christianity is not "indifference to all opinions." "This is the spawn of hell," he declared, "not the offspring of heaven. This unsettledness of thought, this being 'driven to and fro, and tossed about with every wind of doctrine,' is a great curse, not a blessing; an irreconcilable enemy, not a friend, to true catholicism. A man of a truly catholic spirit . . . is fixed as the sun in his judgment concerning the main branches of Christian doctrine. It is true, he is always ready to hear and weigh whatsoever can be offered against his principles; but as this does not show any wavering in his own mind, so neither does it occasion any. He does not halt between two opinions, nor vainly endeavour to blend them into one. Observe this, you who know not what spirit ye are of; who call yourselves men of a catholic spirit, only because you are of a muddy understanding; because your mind is all in a mist; because you have no settled, consistent principles, but are for jumbling all opinions together. Be convinced, that you have quite missed your way; you know not where you are. You think you are got into the very Spirit of Christ; when, in truth, you are nearer the spirit of Antichrist. Go, first, and learn the first elements of the gospel of Christ, and then shall you learn to be of a truly catholic spirit."

[9] Deut. 4:2; Psa. 111:7; 119:9, 89; Isa. 40:8; Ezek. 12:25; Matt. 5:18, 24:35; Luke 21:33; Acts 1:16; Rom. 15:4; 2 Tim. 3:16; 2 Pet. 1:19, 21, 25; Rev. 22:19.

[10] John Wesley's *Complete English Dictionary, Explain most of those Hard Word Which are Found in the Best English Writers* (3rd ed., 1777) defines an infidel as "one that does not believe the Bible."

Christian faith and practice.[11] In this, we are fundamentally distinguished from those of the Roman Church.[12] We believe Christ to be the eternal, supreme God; and herein we are distinguished from the Socinians[13] and Arians.[14] As to all opinions that do not strike at the root of Christianity, we think and let think. Whatever

---

[11] Article VI of the Anglican Articles of religion states, "Holy Scripture containeth all things necessary to salvation: so that whatsoever is not read therein, nor may be proved thereby, is not to be required of any man, that it should be believed as an article of the Faith, or be thought requisite or necessary to salvation. In the name of the Holy Scripture we do understand those canonical Books of the Old and New Testament, of whose authority was never any doubt in the Church." The United Methodist Church affirms the final authority of Scripture in matters of doctrine and life in its Articles of Religion §V, and Confession of Faith §IV.

Those to be ordained as priests and consecrated as bishops in the Anglican Church are asked the following question about the Scriptures: "Are you persuaded that the holy Scriptures contain sufficiently all doctrine required of necessity for eternal salvation through faith in Jesus Christ? And are you determined out of the said Scriptures to instruct the people committed to your charge, and to teach nothing (as required of necessity to eternal salvation) but that which you shall be persuaded may be concluded and proved by the Scripture?" Those to be ordained are expected to answer, "I am so persuaded, and have so determined by God's grace."

The United Methodist Church's Service for the Ordination contains this question: "Are you persuaded that the Scriptures of the Old and New Testaments contain all things necessary for salvation through faith in Jesus Christ and are the unique and authoritative standard for the church's faith and life?" The expected answer is, "I am so persuaded, by God's grace."

The consecration of United Methodist bishops contains this question: "Will you guard the faith, order, liturgy, doctrine, and discipline of the Church against all that is contrary to God's Word?" The expected answer is, "I will, for the love of God.

[12] The sixteenth-century Roman Catholic Council of Trent drew a line between Roman Catholicism and the Protestant reformers. Protestantism defines Scripture as the final source of authority *sola scriptura* (Latin, ablative absolute), "by scripture alone." The Roman Catholic Council of Trent asserted the dual authorities of Scripture *and* certain traditions that accumulated through the centuries (such as purgatory, prayers to saints, transubstantiation, salvation by faith and works together, and the supreme or infallible authority of the papacy). Roman Catholicism posits a theory of "dual revelation" that posits the twin authorities of the Scriptures and accumulated beliefs and customs *(de scriptura et traditione)*.

[13] Socinianism is a sixteenth-century rationalist, anti-Trinitarian movement stemming from Faustus Sozzini (1539–1604). This anti-Trinitarian movement regards Jesus Christ as an exalted man, not the preexistent second person of the Trinity. Socinianism denies the existence of hell, but holds to the annihilation of the wicked. Sozzini rejected the doctrine of original sin (the Fall) and held that we attain salvation by good works. This movement gave rise to modern Unitarianism.

[14] Arianism is a theological doctrine attributed to Arius (c. 250–337), a presbyter from Alexandria, Egypt. Arius taught that Jesus did not always exist, but was created by God the Father, and not fully divine. The teaching of Arius led to the Council of Nicea (325) and the Nicene Creed, which affirms the eternal Holy Trinity—Father, Son, and Holy Spirit.

they are, whether right or wrong, they are not distinguishing marks of a Methodist.

2. Neither is a Methodist characterized by any special kinds of words or phrases. We do not attach our religion, or any part of it, to any particular mode of speaking or any eccentric or unusual set of expressions. Ahead of others, we prefer the most obvious, easy, common words to convey our meanings. We do so regarding commonplace occasions and when we speak of the things of God. Therefore, we never willingly or intentionally deviate from the most common way of speaking. That is so, unless when we express scripture truths in scriptural terms, which, we presume, no Christian will censure. Neither do we try to use any particular expressions of Scripture more frequently than some others do, unless the inspired writers themselves use them. Thus, it is as glaring an error to fix the marks of Methodists in their expressions, as it is in any of their merely human opinions.

3. Nor do Methodists wish to distinguish themselves by actions, customs, or usages that do not matter one way or another. Our religion does not lie in doing what God has not commanded, or abstaining from what he has not forbidden. A Methodist mark does not exist in the clothing, the posture of our bodies, the covering of our heads, abstaining from marriage, or from meats and drinks that are all good if received with thanksgiving.[15] Therefore, neither will any who know what they are talking about locate the mark of a Methodist in any actions or customs wholly unimportant and undetermined by the word of God.

4. In the last place, Methodists do not differentiate themselves by laying the entire stress of religion on any single part of religion. You may say, "Yes, they do, because they think we are saved by faith alone."[16] I answer, "You do not understand the terms." By salvation, Methodists mean holiness of heart and life. They affirm that holiness springs from faith alone. Can even a nominal Christian deny it? Is this placing a part of religion for the whole? Do we then overthrow the law by this faith? By no means! On the contrary, we uphold the law."[17]

We do not place the whole of religion (as too many do, God knows) either in doing no harm, or in doing good, or in using the ordinances of God.[18] No, not even in all these together. We know by personal experience that people may labor for many years, and still have no religion at all. No more than they had at the beginning. Much less does true religion consist of observing any guidelines, or perhaps a fragment of one of them—such as one who imagines herself a virtuous

---

[15] 1 Tim. 4:3–4.

[16] Gen. 15:6; Acts 13:39; Rom. 4:3, 5:1; Gal. 3:6, 24; Eph. 2:8–9; Phil. 3:9.

[17] Rom. 3:31.

[18] These are the three sections of Methodism's General Rules—(1) Doing no harm, (2) Doing good, and (3) Using all the ordinances of God (the means of grace).

woman only because she is not a prostitute, or one who imagines he is an honest man only because he does not rob or steal. May the Lord God of my fathers preserve me from such a poor, starved religion as this! If these were the marks of a Methodist, I would rather choose to be a sincere Jew, Turk, or Pagan.

5. What then *is* the mark of a Methodist? You may ask, "Who is a Methodist, Wesley, according to your own explanation?" I answer that Methodists are those who have God's love poured into their hearts through the Holy Spirit given to us.[19] Methodists love the Lord their God with all their heart, with all their soul, and with their entire mind.[20] God is the joy of the heart and the desire of the soul, which constantly cries, "Whom have I in heaven but you? There is nothing on earth that I desire other than you. My God and my all! You are the strength of my heart and my portion forever."[21]

6. A Methodist is therefore happy in God, yes, always happy, as having within a spring of water gushing up to eternal life,[22] overflowing the soul with peace and joy.[23] Perfection in love has cast out fear.[24] A Methodist delights in the Lord always,[25] always in God as the Savior. Methodists rejoice in the Father, through our Lord Jesus Christ, through whom we have now received reconciliation.[26] Methodists have found redemption through Christ's blood, the forgiveness of trespasses, yes, the forgiveness of sins.[27] When they look back at the horrible pit out of which God has delivered them, they can only express joy.[28] When they see that God has swept away their transgressions like a cloud, and their sins like mist,[29] they can only exult when they consider their present redeemed state. As a gift, God has justified them by his grace, through the redemption that is in Christ Jesus.[30] Those who believe have in their hearts the testimony of this redemption,[31]

---

[19] Rom. 5:5.
[20] Matt. 22:37; Mark 12:30; Luke 1:27.
[21] Psa. 73:25–26.
[22] John 4:14.
[23] Rom. 15:13.
[24] 1 Jn. 4:18.
[25] 1 Thess. 5:16.
[26] Rom. 5:11.
[27] Eph. 1:7; Rom. 5:5; Matt. 22:37; Mark 12:30; Luke 1:27; Psa. 73:25–26; John 4:14; Rom. 15:13; 1 Jn. 4:18; 1 Thess. 5:16; 2 Sam. 22:3; Isa. 43:3; 45:21; Hos. 13:4; Luke 1:47; Acts 5:31; 13:23; 1 Tim. 1:1; 2:3; 4:10; Tit. 1:3–4; 2:10, 13; Tit. 3:4; 2 Pet. 1:1; Jude 1:25; Rom. 5:11.
[28] Job 33:28.
[29] Isa. 44:22.
[30] Rom. 3:24.
[31] 1 Jn. 5:10. The inner witness of the Holy Spirit is an important emphasis of Methodism (Rom. 8:16; Gal. 4:5; 1 Jn. 3:24; 4:13; 5:6).

for they are children of God though faith.[32] Because they are God's children, he has sent the Spirit of his Son into their hearts, crying, "Abba, Father!"[33] In addition, that same Spirit bears witness with our spirit that we are children of God.[34] Methodists also rejoice whenever they look to the future, as those who share in the glory to be revealed."[35] Indeed, their joy is full,[36] and their entire frame cries out,[37] "Blessed is the God and Father of our Lord Jesus Christ. By his great mercy he has given us a new birth into a living hope through the resurrection of Jesus Christ from the dead, and into an inheritance that is imperishable, undefiled, and unfading, kept in heaven for us."[38]

7. Those that have this hope are full of immortality.[39] They give thanks in all situations, for this is the will of God in Christ Jesus for us.[40] Such people cheerfully accept every circumstance, saying, "The will of God is good,"[41] always blessing the name of the Lord whether the Lord gives or takes away.[42] They have learned in all circumstances to be content with whatever they have.[43] The Methodists know what it is to have little, and what it is to have plenty. In all circumstances, they have learned the secret either of being well fed or going hungry, of having plenty and of being in need.[44] Whether in ease or pain, sickness or health, life or death, from the depths of their hearts they give thanks to God who orders everything for good. They know that every generous act of giving, with every perfect gift, is from above, coming down from the Father of lights.[45] They entrust body and soul to the faithful Creator.[46] Therefore, they do not worry about anything,[47] for they have cast all their anxiety on him, because he cares for them.[48] After prayer and

---

[32] Gal. 3:26.
[33] Gal. 4:6.
[34] Rom. 8:16.
[35] 1 Pet. 5:1.
[36] John 15:11, 16:24; Acts 2:28; 1 Pet. 1:8; 1 Jn. 1:4; 2 Jn. 1:12.
[37] Psa. 35:10.
[38] 1 Pet. 1:3–4.
[39] 2 Tim. 1:10.
[40] 1 Thess. 5:18.
[41] 2 Kings 20:18; Psa. 143:10; Isa. 39:8; Jer. 42:6; Rom. 12:2; Phil. 2:13.
[42] Psa. 35:28, 71:6, 14, 104:33, 145:1; Rev. 5:13.
[43] Phil. 4:12; 1 Tim. 6:6; Heb. 13:5.
[44] Phil. 4:11.
[45] James 1:17.
[46] 1 Pet. 4:19.
[47] Phil. 4:6.
[48] 1 Pet. 5:7.

supplication with thanksgiving making their requests known to God, in everything they rest in him.[49]

8. Indeed, the character of a Methodist is to pray without ceasing.[50] It is Methodist practice always to pray and not to lose heart.[51] This does mean that one is always in the house of prayer, although one neglects no opportunity to be there. Neither are Methodists always on their knees, even if they are often on their face before the Lord God. Nor are they always crying aloud to God, or calling on him in words. Often, the Spirit helps us in our weakness—for we do not know how to pray as we ought, but that very Spirit intercedes with sighs beyond words.[52] Yet, at all times the language of the heart is, "O God, the brightness of the eternal glory, my heart comes to you, though without a voice, and my silence speaks to you."[53] This and this alone, is true prayer. At all times and in all places Christians continually lift their hearts to God. In this exercise, they are neither hindered nor disconnected by any person or circumstance.[54] In seclusion or in company, in leisure, in business, or in behavior, the heart is ever with the Lord.[55] Whether lying down or rising up, God is in every thought.[56] A true Methodist walks with God continually, having the loving eye of the mind still fixed upon the Lord.[57] And everywhere, they see God who is invisible.[58]

9. In this way, one always expresses love to God by praying without ceasing, rejoicing always, and giving thanks in all circumstances.[59] This commandment embeds itself in the heart.[60] "Those who love God must love their brothers and

---

[49] Phil 4:6.
[50] 1 Thess. 5:17.
[51] Luke 18:1; Eph. 6:1; James 5:13.
[52] Rom. 8:26.
[53] Possibly, Wesley gathered this line from a contemporary, the Scottish poet. James Thomson (1700–48). Thomson was one of the most celebrated Scottish poets of the eighteenth century. Thomson, in 1725, went to London where he published his masterpiece, *The Seasons*. Wesley's words here may have been an adaptation of the last stanza of Thomson's poem:

> *And better thence again, and better still,*
> *In infinite progression.— But I lose*
> *Myself in Him, in light ineffable!*
> *Come then, expressive silence, muse His praise.*

[54] Wesley is saying that dedicated Christians do not allow people or circumstances to turn them aside from faith in and obedience to God.
[55] 1 Thess. 4:17.
[56] Psa. 19:14, 48:9, 63:6, 119:59, 148; Phil 4:8.
[57] Psa. 57:7; 108:1; 112:7.
[58] Heb. 11:27.
[59] 1 Thess. 5:16–18.
[60] Prov. 10:8.

sisters also."[61] Accordingly, they love their neighbor as they love themselves.[62] They love everyone as they love their own souls.[63] Their hearts are full of love for all people, for every child of the Father of the spirits of all flesh.[64] That we do not know another individual personally is not a barrier to God's love. Not even if another is one of whom we do not approve, and who returns hatred for our goodwill. Such Christians love their enemies, yes, and the enemies of God, the evil and the unthankful.[65] Further, if it is not in their power to do good to them that hate them, Christians do not stop praying for them, even if they continue to spurn love, and despitefully use and persecute them.[66]

10. True Methodists are pure in heart.[67] God's love has cleansed their hearts from all vindictive passions, envy, malice, anger, and every unkind attitude or malicious disposition.[68] This love has cleansed them from a prideful and haughty spirit, the sole source of strife.[69] These Christians have put on compassion, kindness, lowliness, meekness, and patience.[70] They are patient with one another.[71] If they have a complaint against others, they forgive them,[72] even as the Lord has forgiven them.[73] Indeed, as far as they are concerned, they have removed every possible ground for strife. No one can take anything they desire from them, because they do not love the world or the things in the world.[74] The world has been crucified to them, and they are crucified to the world.[75] They are dead to all that is in the world—that is, the desire of the flesh, the desire of the eyes, and the pride of life.[76] Their yearning is for God, and the glory of his name is their souls' desire.[77]

11. Consistent with this one desire is the purpose of the Christian's life, which is wanting not to do one's own will, but the will of him who sent us into the

---

[61] 1 Jn. 4:21.
[62] Mark 12:33.
[63] 1 Sam. 18:1.
[64] Num. 16:22; Heb. 12:9.
[65] Ex. 23:4; Prov. 24:17, 25; Matt. 5:43–44; Luke 6:27, 35; Rom. 12:20; 1 Thess. 5:15.
[66] Matt. 5:44.
[67] Matt. 5:8.
[68] Eph. 4:31; Col. 3:8.
[69] Prov. 13:10.
[70] Col. 3:12.
[71] Gal. 5:22–23.
[72] Matt. 6:12.
[73] Col. 3:13.
[74] 1 Jn. 2:15.
[75] Gal. 6:14.
[76] 1 Jn. 2:16.
[77] Psa. 63:6; Eccl. 12:1; Jonah 2:7; Zech. 10:9; Isa. 26:8.

world.[78] Always, their holy single intention in everything is not to please themselves, but the God they love.[79] Methodists have a single eye, and because the eye is healthy, their whole body is full of light.[80] Indeed, when we fix our soul on the loving eye of God, there can be no darkness at all.[81] The entire soul is light, as when a lamp disperses light with its rays.[82] God alone then reigns.[83] Everything in the soul is holiness to the Lord.[84] There is no stirring in the heart, except what agrees with God's will.[85] Every rising notion points to God,[86] and all thoughts are in obedience to the law of Christ.[87]

12. We know a tree by its fruit,[88] and because Christians love God, they keep his commandments.[89] Not just some or most of them, but all of them from the least to the greatest.[90] Christians are not content to keep the whole law, yet to fail in one point.[91] However, in all points, they have a clear conscience toward God and others.[92] Whatever God has forbidden, they avoid; whatever God has bidden, they do.[93] They do so whether it be little or great, hard or easy, joyful or disagreeable to one's natural desires. They walk the way of God's commandments, for he has set their hearts free.[94] It is their delight to obey God.[95] The Christian's daily crown of rejoicing[96] is to do the will of God on earth, as it is done in heaven.[97] They know that is the highest privilege of God's angels, the mighty ones who do his bidding, and who obey his revealed word.[98]

---

[78] John 6:38.
[79] Song of Sol. 1:7.
[80] Isa. 60:20; Matt. 6:22; Luke 11:34; John 8:12.
[81] Matt. 6:23.
[82] Job 11:17; Luke 11:36; 2 Cor. 3:18; Eph. 1:18; 1 Pet. 2:9.
[83] 1 Cor. 15:25; Rev. 11:5, 22:5.
[84] Ex. 28:36, 39:30.
[85] Mark 3:35; John 7:17, 9:31; Rom. 12:2; Eph. 6:6; Phil. 2:13; Heb. 10:7; 1 Pet. 4:2; 1 Jn. 2:17.
[86] Psa. 63:6.
[87] 2 Cor. 10:5.
[88] Matt. 7:17–18; Luke 6:44.
[89] John 14:15, 21, 15:10; 1 Jn. 5:2–3.
[90] Num. 15:40; Deut. 5:29; 1 Kings 6:12; Psa. 119:172.
[91] James 2:10.
[92] Acts 24:16.
[93] John 14:15, 23; 15:10.
[94] Psa. 119:32.
[95] Psa. 40:8; 119:35.
[96] Sirach 1:11.
[97] Matt. 6:10.
[98] Psa. 103:20.

13. Accordingly, Christians keep all the commandments of God, and they do so with all their strength.[99] Their obedience is in accord with God's love, the source from which it flows. Therefore, loving God with all their heart, they serve him with all their strength.[100] They continually present their bodies as living offerings, holy and acceptable to God.[101] Entirely and without reserve, they devote themselves, all they have, and all they are, to the glory of God. They constantly employ all their God-given talents according to the Master's will. They do so with every power and faculty of their souls, and with every member of bodies. Formerly, they gave themselves over to sin and the devil, as instruments of wickedness. Now, however, as those who have moved from death into life, they present the members of their bodies to God as instruments of righteousness.[102]

14. As a consequence of this commitment, whatever these Christians do is wholly to the glory of God.[103] In all their works, Christians not only *aim* at glorifying God (which having a single eye implies[104]), and they actually *attain* it. All of their business, occasions of relaxation, and prayers serve this great end. Whether they sit in God's house, walk, lie down, or rise up, in their speaking and doing they promote the grand business of their lives, which is God's glory.[105] Whether they dress, work, eat, drink, or rest from tiring labor—everything inclines to the advancement of God's glory, through peace and good will among all people.[106] The Methodists' one invariable rule is this: Whatever they do in word or deed, they do in the name of the Lord Jesus, giving thanks to God the Father through him.[107]

15. The customs of the world do not thwart their running the race that is set before them.[108] They know that evil does not lose its nature, even if wickedness becomes ever so fashionable. They remember that each of us will be accountable to God.[109] Methodists, therefore, cannot follow any majority of others in doing

---

[99] Tobit 14:8; Luke 10:27.
[100] Mark 12:30.
[101] Rom. 12:1.
[102] Rom. 6:13.
[103] Psa. 34:3; Isa. 25:1; Matt. 5:16; Rom. 15:6; 1 Cor. 6:20; 10:31; Rev. 19:7.
[104] Matt. 6:22.
[105] Deut. 6:7; 11:19.
[106] Luke 2:14.
[107] Col. 3:17.
[108] Heb. 12:1.
[109] Matt. 12:36; Rom. 14:12; 1 Pet. 4:5. Wesley's sermon, "The Great Assize," speaks forthrightly about God's final judgment. (The word *assize* means a court that tries civil and criminal cases.) In that sermon Wesley said, "Suffer me to add a few words to all of you who are at this day present before the Lord. . . . [W]e shall all . . . stand at the judgment-

wrong.[110] Methodists cannot feast sumptuously every day[111] or make provision for the flesh, to gratify its desires.[112] They cannot store up treasures on earth,[113] any more than they can carry fire to their bosom.[114] They cannot dress themselves pretentiously with gold or expensive clothes.[115] They cannot participate in or tolerate any amusement that has the slightest tendency toward any sort of immorality.[116] They cannot speak evil of their neighbor,[117] any more than they can lie for

---

seat of Christ..... Here [in human courts] a man is questioned concerning one or two facts, which he is supposed to have committed: There [in the final judgment] we are to give an account of all our works, from the cradle to the grave; of all our words; of all our desires and tempers [attitudes], all the thoughts and intents of our hearts; of all the use we have made of our various talents, whether of mind body, or fortune, till God said, 'Give an account of thy stewardship, for thou mayest be no longer steward.' In this [earthly] court, it is possible, some who are guilty may escape for want of evidence; but there is no want of evidence in [God's] court. All men, with whom you had the most secret intercourse, who were privy to all your designs and actions, are ready before your face. So are all the spirits of darkness, who inspired evil designs, and assisted in the execution of them. So are all the angels of God; those eyes of the Lord, that run to and fro over all the earth, who watched over your soul, and laboured for your good, so far as you would permit. So is your own conscience, a thousand witnesses in one, now no more capable of being either blinded or silenced, but constrained to know and to speak the naked truth, touching all your thoughts, and words, and actions. And is conscience as a thousand witnesses? — yea, but God is as a thousand consciences! O, who can stand before the face of the great God, even our Saviour Jesus Christ!"

[110] Exod. 23:2; 34:12; Psa. 1:1; Prov. 4:14; 2 Cor. 6:14.

[111] Luke 16:19.

[112] Rom. 13:14. Here, the New Testament word for *desire* is ἐπιθυμίας, which means a craving, mostly of evil desires. The word can be translated as *concupiscence*, *lust*, or *impure desire*.

[113] Matt. 6:19.

[114] Prov. 6:27.

[115] 1 Tim. 2:9.

[116] 1 Thess. 5:22.

[117] The New Testament speaks strongly against "evil speaking." We can translate the verb καταλαλέω and the noun καταλαλιά as *evil speech*, *railing*, or *slander*. The Geneva Bible and the KJV translated this term as *backbiter*; the RSV, the NRS, and the NIV use the word *slanderer*. In one form or another, this word appears in such passages Rom. 1:30; 2 Cor. 12:20; James 4:11; 1 Pet. 2:12, 3:16.

John Wesley's *Notes upon the New Testament* translates καταλάλους as *backbiters*, and comments that such people "speak against others behind their back." Wesley said that evil speaking is "the bane of religion." He said in a Sermon, *The cure of Evil Speaking*, "Speak evil of no man' ... [is] as plain a command as, 'Thou shalt do no murder.'.... Yea, how few are there that so much as understand it! What is evil speaking? It is not, as some suppose, the same with lying or slandering. All a man says may be as true as the Bible; and yet the saying of it is evil speaking. For evil-speaking is neither more nor less than speaking evil of an absent person; relating something evil, which was really done or said by one that is not present when it is related. Suppose, having seen a man drunk, or heard him curse or swear, I tell this when he is absent; it is evil speaking. In our language, the proper term is *backbiting*. Nor is there any material difference between this term and what we commonly

God or any person.[118] They cannot utter an unkind word about anyone, because love guards the door of their lips.[119] They cannot speak idle words.[120] No evil talk comes out of their mouths.[121] They say only what is useful for edifying, so that their words impart grace to those who hear.[122] They think, speak, and do whatever is true, honorable, just, pure, pleasing, and commendable.[123] They are an ornament to the doctrine of God our Savior.[124]

16. Finally, regarding the character of a Methodist, as time allows, he or she, works for the good of all[125]—whether neighbors, strangers, friends, or enemies.[126] They do so in every possible way to their bodies, by feeding the hungry, clothing the needy, and visiting those who are sick or in prison.[127] So much the more, does the Methodist labor to do good to people's souls. This work requires the ability that God gives us[128] to awaken those that sleep in spiritual death,[129] to bring those whom God awakens to Christ's atoning blood.[130] Being justified by faith, these people may have peace with God through our Lord Jesus Christ.[131] A Methodist also encourages those who have peace with God to abound more in love and in

---

call *gossip*. If one delivers the account in a soft and quiet manner, (perhaps with expressions of good will to the person, and of hope that things may not be quite so bad,) then we call it whispering. In whatever manner we might speak, the thing is the same. . . . Still it is evil-speaking; still this command, 'Speak evil of no man,' is trampled underfoot; if we relate to another the fault of a third person, when he is not present to answer for himself."

[118] Ex. 20:16; 23:1; Prov. 12:17; 19:9; 25:18; Matt. 19:18.

[119] Psa. 141:3; Prov. 21:23; James 1:26; 1 Pet. 3:10.

[120] Matt. 12:36, (ῥῆμα ἀργὸν *idle word*) means conversation that is *empty, unprofitable, hollow,* or *injurious*. In Wesley's *Notes upon the New Testament*, he said, "Ye may perhaps think, God does not so much regard your words. . . . That not for blasphemous and profane words only, but for every idle word . . . . For want of seriousness or caution; for every discourse which is not conducive to the glory of God, [you] shall give account in the day of judgment. For by your words (as well as your tempers and works) thou shalt then be either acquitted or condemned."

[121] Psa. 34:13; Eph. 4:31.

[122] Eph. 4:29.

[123] Phil. 4:8.

[124] Tit. 2:10.

[125] Gal. 6:10.

[126] Exod. 23:4; Prov. 24:17; 25:21; Matt. 5:44; Rom. 12:20.

[127] Matt. 25:35–36. Wesley states in his *Notes upon the New Testament*, "All these works of outward mercy suppose faith and love, and must needs be accompanied with works of spiritual mercy."

[128] 1 Pet. 4:11.

[129] Rom. 13:11.

[130] Lev. 17:11.

[131] Rom. 5:1.

good works.[132] A Methodist is willing to spend and be spent in this work,[133] even being poured out as a libation over the sacrifice and the offering of their faith,[134] so that others may come to the measure of the full stature of Christ.[135]

17. These are the *principles* and *practices* of our people; they are the marks of a true Methodist. By these signs alone do we (who some derisively call *Methodists*) want to be distinguished from others. Someone may say, "Why, these are only the common fundamental principles of Christianity!" Correctly, you have said so![136] Christianity is what I mean to describe. It is the very truth, and I know there are no other true marks of Christianity.[137] I would to God that you and everyone else knew that I, and all who follow my judgment, fervently refuse to be distinguished from other people, except by these common principles of Christianity. This is the plain, historical Christianity that I teach, while renouncing and abhorring all other marks of distinction.

All who embody what I preach are Christians. Let others call them what they will. Names change, but not the nature of things. These are Christians not only in name, but also in heart and in life. Inwardly and outwardly, they are conformed to the will of God, as revealed in the written word.[138] They think, speak, and live according to the "method" laid down in the revelation of Jesus Christ. Their souls are renewed in knowledge according to the image of God.[139] And this is according to the likeness of God's true righteousness and holiness.[140] True Methodists have the mind that was in Christ,[141] and they walk just as Christ walked.[142]

18. By these marks and fruits of a living faith, we strive to distinguish ourselves from the unbelieving world—that is, from all those whose minds or lives do not concur with the gospel of Christ.[143] However, we earnestly desire *not* to be distinguished in any way from real Christians, of whatever denomination they may be. We are at one with all who sincerely follow after what they know they have not yet attained.[144] Whoever does the will of my Father in heaven is my brother, sister,

---

[132] Eph. 2:10; 1 Tim. 6:18; 2 Tim. 3:17; Tit. 2:7, 14; 3:8, 14; Heb. 10:24; 1 Pet. 2:12.
[133] 2 Cor. 12:15.
[134] Phil. 2:17.
[135] Eph. 4:13.
[136] Matt. 26:64.
[137] 1 Jn. 3:18.
[138] Rom. 12:2.
[139] Col. 3:10.
[140] Eph. 4:24.
[141] Phil. 2:5.
[142] 1 Jn. 2:6.
[143] Gal. 2:14.
[144] Phil. 3:12.

and mother.[145] Brothers and sisters, I beseech you, by the mercies of God:[146] Let us not allow divisions among ourselves.[147] Is your heart as true to mine as mine is to yours? If it is, give me your hand.[148] Concerning opinions or terms, let us not destroy the work of God.[149] Do you love and serve God? That is enough. I give you the right hand of fellowship. If there is any encouragement in Christ, any consolation from love, any sharing in the Spirit, any compassion and sympathy,[150] let us strive together for the faith of the Gospel.[151] Let us walk worthily, with all humility and gentleness, with patience, bearing with one another in love, making every effort to maintain the unity of the Spirit in the bond of peace.[152] Let us remember there is one body and one Spirit, just as you were called to the one hope of your calling. There is one Lord, one faith, one baptism, one God and Father of all, who is above all, and through all and in all.[153]

---

[145] Matt. 12:50. Wesley said in his Sermon #39, *Catholic Spirit*, "Although a difference in opinions or modes of worship may prevent an entire external union; yet need it prevent our union in affection? Though we cannot think alike, may we not love alike? May we not be of one heart, though we are not of one opinion? Without all doubt, we may. Herein all the children of God may unite, notwithstanding these smaller differences. These remaining as they are, they may forward one another in love and in good works."

[146] Rom. 12:1.

[147] 1 Cor. 1:13.

[148] 2 Kings 10:15.

[149] Wesley's sermon "Catholic Spirit, rejected doctrinal unconcern or heterodoxy. He said, "A catholic spirit is not speculative latitudinarianism. It is not an indifference to all opinions: This is the spawn of hell, not the offspring of heaven. This unsettledness of thought, this being 'driven to and fro, and tossed about with every wind of doctrine,' is a great curse, not a blessing; an irreconcilable enemy, not a friend, to true catholicism. A man of a truly catholic spirit, has not now his religion to seek. He is fixed as the sun in his judgment concerning the main branches of Christian doctrine. It is true, he is always ready to hear and weigh whatsoever can be offered against his principles; but as this does not show any wavering in his own mind, so neither does it occasion any. He does not halt between two opinions, nor vainly endeavour to blend them into one. Observe this, you who know not what spirit ye are of; who call yourselves men of a catholic spirit, only because you are of a muddy understanding; because your mind is all in a mist; because you have no settled, consistent principles, but are for jumbling all opinions together. Be convinced, that you have quite missed your way; you know not where you are. You think you are got into the very Spirit of Christ; when, in truth, you are nearer the spirit of Antichrist. Go, first, and learn the first elements of the gospel of Christ, and then shall you learn to be of a truly catholic spirit."

[150] Phil. 2:1.

[151] Phil 1:27.

[152] Eph. 4:1–3.

[153] Eph. 4:4–6.

Editor's Introduction

The Whole Armor of God
(Soldiers of Christ, Arise)

The following hymn, written by Charles Wesley, first appeared at the end of the first three editions of John Wesley's *The Character of a Methodist* (1742). These verses also appeared separately on a large sheet of paper, called a broadside. The first four stanzas of this sixteen-stanza hymn next appeared in 1749 in the Wesleys' *Hymns and Spiritual Songs*, with the title "The Whole Armour of God; Ephesians 6." Additional stanzas followed in the two succeeding hymns.

Wesley's 1780 hymnal, *A Collection of Hymns, For the Use of the People Called Methodists* was first-generation Methodism's definitive hymnal. Twelve stanzas of *The Whole Armour of God* appeared in that hymnal in three successive divisions—#258, part one; #259, part two; and #260, part three. The original hymn tune, sung by the eighteenth-century Methodists was *Aynhoe*, composed by James Nares (1715–83). The 1989 United Methodist Hymnal (#513) contains four stanzas of this hymn under the title, *Soldiers of Christ Arise*, with the hymn tune *Diademata*, composed by George J. Elvey in 1868. Over the years, Christians have also sung these verses (SMD meter) to *Handel's March*. Composed by George Frederick Handel (1686–1759); *Silver Street*, composed by Isaac Smith (1735–1800); *Kirk-*

wood, composed by William Batchelder Bradbury (1816–68); *St. Ethelwald*, composed by William Henry Monk (1823–89); and *From Strength to Strength*, composed by Edward W. Naylor (1867–1934).

Soldiers of Christ Arise

Soldiers of Christ, arise,
    And put your armor on,[1]
Strong in the strength which God supplies
    Through His eternal Son.[2]
    Strong in the Lord of Hosts,[3]
    And in His mighty power,[4]
Who in the strength of Jesus trusts[5]
    Is more than conqueror.[6]

    Stand then in His great might[7]
    With all His strength endued,[8]
But take, to arm you for the fight,[9]
    The panoply of God;[10]
    That, having all things done,[11]
    And all your conflicts passed,[12]
Ye may o'ercome through Christ alone,[13]
    And stand entire at last.[14]

    Stand then against your foes,[15]
    In close and firm array;[16]
Legions of wily fiends oppose[17]
    Throughout the evil day.[18]

---

[1] Eph. 6:10–18; 2 Tim. 2:3–4.
[2] 1 Pet. 4:11
[3] Jer. 50:34; Hag. 2:4; Zech. 8:9.
[4] Eph. 6:10–11.
[5] Rev. 12:10.
[6] Psa. 44:5; Rom. 8:37; 1 Jn. 5:4.
[7] Mich. 5:4.
[8] Psa. 68:35.
[9] 1 Pet. 4:1.
[10] Eph. 6:11.
[11] Phil. 4:13.
[12] 1 Cor. 15:57; 1 Jn. 5:4; Rev. 15:2.
[13] Rom. 12:21; 1 Jn. 2:13–14; 4:4
[14] Rom. 5:2; 1 Cor. 15:1; 16:13; 2 Cor. 1:24; Gal. 5:1; Eph. 6:11, 13–14; Phil. 1:27; 4:1; Col. 4:12; 1 Thess. 3:8; 2 Thess. 2:15; 1 Pet. 5:12.
[15] Psa. 89:23.
[16] Joel 2:5.
[17] Eph. 6:11.
[18] Eph. 6:13.

But meet the sons of night,[19]
And mock their vain design,[20]
Armed in the arms of heavenly light,[21]
Of righteousness divine.[22]

Leave no unguarded place,[23]
No weakness of the soul,
Take every virtue, every grace,
And fortify the whole;
Indissolubly joined,[24]
To battle all proceed;[25]
But arm yourselves with all the mind[26]
That was in Christ, your Head.[27]

But, above all, lay hold
On faith's victorious shield;[28]
Armed with that adamant and gold,[29]
Be sure to win the field:
If faith surround your heart,
Satan shall be subdued,[30]
Repelled his every fiery dart,[31]
And quenched with Jesu's blood.[32]

Jesus hath died for you![33]
What can His love withstand?
Believe, hold fast your shield,[34]

---

[19] 1 Thess. 5:5; 1 Pet. 2:9.
[20] 2 Cor. 11:14; 2 Thess. 2:9; Rev. 12:9.
[21] Rom. 13:12; Eph. 5:8; 1 Jn. 1:7.
[22] Rom. 5:17; 14:17; 1 Cor. 1:30; 2 Cor. 5:21; Eph. 4:24; Phil. 3:9; 1 Pet. 2:24; 1 Jn. 3:10.
[23] Matt. 26:41; Mark 13:33; 14:38; Luke 21:36.
[24] 1 Cor. 1:10; Eph. 4:16.
[25] Josh. 10:25; 1 Tim. 6:12.
[26] Rom. 13:12; 2 Cor. 6:7; Eph. 6:11, 13.
[27] 1 Pet. 4:1.
[28] Psa. 3:3; 18:35; 28:7; 84:11; 91:4; Prov. 30:5; Eph. 6–17.
[29] 1 Pet. 4:1.
[30] 1 Jn. 5:4.
[31] Eph. 6:16.
[32] Rev. 12:11.
[33] 1 Cor. 15:3.
[34] Eph. 6:16.

And who shall pluck you from His hand?[35]
Believe that Jesus reigns;[36]
   All power to Him is giv'n:[37]
Believe, till freed from sin's remains;[38]
   Believe yourselves to Heav'n.[39]

To keep your armor bright,[40]
   Attend with constant care,[41]
Still walking in your Captain's sight,[42]
   And watching unto prayer.[43]
   Ready for all alarms,
   Steadfastly set your face,[44]
And always exercise your arms,
   And use your every grace.[45]

Pray without ceasing, pray,[46]
   (Your Captain gives the word;)
His summons cheerfully obey[47]
   And call upon the Lord;[48]
   To God your every want[49]
   In instant prayer display,[50]
Pray always; pray and never faint;[51]
   Pray, without ceasing, pray![52]

---

[35] John 10:28–29.
[36] Rom. 5:17.
[37] Matt. 28:18; John 17:2; 2 Pet. 1:3; Rev. 17:14; 19:16.
[38] Rom. 6:18, 22; 8:2.
[39] John 20:31; 1 Tim. 1:16; 1 Jn. 5:13.
[40] Rom. 13:12; 2 Cor. 6:7; Eph. 6:11, 13.
[41] Rev. 3:2.
[42] 1 Pet. 2:25.
[43] Matt. 26:41; Acts 20:31; 1 Cor. 10:12; 16:13; Eph. 6:18; Col. 4:2; 1 Pet. 5:8.
[44] Luke 9:51; 1 Cor. 15:58; Gal. 5:1; Phil. 1:27; 1 Pet. 5:9; 2 Pet. 3:17.
[45] 2 Pet. 3:18.
[46] 1 Chron. 16:11; Matt. 26:41; Luke 18:1; John 16:24; Eph. 6:18; 1 Thess. 5:17; James 5:13.
[47] Heb, 5:9.
[48] Rom. 10:12.
[49] 1 Pet. 5:7.
[50] Psa. 62:8.
[51] Luke 18:1; 21:36.
[52] 1 Thess. 5:17.

> In fellowship alone,
> To God with faith draw near;[53]
> Approach His courts, besiege His throne[54]
> With all the powers of prayer:[55]
> Go to His temple, go,[56]
> Nor from His altar move;[57]
> Let every house His worship know,
> And every heart His love.[58]
>
> To God your spirits dart,
> Your souls in words declare,
> Or groan, to Him Who reads the heart,
> The unutterable prayer:[59]
> His mercy now implore,[60]
> And now show forth His praise,[61]
> In shouts, or silent awe,
> Adore His miracles of grace.
>
> Pour out your souls to God,[62]
> And bow them with your knees,[63]
> And spread your hearts and hands abroad,[64]
> And pray for Zion's peace;[65]
> Your guides and brethren bear
> Forever on your mind;[66]
> Extend the arms of mighty prayer,

---

[53] Heb. 10:22.
[54] Psa. 100:4.
[55] Psa. 84:10; 96:8; 100:4.
[56] Psa. 5:7; 18:6; 27:4; 48:9; 64:4; 138:2; Isa. 6:1; Hab. 2:20.
[57] Psa. 84:10.
[58] Deut. 6:5.
[59] Rom. 8:26.
[60] Psa. 26:11; 41:4, 10; 56:1; 57:1; 67:1; 86:3; 119:58, 76 132; Luke 18:13; Heb. 8:12.
[61] Psa. 7:17; 9:1–2, 14; 22:6; 28:7; 30:12; Isa. 12:4; 51:1; Jer. 17:26; Dan. 2:23; Rom. 15:11; Eph. 1:6; Heb. 2:12; 1 Pet. 4:11; Rev. 19:5.
[62] 1 Sam. 1:15; Psa. 42:4; 62:8; Lam. 2:19.
[63] Eph. 3:14.
[64] Lam. 3:41.
[65] Psa. 122:6; Ezek. 13:16.
[66] Prov. 15:22.

In grasping all mankind.[67]

From strength to strength go on,[68]
Wrestle and fight and pray,[69]
Tread all the powers of darkness down[70]
And win the well-fought day.[71]
Still let the Spirit cry[72]
In all His soldiers, "Come!"[73]
Till Christ the Lord descends from high[74]
And takes the conquerors home.[75]

---

[67] Eph. 6:18.
[68] Psa. 84:7.
[69] Eph. 6:12.
[70] Luke 22:53; Acts 26:18; Col. 1:13.
[71] Rev. 3:21.
[72] Rom. 8:15.
[73] Rev. 22:20.
[74] 1 Thess. 4:16.
[75] 1 Thess. 4:17.

Selection 3

A Letter to a Clergyman

Editor's Introduction

A Letter to a Clergyman

In 1745, an unidentified British soldier organized a Methodist society in Dublin, Ireland. In Wesley's day, Ireland's religious needs were serious. Irish Anglican and Roman Catholic priests neglected the people. Most churches were open only once a week, and less than one-fourth of the Irish people attended worship services. A British Methodist historian assessed the eighteenth-century state of Protestant religion in Ireland:

> The established [Anglican] Church presented a melancholy spectacle. . . . Considered by British statesmen rather as a political engine than an instrument of instruction in evangelical truth, [Ireland's] dignities and benefices were bestowed as the reward of political desert rather than of moral and religious worth. . . . Scarcely one bishop can be named who labored to promote the spiritual interests of his diocese. . . . What must have been the character and conduct of the clergy in general? They were comparatively few in number, badly paid, and ill-fitted for their work.[1]

During George Whitefield's third visit to Ireland, he wrote, "Not one clergyman in all Ireland is yet stirred up to come out singularly for God." Another observer said, "A cold formal, worldly spirit crept down, like a mountain mist, from the high places of the church, and spread itself everywhere."

---

[1] Charles H. Crookshank, "Methodism Beyond the Seas: Ireland," in W. J. Townsend, H.B. Workman, and George Eayrs, eds., *A New History of Methodism*, 2 vols. (London: Hodder and Stoughton, 1909), II:4.

In 1746, Wesley's conference of Methodist preachers met at Bristol, and the conference considered a mission to Ireland:

> What is a sufficient call of Providence to [go to] a new place—suppose Edinburg or Dublin?
> (1) An invitation from someone that is worthy, a serious man, fearing God who has a house to receive us;
> (2) A probability of doing more good by going thither than by staying longer where we are.

That 1746 conference of Methodist preachers agreed to launch a Methodist mission to Ireland. A Methodist lay preacher, Thomas Williams, went to Ireland to begin preaching—first in an old Lutheran Church and soon in the open air. Williams formed his converts into a Methodist society, and he wrote John Wesley for guidance and assistance. Wesley embarked for Ireland on 8 August 1747. He arrived on 10 August, and wrote in his journal,

> I met the society at five, and at six preached on 'Repent and believe the gospel.' The room, large as it was, would not contain the people who seemed to taste the good word. Between eight and nine I went to Mr. R [Moses Roquier,] (the Anglican curate of St. Mary's); he professed abundance of goodwill, commended my sermon in strong terms, and begged he might see me again the next morning. But at the same time he expressed the most rooted prejudice against lay preachers or preaching out of a church, and said the [Anglican] Archbishop of Dublin was resolved to suffer no such irregularities in his diocese.[2]

The next day, Wesley preached to a large crowd. He added to his journal,

> The house wherein we then preached was originally designed . . . [to] contain about four hundred people. But four or five times the number may stand in the yard. Many of the rich were there, and many ministers of every denomination. . . . I spoke closely and strongly. But none at all seemed to be offended. If my brother or I could have been here for a few months, I question if there might not have been a larger society here than even in London itself.[3]

---

[2] Journal, Bicentennial ed., 10 August, 1747, 20:187–88.
[3] Ibid.

During that preaching tour, Wesley bonded with the Irish people, and warm-hearted listeners from all strata of society expressed exuberant demonstrations of affection for him. In a letter to his friend, Ebenezer Blackwell, Wesley wrote from Dublin about that first visit to Ireland:

> I have found a home in this strange land. . . . For natural sweetness of temper, for courtesy and hospitality, I have never seen any people like the Irish. Indeed, all I converse with are only English transplanted into another soil; and they are much mended by the removal, having left all their roughness and surliness behind them. They receive the word of God with all gladness and readiness of mind. The danger is, that it should not take deep root; that it should be as seed falling on stony ground. But is there not the same danger in England also? Do not you find it in London? . . . . [The gospel] does not properly take root till we are convinced of inward sin; till we begin to feel the entire corruption of our nature.[4]

Under Wesley's supervision, Irish Methodism grew through the ministries of lay preachers. All told, Wesley sailed across the Irish Channel forty-two times, and he presided over the Irish Methodist Conference twenty-one times.

Irish converts to Methodism produced some remarkable Christians, one of which was Adam Clarke (1766–1832), who became a renowned scholar, a compelling preacher, and a widely read biblical commentator. Clarke worked confidently with Hebrew, Samaritan, Chaldee, Syriac, Greek, and Latin versions of the Old and New Testaments. He also knew several modern European languages and almost every branch of literature and science. He held memberships in several scholarly societies, and universities showered degrees upon him. Clarke was also a preacher of exceptional power. Eyewitnesses reported that sometimes he held congregations in rapt attention for as long as two or three hours. His sermons reached the hearts of common people, and he brought many coal miners and soldiers to saving faith in Jesus Christ. Clarke's multi-volume commentary on the entire Bible became a standard in British and American Methodism's Courses of Study for preachers.

---

[4] Letters, 13 August 1747.

Another famed Irish Methodist convert was Henry Moore (1751–1844), whom Wesley later designated as one of the three custodians of his manuscripts.[5] Moore, with Thomas Coke[6], co-authored, *The Life of the Rev. John Wesley* (1792). Moore's theological writings and sermons helped shape that generation of Methodists. Twice, British Methodism elected him President of the Methodist Conference. On one occasion, Wesley said to Moore, "No man in England has contradicted me more than you have done; and yet, Henry, I love you still. You are right." Moore died at age ninety-three, having preached for sixty-five years.[7]

Still another Irish Methodist who significantly contributed to Methodism was Thomas Walsh (1730–59). When Walsh was nineteen, he sensed a growing dissatisfaction with his spiritual life. His older brother, a Member of Parliament, advised him to read the Bible. By doing so, Walsh came to see that the only mediator between humanity and God is Jesus Christ, who is the sole source of our salvation. Walsh's firm belief in Christ as savior led him to leave the Roman Catholic Church. Under Wesley's tutelage, Walsh became a Methodist preacher in his native Ireland. Wesley wrote in his journal, "What a pity that all our Preachers in every place have not the zeal and wisdom to follow his example!"[8]

The saintly Thomas Walsh was also a scholar and a poet. Wesley reported, "[Walsh] was so thoroughly acquainted with the Bible, that if he was questioned concerning any Hebrew word in the Old, or any Greek word in the New Testament, he would tell, after a little pause, not only how often the one or the other occurred in the Bible, but also what it meant in every place. . . . Such a master of Biblic knowledge I never saw before, and never expect to see again."[9] Walsh preached both in English and in the Irish language, his mother tongue. Wesley said of him, "Give me half-a-dozen men like Tommy Walsh, and I'll turn the kingdom upside down." It was said of Walsh that his feet touched the earth, but his spirit was in the celestial world, and that when he preached he came out from

---

[5] The other custodians were Thomas Coke and John Whitehead. Coke became American Methodism's first bishop, and Whitehead, a physician, attended both John and Charles Wesley in their final illnesses.

[6] In 1784, Thomas Coke, American Methodism's first superintendent (bishop), ordained Francis Asbury and consecrated him a bishop.

[7] Moore reported that on one Sunday morning John Wesley, on entering the pulpit, instead of announcing the hymn immediately, to the great surprise of the congregation, stood silent, with his eyes closed, for the space of at least ten minutes, rapt in thought; and then, with a feeling which at once conveyed to all present the subject which had so absorbed his attention, gave out the hymn beginning with the lines, *Come, let us join our friends above, Who have obtain'd the prize.*

[8] Journal, 11 April 1756.

[9] Sermon, "On Charity," II, §5.

the immediate presence of God as Moses did when he descended from the mountain with his face shining as an angel. Rabbles attacked him, but he persevered and won many to Christ. 1789, John Wesley, assisted by two other Anglican priests[10] ordained him and two other preachers, the first to be ordained for the Methodist ministry in England. Overwork and persecution by priest-inspired mobs compromised Walsh's health, and he died at the age of twenty-eight.

Of particular importance to American Methodism were two Irish preachers, Robert Strawbridge and Philip Embury. Robert Strawbridge [or Strobridge] (c. 1732–1783) came to Christ under the preaching of one of Wesley's preachers in Ireland, and he became a Methodist lay preacher. In the early 1760s, he immigrated to Maryland, where he built a log cabin near Sam's Creek, in Frederick County. His ministry led to the construction of the first Methodist chapel in the American colonies. Wherever Strawbridge preached, he raised up young preachers. Strawbridge led Richard Owings to Jesus Christ, and Owings became the first American-born Methodist preacher. Bishop Francis Asbury said in his journal, "Mr. Strawbridge formed the first society in Maryland—and *America*."[11] Methodist scholar Frank Baker was just in his pronouncement that Strawbridge was "the outstanding lay pioneer of early American Methodism."[12]

The second Irish lay preacher to bring Methodism to the American colonies was Philip Embury (1728–c.1773), who had become a Christian due to the influence of John Wesley's preaching in Limerick. Wesley appointed him a class leader and lay preacher. In the mid-1760s Strawbridge immigrated to New York City, where he founded a Methodist society. The congregation eventually constructed a chapel on John Street. Letters from these New York Methodists prompted John Wesley, over several years, to send eight "missionaries" to America, one of whom was Francis Asbury, who arrived in America in 1771. Embury served the Methodist congregation in New York without pay. Only occasionally did the congregation give him a donation with which to purchase clothing. When he left New York City, the church trustees gave him just over £2 so he could buy a Bible concordance as a memento of his years of faithful service to the congregation as its carpenter, custodian, pastor, and preacher. Later, an American bishop, Matthew Simpson, said of Embury, "He evinced deep feeling, was earnest in his appeals, and he manifested the beauty of deep Christian piety. The Methodists of America everywhere honor his memory."

---

[10] James Creighton and Peard Dickinson.
[11] Asbury's journal, 30 April 1801, italics in the original text.
[12] Frank Baker, *From Wesley to Asbury: Studies in Early American Methodism* (Durham, NC: Duke University Press, 1976), 39.

As Methodism grew in Ireland, Roman Catholic and Anglican persecution against the Methodists became severe. Numbers of priests recruited troublemakers to beat drums to drown out the Methodist preachers' sermons. Rowdies physically attacked Methodist preachers. After preaching in Ireland, Charles Wesley journalized,

> A mob . . . assaulted the house where the [Methodist] society was met after evening service. They met them going out with sticks and stones, knocked down several, both men and women, and beat them in a barbarous manner. . . . The mob broke [the door] open, and . . . tore down the desk and forms, carried two large counters, chairs, and part of the wainscoting into the street, and openly burnt all but what they stole. . . . They have often threatened our lives."

In 1762, in response to persecutions of the Methodists, John Wesley wrote *A Short Address to the Inhabitants of Ireland, Occasioned by Some Late Occurrences*. Opening that tract, Wesley said,

> There has lately appeared . . . a set of men preaching up and down several parts of this kingdom who for ten or twelve years have been known in England by the title of 'Methodists'. The vulgar in Ireland term them 'Swaddlers'—a name first given them in Dublin, from one of them preaching on those words, 'Ye shall find the young child wrapped in swaddling clothes, lying in a manger.'
>
> Extremely various have been the reports concerning them. Some persons have spoken favourably; but the generality of men treat them in a different manner, with utter contempt, if not detestation; and relate abundance of things in order to prove that they are not fit to live upon the earth.[13]

Wesley explained what the Methodists believed, assured his readers that the Methodist preachers were loyal to the king, and called for charity and good will among Christians. Specifically, he asked for tolerance toward Methodist preachers whose only aim was to bring people to faith in Jesus Christ and to help nurture their Christian lives. Wesley closed that tract with a plea:

---

[13] "A Short Address to the Inhabitants of Ireland, Occasioned by Some late Occurrences," *The Works of John Wesley*, Bicentennial ed. Vol. 9 (Nashville: Abingdon Press, 1989), 282–87.

> Ye men of Ireland, help! Come all, as one man, all men of religion and reason, all lovers of God and of mankind, and all lovers of your country.... Open your eyes; look around and judge for yourselves; see plain and undeniable facts; be convinced by the force of truth and love that the [Methodist] work is indeed of God.... Beware you do not oppose, or speak or think evil of, what God hath done in the earth. Rather ... join hearts and hands in the work, till holiness and happiness cover our land as the waters cover the sea.[14]

A major complaint against the Methodist preachers was that they were lay people who lacked ordination by a bishop. Concerning this critique, in 1750 Wesley wrote a sermon titled, "A Caution against Bigotry," in which he said,

> But what, if [one] be only a layman, who casts out devils? .... Is there reasonable proof that this man has or does cast out devils? If there is, forbid him not; no, not at the peril of your soul. Shall not God work by whom he will work? No man can do these works unless God is with him; unless God hath sent him for this very thing. But if God hath sent him, will you call him back? Will you forbid him to go?[15]

In his sermon titled "On the Ministerial Office," Wesley elucidated his views on lay preaching:

> In 1744, all the Methodist Preachers had their first Conference. But none of them dreamed that being called to preach gave them any right to administer sacraments. And when that question was proposed, "In what light are we to consider ourselves?" it was answered, "As extraordinary [non-ordained] messengers, raised up to provoke the ordinary [ordained] ones to jealousy."[16] In order hereto, one of our first rules was given to each Preacher, "You are to do that part of the work which we appoint." But what work was this? Did we ever appoint you to administer sacraments; to

---

[14] Ibid, 87.
[15] Sermon, "A Caution Against Bigotry," III, 5.
[16] A reference to Rom. 11:11. "So, I ask, have they stumbled so as to fall? By no means! But through their trespass salvation has come to the Gentiles, so as to make Israel jealous."

exercise the priestly office? Such a design never entered into our mind; it was the farthest from our thoughts.[17]

An unidentified Irish Roman Catholic priest objected to Wesley that it was "harmful, disgraceful, and pernicious" for un-ordained lay persons to preach.[18] Wesley and this interlocutor debated the issue of lay preaching. This discussion led Wesley to write *A Letter to a Clergyman*. A publisher printed it in Dublin in May 1748, and it appears below. In this tract Wesley argues that if preachers have an effective ministry of saving souls they are true ministers—even if they lack a university education, extensive learning, ordination, or salary. Wesley declares, "Every Christian, if he is able to do it, has authority to save a dying soul."

Objections to lay preaching continued in Ireland and England. Years later, in a letter to Anglican Archdeacon George Fleury of Waterford, Wesley said, "This is all harping upon the same string, the grand objection [to] Lay Preachers. We have it again and again, ten, twenty times over. I shall answer it once for all. Not by anything new,—that is utterly needless; but barely [openly] by repeating the answer which convinced a serious Clergyman many years ago."[19] That *Letter to a Clergyman* follows.

---

[17] Sermon, "Prophets and Priests," §11. This sermon is sometimes titled, "On the Ministerial Office."

[18] For that matter, the Anglican bishops and most of the clergy held the same opinion.

[19] Wesley's logic in this tract silenced the priest on the matter of lay preaching.

A Letter to a Clergyman

Tullamore, Ireland
4 May 1748

Reverend Sir,

Presently I have no spare time or inclination to enter into a formal controversy with you. However, I trust you will permit me to offer only a few loose suggestions related to our conversation last evening.

I.

1. Granting that physical life and health are matters of such great importance, undoubtedly it is most fitting that physicians should have all possible advantages of learning and education.

2. Certainly, competent examiners should evaluate them before they begin a public practice.

3. After such assessments, those who are empowered to convey the authorization should certify them to practice medicine.

4. Furthermore, while these doctors are preserving the lives of others, they should have an adequate income to sustain their own lives.

5. Let us suppose that a man bred at the University in Dublin with all the advantages of a medical education, after he has undergone all the usual examinations, receives authorization to practice his vocation.

6. Then, suppose this physician settles at —— for some years, but he cures no one at all. After trying his skill on five-hundred people, he cannot demonstrate that he has healed one person. Many patients died under his hands, and the rest of them remain just as they were before he came.

7. Would you condemn someone who has some lesser skill in the practice of medicine, but a tender compassion for those who are sick or dying all around him, for curing many of them? He asks for no fee or reward for helping those whom the certified doctor could not cure.

8. At least that person did not ask for money (which is the same thing in this example). The certified doctor did not go to the people, and they would not come to him.

9. Will you condemn the one who heals because he lacks formal learning, or because he does not have a university education? Think about it. He cures those whom the man of learning and education cannot cure!

10. Will you object, "He is no physician, nor does he have any right to cure others?" I cannot come to such an opinion. I think, *Medicus est qui medetur* [*He who heals is a physician*]. I also think that everyone has the license to save the life of a dying man. However, if you think only that the healer has no authority to take fees, I do not contest the issue. The effective healer takes no fees at all.

11. Indeed, on the other hand, I fear that it will also hold that *Medicus non est qui non medetur* [*He who does not heal is not a physician*]. To use polite language, I fear that he is no physician who works no cure.

12. You might object, "O, but he has taken his degree of Doctor of Physic, and therefore he has authority."

I answer, "Authority to do what?"

Perhaps you may say, "Why, he has authority to heal all the sick that will employ him."

Now (to set aside the case of those who will not employ him), would you sanction throwing away people's very lives? I answer that he does not heal those that do employ him. Those that were already sick are still sick, or else they have passed away and are seen no more. Therefore, the certified doctor's authority is not worth a rush.[1] The certification does not serve its intended purpose.

13. Surely, the doctor, by hindering someone else from saving people's lives, has no authority to kill them!

14. If such a doctor were to attempt or wish to hinder the healer and condemns or disapproves of the one who cures others, it is clear to all thinking people that the doctor values his own fees more than the lives of his patients.

---

[1] The adage "Not worth a rush" meant "worthless," an allusion is to the practice of strewing floors with rushes, fit only to step on, and afterward to be discarded.

II.

Now I will apply my illustration to our conversation of last evening.

1. Everlasting life, holiness, and the health of souls, are matters of the greatest importance. It is most fitting that Christian ministers, being physicians of the soul, should have all the advantages of education and learning.[2]

2. It is proper that the most competent judges conduct a full examination of them in all respects. This assessment should take place before ministers enter into the public exercise of their office—the salvation of souls.

3. After a proper examination, those who are empowered to convey that authority should authorize these ministers to exercise that office. I believe Bishops are empowered to do this work, and have been so from the apostolic age.[3]

---

[2] John Wesley selected his lay preachers on the basis of their experiential knowledge of God, their natural gifts and abilities, and their effectiveness in ministry. He also required his Methodist preachers to devote themselves to diligent self-culture and self-education. He developed courses of reading for them, including classic works on biblical studies, historical studies, theology, and subjects in other areas as well. He wrote, "(1.) Read the most useful books, and that regularly and constantly. Steadily spend all the morning in this employ, or, at least, five hours in four-and-twenty. . . . If you need no book but the Bible, you are got above St. Paul. . . . Contract a taste for [reading] by use, or return to your trade. . . . No Preacher will stay with us who is as salt that has lost its savour." (*Minutes of Several Conversations*, Q. 32, 1).

In time, Wesley set a standard that required his lay preachers to become equal in understanding to university graduates. Writing about these preachers, he claimed, "I trust there is not one of them who is not able to go through such an examination, in substantial, practical, experimental Divinity, as few of our candidates for holy orders, even in the University, (I speak it with sorrow and shame, and in tender love,) are able to do. But, O! what manner of examination do most of those candidates go through! And what proof are the testimonials commonly brought . . . either of their piety or knowledge to whom are entrusted those sheep which God hath purchased with his own blood!" (*A Farther Appeal to Men of Reason and Religion*, §10).

[3] Christian ordination began when Jesus commissioned the twelve disciples (Matt. 10:1–5) and the Seventy-two for kingdom work in the harvest field (Luke 10:1). After Pentecost, the Twelve directed the Christian community (Acts 2:14; 3:1. 10). In the early church, the chief instances of investiture (ordination) for ministry were (i) The appointment of seven deacons by the laying on of hands (Acts 6). (ii) The prophets and teachers at Antioch commissioning Paul and Barnabas for missionary work (Acts 13:1–3). (iii) St. Paul's reference to *overseers* (ἐπισκόπους), who were to shepherd (ποιμαίνειν) the Church of God (Acts 20:28). (iv) St. Paul's encouraging letter to Timothy to exercise the gift authority given to him by the laying on of hands of the presbytery (1 Tim. 4:14), and the gift that God gave him when St. Paul laid hands on him (2 Tim. 1:6). Further, St. Paul warned Timothy not to commission anyone hastily (1 Tim. 5:22). The apostle outlined the qualifications for elders in the books of 1 Timothy and Titus. In apostolic times and up to the present, ordination is by the entire church, through the church's existing ministers. Self-ordination is not proper.

4. Furthermore, those who save souls should receive what they need to provide for their material needs.[4]

5. Suppose a man bred at the University in Dublin, with all the advantages of education, has undergone the usual examinations and received proper authorization [ordination] to save souls from spiritual death.

6. Suppose, this minister settles at —— for some years, and yet saves no souls whatever. He has rescued no sinners from their sins. After he has preached all this time to five- or six-hundred people, he cannot show that he has converted any of them from the error of their ways. Many of his parishioners die as they lived, and the rest remain just as they were before he came.

7. Will you condemn those who have compassion for dying souls and who possess some knowledge of the gospel of Christ for preaching? They do so without any temporal reward, and save people from their sins, those whom the ordained minister could not save.

8. At least, the ordained minister has not yet saved any souls, nor is he ever likely to do so. He did not go to the people, and they would not come to him.

9. Will you condemn such lay preachers because they lack a formal learning or a university education? Think about it. They save those sinners from their sins, whom the man of learning and education cannot save.

Once, a peasant came before the College of Physicians at Paris. A learned doctor accosted him, "I beg your pardon, friend, do you pretend to prescribe to people that have agues? Do you know what an ague is?"[5] The peasant replied, "Yes, Sir; an ague is what I can cure, and you cannot cure."

10. Will you object, "But he is no minister, and he has no authority to save souls?" I must beg permission to dissent from your view. I think he is a true, evangelical Minister, a διάκονος, [*a servant*] of Christ and his Church, who οὕτως διακονεῖ [*thus ministers*] to save souls from death and to reclaim sinners from their sins. All Christians, if they are able, have the authority to save dying souls. If you mean only that the lay preacher has no authority to take tithes, I grant it. He takes none. As he has freely received, so he freely gives.[6]

11. To carry the matter a little further, I fear, on the other hand, that this view will apply to the soul as well as the body: *Medicus non est qui non medetur* [*He who does not heal is not a physician*]. I am afraid that reasonable people will be much inclined to think that the one who saves no souls is no minister of Christ.

---

[4] 1 Cor. 9:14.
[5] A fever characterized by regularly returning paroxysms, marked by successive cold, hot, and sweating fits.
[6] Matt. 10:8.

12. One might say, "O, but he is ordained, and therefore has authority."

I answer, "Authority to do what? To save all the souls that will put themselves under his care?" That is true; but (to wave the case of them that will not come to him) would you want them to perish? In fact, such a minister does not save those that are under his care: Therefore, what purpose does his authority serve? Among his flock, he that was a drunkard is still a drunkard. The same is true of the Sabbath-breaker, the thief, and the common swearer. This is the best of the case, for many have died in their iniquity. God will require their blood at the watchman's hand.[7]

13. Surely, such a minister has no authority to murder souls by his neglect, his easy if not false doctrine, or his hindering another preacher from plucking souls out of the fire[8] and his bringing them to everlasting life.[9]

14. If the one who objects to the effective minister or attempts or wants to hinder him, if he condemns or is displeased with him for saving souls, how strong are the reasons to fear that he regards his own profit more than the salvation of souls!

I am, Reverend Sir,
Your affectionate brother,
John Wesley

---

[7] Ezek. 33:6; Heb. 13:17; James 3:1.
[8] Zech. 3:2.
[9] John 6:47; 1 Tim. 1:16.

Selection 4

Advice to the People Called Methodists

Editor's Introduction

Advice to the People Called Methodists

In 1745, John Wesley wrote *Advice to the People Called Methodists* to define the ideal character of a devout Christian. Wesley states that Methodism aims at nothing more than holiness of heart and life that leads in all things to inward and outward conformity to God's will revealed in Scripture.

Assuming this standard, Wesley gives the Methodists his advice, much as a second-century bishop might have addressed his flock. Wesley tells the Methodists to keep to the path they have chosen. "Be true to your principles," he declares. "Never rest again in the dead formality of religion. Pursue with your might both inward and outward holiness; a steady imitation of Him you worship; a still increasing resemblance of his perfections, his justice, mercy, and truth."

Wesley's vision harmonizes with the aims and experiences of sincere Christians through the centuries. Among Roman Catholics, Eastern Orthodoxy, Lutherans, Anabaptists, Calvinists, Anglicans, Puritans, Baptists, Quakers, Presbyterians, and others there are examples of men and women who exemplified the principles and practices that Wesley describes in this tract. These Christians have not necessarily used Wesley's terminology. However, they were "a people who quietly trimmed the golden lamps of personal piety, and shed radiance over their own narrow sphere."[1]

These godly men and women, however, often lacked the degree of connection with each other that Wesley deemed important for Christians. A mark of the Methodist heritage is that it gathered committed Christians into united societies whose aim was to make biblical principles and practices a pattern for their lives. In this tract, Wesley told the Methodists that they were a "new people." Their name was new and, to many whom the church had failed to reach, their principles were new. In that day, they were a new people with regard to their commitments to abstain from every form of evil, and their mutual determination to live fully for God, with a view to eternity embedded in their souls.

Methodism's power was impressive, and its influence was astonishingly effective. The Methodists encouraged the abolition slavery, advanced the education of the masses, grew Sunday schools, helped humanize the prison system, worked to end child labor, assisted in the emancipation of oppressed workers, improved national politics, and brought untold numbers of lost people to a saving knowledge of Jesus Christ. As logs are placed closely together in a fireplace, the concentrated and reciprocal light and warmth of the Methodists reached throughout the British Commonwealth, into the American colonies, and, eventually, around the world.

This tract, *Advice to the People Called Methodists*, reminds us that throughout Christian history it is normal for Christ's devoted followers to encounter opposition. Jesus said to his disciples, "Servants are not greater than their master. If they persecuted me, they will persecute you."[2] St. Paul predicted, "All who want to live a godly life in Christ Jesus will be persecuted."[3] Serious Christians can expect the disapproval of others. As to be expected, from the beginning of the Wesleyan movement, people ridiculed and physically persecuted the Methodists.[4]

From a logical standpoint, the strength and fury of Methodism's enemies seems inexplicable. The majority of the Methodists were honest, orderly, industrious, and law-abiding. They helped their neighbors and did works of charity and mercy. Indeed, membership in a Methodist society required a commitment to upright living and service to others. Wesley did not disparage the Church of England or the nation's government. He urged the Methodists to remain loyal to both

---

[1] John S. Simon, *The Revival of Religion in England in the Eighteenth Century* (London: Robert Cullley, n. d.) 308.
[2] John 15:20.
[3] 2 Tim. 3:12.
[4] Josiah Henry Barr, *Early Methodists Under Persecution* (Salem, OH: Schmul Publishers, reprint, 1978).

church and state.[5] Wesley's sermons were charitable, temperate, sensible, and accepting of others. He never sought to inflame his hearers to engage in rash or revolutionary acts. It is perplexing that civil authorities failed to protect the Methodists from persecution and violence at the hands of ruffians, rowdies, and religious leaders.

Wesley spoke about persecution in Discourse Three of his series of thirteen sermons on Christ's Sermon on the Mount, He asked, rhetorically, "Why are Christ's followers persecuted?" He said, "The answer is equally plain and obvious. It is for righteousness' sake . . . because they 'will live godly in Christ Jesus'[6] because they 'are not of the world.'[7] . . . . If it were not for this, they would be tolerated, and the world would love its own.[8] They are persecuted, because they are poor in spirit.[9] . . . they hunger and thirst after righteousness[10] . . . they are merciful,[11] lovers of all, including evil and unthankful people."

Wesley said, "The persecution which attends all the children of God is that our Lord describes in the following words:

> Blessed are ye when men shall revile you, and persecute you,—shall persecute by reviling you,—and say all manner of evil against you, falsely, for my sake.[12] This cannot fail; it is the very badge of our discipleship; it is one of the seals of our calling; it is a sure portion entailed on all the children of God: If we have it not, we are bastards and not sons. Straight through evil report, as well as

---

[5] In 1758, John Wesley wrote a tract, *Reasons Against A Separation From the Church of England.* "Such a separation," he said "should not only throw away the peculiar glorying which God has given us, that we do and will suffer all things for our brethren's sake, though the more we love them, the less we be loved; but should act in direct contradiction to that very end for which we believe God hath raised us up. The chief design of His providence in sending us [Methodists] out is, undoubtedly, to quicken our brethren. And the first message of all our Preachers is, to the lost sheep of the Church of England. Now, would it not be a flat contradiction to this design, to separate from the Church."

Wesley's brother, Charles, added, "I think myself bound in duty to add my testimony to my brother's. His twelve reasons against our ever separating from the Church of England are mine also. . . . I am quite clear that it is neither expedient nor lawful for me to separate; and I never had the least inclination or temptation so to do. My affection for the Church is as strong as ever; and I clearly see my calling; which is, to live and to die in her communion. This, therefore, I am determined to do, the Lord being my Helper."

[6] 2 Tim. 3:12.
[7] John 15:19; 17:14, 16; 18:36; Rom. 12:2; 1 Cor. 2:12.
[8] John 15:19.
[9] Matt. 5:3.
[10] Matt. 5:6.
[11] Matt. 5:7.
[12] Matt. 5:10.

good report, lies the only way to the kingdom. The meek, serious, humble, zealous lovers of God and their fellow beings are of good report among their brethren. However, they are of evil report with the world, which counts and treats them as the filth and offscouring of all things.[13]

John Wesley wrote *Advice to the People Called Methodists* to advise the Methodists that the proper response to antagonism is to live without duplicity, remain tolerant of others, keep consistent, and continue their strong trust in God.

---

[13] Wesley's "Sermon on the Mount, Discourse 3," III, §7. The quotation "the filth and offscouring of all things" comes from 1 Cor. 4:13. *Offscouring* is an older English word that means *refuse, filth, scum, garbage,* or *rubbish*. In 1526, William Tyndale translated 1 Cor. 4:13, "We are evyll spoken of and we praye. We are made as it were the filthynes of the worlde the ofscowringe of all thinges even vnto this tyme."

Advice to the People Called Methodists

(Written in 1745)

Disce, docendus adhuc quae censet amiculus.[1]

1. It may be necessary to identify who I mean by the indistinct term, *Methodists*. It would be a waste of energy to speak to them without first describing them.

2. By Methodists, I mean those who profess to pursue holiness of heart and life (in whatever measure they have attained it). Methodists seek inward and outward conformity to God's revealed will in all things. They want their religion consistently to resemble its great purpose, which is an unceasing imitation of the God they worship, in all his replicated perfections. Particularly, they desire that justice,[2] mercy,[3] truth,[4] and universal love[5] fill their hearts and govern their lives.[6]

3. You Methodists, to whom I now speak, believe such love for humankind cannot rise from any source other than the love of God. You know that there can be no example of one whose tender affection embraces everyone (though not linked to you by ties of blood or any natural or civil bond) unless that affection flows from a grateful, devoted love to the common Father of everyone.[7] That is,

---

[1] This line is from Horace [Quintus Horatius Flaccus (65 BC– 8 BC)], *Epistles*, I.xvii.3. "Yet learn the views of your humble friend, who still needs some teaching."

[2] Psa. 103:6; Zeph. 3:5; John 5:30; Rom. 2:2; Rev. 15:13, 16:7.

[3] Gen. 18:26, 19:16; Ex. 34:6; Deut. 4:31, 32:33; 2 Chron. 30:9; Ezra 9:13; Neh.9:17, 31; Psa. 37:26, 103:8, 116:5, 117:2, 119:76; Jer. 3:12; Joel. 2:13; Jonah 4:2; Luke 6:36; Heb. 8:12.

[4] 2 Sam. 7:28; Matt. 22:16; Mark 12:14; John 1:14, 3:33, 14:6, 18:37; Rom. 3:4; 2 Cor. 1:18; 1 Thess. 1:9; Heb. 6:18; 1 Jn.5:20; Rev. 3:14; 15:13, 19:19, 22:6.

[5] Psa. 103:11; Zeph. 3:17; Rom. 5:5, 8:39; Eph. 2:4; 1 Jn. 4:7–8, 10, 16.

[6] Psa. 25:9, 31:3, 32:8, 48:14, 73:24; Isa. 49:10; 58:11; Luke 1:79; John 16:13.

[7] John Wesley sometimes uses the word *Father* to indicate God as *creator*. By no means did Wesley that all people on earth are children of God, although God *created* everyone.

to God, who is not only a personal Father, but the Father of the spirits of all flesh.[8] Indeed, God is the common parent and friend of all the families of both heaven and earth.[9]

4. Let us understand that this filial love flows only from faith, which is the assurance of things hoped for and the conviction of things not seen.[10] To those who accept this principle, we can say,

> *The things unknown to feeble sense,*[11]
> *Unseen by reason's glimmering ray,*
> *With strong commanding evidence*[12]
> *Their heavenly origin display.*[13]

In Wesley's sermon, "The Marks of the New Birth," (II. §3), he said, "Say not then in your heart, 'I was once baptized, therefore I am now a child of God.' Alas, that consequence will by no means hold. How many are the baptized gluttons and drunkards, the baptized liars and common swearers, the baptized railers and evil-speakers, the baptized whoremongers, thieves, extortioners? What think you? Are these now the children of God? Verily, I say unto you, whosoever you are, unto whom any one of the preceding characters belongs, 'Ye are of your father the devil, and the works of your father ye do.'"

[8] Num. 16:22, 27:16.

[9] The biblical revelation of God as Father runs in two parallel streams: (1) In a general sense, by God's creation, he is the Maker "of all flesh." In this sense, we can speak of the universal fatherhood of God. (2) In a qualified and restricted sense, God is the heavenly Father of the Lord's Prayer. In this context, God is the heavenly parent only of those who through grace have placed their faith in Christ and are committed to his Lordship in their lives.

The following scriptures speak of the Creator-God in the universal sense as the father of all humankind: Deut. 32:6; Mal. 2:10; Matt. 23:9; Rom. 3:29; 1 Cor. 8:6; Eph. 4:6; Heb. 12:9; 1 Jn. 5:7. The Pharisees claimed God as their father. God was their creator, but they refused to surrender their lives to God or to obey his commands. Jesus announced to the Pharisees, "You are from your father the devil, and you choose to do your father's desires. He was a murderer from the beginning and does not stand in the truth, because there is no truth in him. When he lies, he speaks according to his own nature, for he is a liar and the father of lies" (John 8:44). God was their creator; Satan was their father.

These scriptures speak of God in the Christian sense as the Heavenly Father of the followers of Jesus Christ: John 1:18, 6:27, 45–46, 8:42, 16:27; Rom. 1:7, 15:6; 1 Cor. 1:3, 8:6, 15:24; 2 Cor. 1:2–4, 11:31; Gal 1:1–6; Eph. 1:2–3, 17, 5:20, 6:23; Phil. 1:2, 2:11, 4:20; Col. 1:2–3, 2:2, 3:17; 1 Thess. 1:1–3, 3:11–13; 2 Thess. 1:1–2, 2:16; 1 Tim. 1:2; 2 Tim. 1:2; Tit. 1:4; Philem. 1:3; James 1:7; 1 Pet. 1:2–3; 1 Jn. 3:1; 2 Jn. 1:3, 9; Jude 1:1; Rev. 2:6. Jesus said, "I am the way, and the truth, and the life. No one comes to the Father except through me (John 14:6). He promised, "Everything that the Father gives me will come to me, and anyone who comes to me I will never drive away" (John 6:37).

[10] Heb. 11:1.
[11] Eccl. 11:5; Acts 17:23.
[12] Heb., 11:1.
[13] Psa. 19:1.

> *Faith lends its realizing light,*[14]
> *The clouds disperse, the shadows fly;*[15]
> *Th' Invisible appears in sight,*[16]
> *And God is seen by mortal eye.*[17]

5. Methodists believe this kind of faith infers the evidence that God is merciful to us as sinners,[18] that we become reconciled by the death of his Son,[19] and that God accepts us for Christ's sake. Accordingly, in addition to your acceptance of Scripture, you describe the faith of a real Christian as a certain trust and sure confidence that God has forgiven our sins; and that through the merits of Christ we are reconciled to God's the favor.[20]

6. Furthermore, you believe that the Spirit of God works this faith and love in us. Truly, there cannot be in any one of us a good attitude, desire, or even a good thought, except by the almighty power of God through the inspiration and influence of the Holy Spirit.[21]

7. I encourage all Methodists to live by the following rule: Continually endeavor to know, love, and resemble, the great God and Father of our Lord Jesus Christ,[22] who is the God of love and pardoning mercy.[23] From this principle of loving and obedient faith, carefully abstain from all evil,[24] and, as you have opportunity, strive to do good to all people[25] (friends or enemies), and unite together to

---

[14] 2 Pet. 1:19.

[15] Song of Songs, 2:17.

[16] John 1:18; Heb. 11:27.

[17] These verses come from Charles Wesley's hymn, "The Life of Faith, Exemplified in the Eleventh Chapter of St. Paul's Epistle to the Hebrews," in sixteen parts. It first appeared in 1740 as a twelve-page broadside and in *Hymns and Sacred Poems*, pp., 6–20. The 1780 Wesleyan hymnal, *A Collection of Hymns for the Use of The People Called Methodists*, includes six of the stanzas (Hymn # 92). Here, John Wesley quotes stanzas five and six of this hymn.

[18] Psa. 6:2; 27:7; 51:1; 119:77; 123:3; Luke 18:3.

[19] Rom. 5:10; 2 Cor. 5:18, 20; Col. 1:21.

[20] 2 Cor. 5:18; Eph. 2:16; Col. 1:12; Heb. 2:17.

[21] The Anglican Book of Common Prayer contains a Collect for Purity that includes the prayer, "Cleanse the thoughts of our hearts by the inspiration of your Holy Spirit, that we may perfectly love you, and worthily magnify your name, through Christ our Lord."

[22] 2 Cor. 11:31.

[23] Psa. 86:5.

[24] 1 Thess. 4:3, 5:22; 1 Pet. 2:11.

[25] Psa. 34:13; 37:3; Luke 6:35; Gal. 6:10; Heb. 13:16; James 4:17.

encourage and help each other in working out your salvation,[26] and watch over one another in love.[27] This description is what I mean by being a Methodist.

8. As one who loves your souls, this is the *first* general advice I would earnestly recommend to every Methodist: *With deep and frequent attention, consider the particular circumstances in which you stand.*[28]

9. One of these circumstances is that you are new creations in Christ.[29] Your name Methodist is new, at least, as used in a religious sense.[30] Until a few years ago, the term Methodist was unheard of in our own or any other nation.[31] Your principles are new. In this regard, there is no other set of people among us (and, possibly, not in the Christian world) who hold them all in the same degree and in such unity. The Methodists strenuously and continually insist on the absolute necessity of complete holiness in heart and life. Methodists have a peaceful, joyous love for God and a supernatural evidence of things not seen.[32] They have an inner witness that they are the children of God.[33] The Holy Spirit inspires them to every good thought, word, and deed. Perhaps there is no other group of people, (at least, not visibly united together) who lay as much or more stress than you Methodists do on rightness of opinions, forms of worship, and the use of those ordinances

---

[26] Phil. 2:12. We are not to work to earn salvation, which comes only by grace through faith. However, Christians are to embrace fully their salvation by becoming and doing all to which God summons them. "It is God who is at work in you, enabling you both to will and to work for his good pleasure" (Phil 2:13).

[27] Rom. 15:14; 1 Cor. 12:25; Gal. 5:13; Eph. 4:32; Col. 3:16; 1 Thess. 5:11; Heb. 3:13, 10:25; 1 Pet. 1:22; 1 Jn. 3:11.

[28] 2 Thess. 2:15.

[29] Wesley's *Notes upon the New Testament* translates 2 Cor. 5:17, "If anyone be in Christ, there is a new creation: the old things are passed away; behold, all things are become new." Commenting on this verse, he said, "Only the power that makes a world can make a Christian.... Behold! The present, visible, undeniable change!.... He has new life, new senses, new faculties, new affections, new appetites, new ideas and conceptions. His whole tenor of action and conversation [conduct] is new, and he lives, as it were, in a new world."

[30] Rev. 2:17, 3:12.

[31] Wesley wrote in his journal on 13–14 October 1739, "Upon a pressing invitation, some time since received, I set out for Wales. About four in the afternoon, I preached on a little green ... to three or four hundred plain people, on, 'Christ our wisdom, righteousness, sanctification, and redemption.' After sermon, one who I trust is an old disciple of Christ, willingly received us into his house: Whither many following, I showed them their need of a Savior, from these words, 'Blessed are the poor in spirit.' In the morning, I described more fully the way to salvation, — 'Believe in the Lord Jesus, and thou shalt be saved'....

I simply described the plain, old religion of the Church of England, which is now almost everywhere spoken against, under the new name of Methodism."

[32] Heb. 11:1.

[33] Rom. 8:16; Gal. 4:6; 1 Jn. 3:24; 4:13; 5:6.

that you acknowledge God has given.³⁴ You lay so much stress on right opinions that you are glad to use every means you know to believe and develop them.³⁵ Yet, you do not condemn any person on earth merely for thinking differently than you think. Certainly, you do not presume that God condemns people for this, so long as they are upright and sincere in heart. You lay much weight on the outward forms of worship through which you receive nurture, and you approve them highly.³⁶ Still, your zeal does not lessen your love for those who conscientiously differ from your style of worship. In the same way, you lay so much emphasis on the use of those ordinances you believe that God gave that you acknowledge there is no salvation for you if you willfully neglect them. Still, you do not judge those who think differently. If others do not believe these ordinances [means of grace] are from God, and consequently do not use them, you do not criticize them.³⁷

10. Taking everything together, we may account your disciplined lives to be new today. (i) You make it a rule, to abstain from fashionable entertainments, reading plays, romances or books of humor, and from singing frivolous songs. (ii)

---

³⁴ Wesley said in his sermon "Causes of the Inefficacy of Christianity" (Sermon #122). "Here I am: I and my Bible. I will not, I dare not, vary from this book, either in great things or small. I have no power to dispense with one jot or tittle of what is contained therein. I am determined to be a Bible Christian, not almost, but altogether. Who will meet me on this ground? Join me on this, or not at all."

³⁵ The Anglican Collect for Whit-Sunday reads, "God, who as at this time didst teach the hearts of thy faithful people, by the sending to them the light of thy Holy Spirit: Grant us by the same Spirit to have a right judgment in all things, and evermore to rejoice in his holy comfort."

³⁶ The Methodists valued congregational singing, the sermon, and individual public testimonies, components of worship often lacking in Anglican services. Frank Baker notes, "Methodists realize their full spiritual stature not as individual worshipers, but as a family. They assemble for fellowship, with each other as well as with God. . . . The essence of Methodist devotion is the fellowship of believers." [*A Charge to Keep: An Introduction to the People Called Methodists* (London: The Epworth Press, 1947), 118–19.]

³⁷ Wesley emphasized the usefulness of "ordinances," such as searching the Scripture, prayer, attending public worship, observing the Lord's Supper, meeting with other believers, fasting, abstinence, and class meetings. He believed that people should use these means of grace, whether or not they felt like it. He disagreed with those who waited for the Holy Spirit to impel them to pray, fast, or attend public worship. He wrote in his journal, "About September, 1739, while my brother and I were absent, certain men crept in among them [the Methodists) unawares, greatly troubling and subverting their souls; telling them, they were in a delusion, that they had deceived themselves, and had no true faith at all. 'For,' said they, 'none has any justifying faith, who has ever any doubt or fear, which you know you have; or who has not a clean heart, which you know you have not: Nor will you ever have it, till you leave off using the means of grace; (so called;) till you leave off running to church and sacrament, and praying, and singing, and reading either the Bible, or any other book; for you cannot use these things without trusting in them Therefore, till you leave them off, you can never have true faith; you can never till then trust in the blood of Christ.'"

You avoid talking in laughing, frivolous, exuberant, distracting manner. (iii) You dress plainly, without superfluous adornment. (iv) You have an honest method in business. (v) You faithfully observe the Lord's Day. (vi) You scrupulously pay the taxes you owe. (vii) You abstain from distilled alcoholic drinks (except in cases of medical necessity). (viii) You observe the rule not to mention the fault of an absent person, in particular of ministers or of those in authority. We can describe this kind of disciplined living as "new."

I recognize that certain Christians are scrupulous in *some* of these things, and others are strict about other matters. However, excepting the Methodists, we do not find any other body of people who insist on observing *all* these rules. Therefore, with respect to your *name*, *principles*, and *practice*, you may be considered a new people.

11. Another distinctive circumstance of your present state is that you are newly united together. That is, you are recently gathered (or gathering) out of other societies or congregations. Also, you have been, and still are, living without a position of authority (because you are underprivileged and unimportant people who lack wealth). Almost all of you are poor and without anything but the necessities of life. You live without any extraordinary gifts of nature or advantages of education. Even most of your teachers are not well educated, and in many areas, they are ignorant.[38]

12. There is still another unique fact about you. Every other group of religious people separated themselves from their former societies or congregations, as soon as they joined together. By contrast, you did not do this. Indeed, you utterly disavowed any desire to separate from others.[39] You openly and continually declare

---

[38] No eighteenth-century British parliament ever adopted a plan for compulsory public education. An exception to the government's disregard for the ignorance of the common people was that in 1699 the Anglican Society for the Promotion of Christian Knowledge's established charity schools for poor children. These schools taught those, between the ages of seven and twelve, the subjects of reading, writing, arithmetic, and the catechism. To correct the lack of public education, Wesley wrote numerous penny tracts containing his sermons, social admonitions, moral teachings, and Charles Wesley's hymns—all printed in clear type on good paper.

[39] In this paragraph, Wesley makes the point that the original Methodists did not plan to leave the Anglican Church. From Methodism's beginnings in America, the movement grew rapidly. However, few Anglican priests in the colonies were willing to give the sacraments to the Methodists. With the start of America's War of Independence and the subsequent formation of the United States of America, most Anglican priests returned to England. As a consequence, the Methodists in America had no access to the sacraments. Wesley implored Robert Lowth, the Anglican Bishop of London, to ordain a ministry for America. Lowth refused Wesley's request. Seeing no alternative, Wesley consecrated

that you have not, nor ever have had, such an intention. Whereas, the congregations to which separatists have belonged have usually spared no efforts to prevent a separation from the Church of England.[40] However, those [Anglican] congregations to which you belong spare no pains to force you to separate from them. They want to drive you out from them and to force you into a division to which you affirm you have the strongest aversion.

13. Considering these particular circumstances, you will see the appropriateness of a *second* word of advice I will recommend to you: *Do not assume that you can avoid giving offence.* Your very name, *Methodist*, renders it impossible to avoid upsetting some people. Possibly, not one in a hundred of those who use the term Methodist have any idea what it means. To ninety-nine of a hundred people, *Methodist* is as obscure as a Greek word, except they believe the term *Methodist* denotes something very bad. They think the word means such things as a Papist, a heretic, a destabilizer of the Church, or some unknown monster. In all probability, the further such rumors spread, they lead more and more people to suspect evil of the Methodists. Thus, it is futile for any Methodist to think of avoiding giving offense.

14. As much offence as you give by your name, you will give still more offense by your principles. (i) You will offend the bigots who favor certain opinions, modes of worship, and ordinances because you do not stress them enough.[41] (ii) You will offend other bigots because you stress them too much. (iii) You will offend people whose religion is mere outward form by insisting so frequently and strongly on the inward power of religion.[42] (iv) You will offend moral people (so called) because you proclaim the absolute necessity of faith for receiving God's

---

Thomas Coke, an ordained Anglican priest, as superintendent of the American Methodists. Wesley also ordained two English lay preachers for work in America. In 1784, the American Methodists formed the Methodist Episcopal Church, formalizing a break from the Anglican Church. British Methodism remained a society within Anglicanism during Wesley's lifetime. After Wesley's death (1791), the British Methodists also formed a new denomination (1795).

[40] During the years of Queen Elizabeth's reign (1558–1603), certain Christians believed that the English Reformation had not sufficiently shed all the "rags of popery." These "Puritans" wanted further to purify the Church of England from all "popish forms." The Puritans promoted a strict Calvinism, and they opposed Roman Catholic clerical vestments, purgatory, limbo for deceased infants lacking baptism, prayers for the dead, prayers to departed saints, the mass as a sacrifice to God, making the sign of the cross ("sign of the Lord"), and ecclesiastical courts. Many Puritans remained within the national church, but some broke away to form small independent, autonomous congregations with congregational governments. These were called Separatists.

[41] Eph. 2:13-15.
[42] 2 Tim. 3:5.

acceptance.⁴³ (v) You will offend rationalists because you talk of inspiration and of receiving the Holy Spirit.⁴⁴ (vi) You will offend drunkards, Sabbath-breakers, common blasphemers, and other bold sinners, by avoiding their company and your censure of their behavior, which you will often need to express.⁴⁵

Indeed, your lives will always offend these people. Your sobriety severely offends the drunkard; your serious conduct is equally intolerable to merry-making, brazen people. Others dislike you because you have become so conscientious, singular, and "monstrously strict beyond sense and reason."⁴⁶ You have scruples about many alleged "harmless things," and you assume that you are obligated to do so many other things that are not required. You cannot avoid offending many people, especially your friends and relatives. Therefore, you must decide whether to give up your principles or your hope of pleasing others.⁴⁷

15. Those who take offense at your principles, regard it even more offensive that you are united together. This union causes you to be more conspicuous, making you even more suspicious in the eyes of others. I mean that you become more liable to draw the suspicion of carrying on some sinister scheme, especially in the eyes of those who do not, or will not, know your holy attachment to the majesty of God. You become even more frightful to those of a distrustful frame of mind, and they imagine you have evil plans. You become more abhorrent to zealous people, if their intensity is anything other than the fervent love of God and their fellow beings.

16. This offence will sink all the deeper because you are gathered out of so many congregations. For the excitable people in these congregations will not easily keep from believing that you despise them or their teachers. Actually, they will

---

⁴³ It is a natural tendency of many people to rely on themselves and their good deeds. They overestimate their own goodness and underestimate their need for the grace of God.

⁴⁴ Rationalists were uncomfortable with spiritual realities and the idea of a conscious presence of God in one's life. They lived on the horizontal plane of the present world, without acknowledging an eternal world and a future final judgment.

⁴⁵ Wesley believed that it is sometimes necessary to speak against and oppose evil. In his 1787 sermon, "The Duty of Reproving Your Neighbor," he used portions of Leviticus: "You shall not hate in your heart anyone of your kin; you shall reprove your neighbor, or you will incur guilt yourself. You shall not take vengeance or bear a grudge against any of your people, but you shall love your neighbor as yourself: I am the LORD. You shall keep my statutes" (Lev. 19:17–19). In that sermon, Wesley said, "Love indeed requires us to warn him, not only of sin, (although of this chiefly,) but likewise of any error which, if it were persisted in, would naturally lead to sin. If we do not 'hate him in our heart,' if we love our neighbour as ourselves, this will be our constant endeavour; to warn him of every evil way, and of every mistake which tends to evil."

⁴⁶ This criticism of the Methodists was likely a common phrase.

⁴⁷ John 12:43; Gal. 1:10.

probably imagine that you utterly condemn them, as if they cannot be saved. Presently, this occasion of offence is now at its height because you have just joined with the Methodists, or you are planning to do so. The critics do not know where Methodism will end. Their fear of losing more of their members (so they think) gives sharpness to their zeal. Their alarm keeps their anger and resentment at full strength.

17. Add to this the fear that you have not exactly left them, because you still rank yourselves as a part of their membership.[48] Those who do not know that your loyalty to the Church of England is a matter of conscience become annoyed by your presence among them. They wish you would get out of their sight! As long as you remain with them, you are a continuing thorn in their side.

18. Your presence among your critics angers them all the more because you possess no power, riches, or learning. Yet, with all their power, money, and wisdom, they can gain no ground against you.

19. You can expect that the offence that continually arises from such a variety of provocations will gradually grow into hatred, malice, and all manner of unkind attitudes. Those who regard you in a hostile way will not fail to represent you to others in the same light that you appear to them. They see you sometimes as maniacs and fools, sometimes as wicked people, people not fit to live on the earth. Humanly speaking, the consequence must be that, along with your reputation, you first will lose the love of your friends, relatives, and acquaintances, even those who once loved you the most affectionately. You will also lose your employment, for many will hire you no longer or purchase from such a person as you. In due time (unless God who governs the world intervenes), you may forfeit your health, freedom, and life.

20. What is the correct counsel for people in such a situation? I can only offer my *third* word of advice to the people called Methodists. Consider deeply with

---

[48] Throughout Wesley's lifetime, he insisted that he was "a Church of England man." He wanted Methodism to serve as a society with the church to call it back to its stated doctrines (of which many in the church were ignorant or neglectful). A year before Wesley died, he wrote in the *Arminian Magazine*, "I never had any design of separating from the Church. I have no such design now. I do not believe the Methodists in general design it, when I am no longer seen. I do, and will do, all that is in my power to prevent such an event. Nevertheless, in spite of all that I can do, many of them will separate from it. . . . I declare once more, that I live and die a member of the Church of England; and that none who regard my judgment or advice will ever separate from it." Wesley died in 1791, and in 1795, the British Methodists formed a new denomination. Earlier, in 1784, the American Methodists had formed the Methodist Episcopal Church, with two bishops, Thomas Coke and Francis Asbury.

yourself, *"Is the God whom I serve able to deliver me?"*[49] You may think, "I am not able to deliver myself out of these difficulties, much less am I able to bear them. I do not know how to surrender my reputation, friends, substance, liberty, and life. Can God enable me to rejoice in doing this; and can I depend on him to do so?[50] Are the hairs of my head all numbered?[51] "Does God ever fail those who trust in him?"[52] Weigh these questions thoroughly. If you can trust God with everything, then go on in the power of his might.[53]

21. To go forward, my *fourth* word of advice to the people called Methodists is, *Keep in the same path on which you now tread. Be true to your principles. Rest no more in the formality of dead religion.*[54] With all your might, pursue both inward and outward holiness. Seek a steady imitation of the God you worship, an ever-growing resemblance of his perfections worthy of imitation[55]—his justice, mercy, and truth.[56]

22. Let this be your robust, noble, generous religion, detached from shabby superstition that sees religion as doing what God has not instructed, or abstaining from what he has not forbidden.[57] Avoid the unkindness of bigotry that limits your affection to your own party, sect, or opinion. Above all, stand firm in obedient faith[58]—that is, faith in the God of pardoning mercy, the God and Father of

---

[49] 2 Sam. 22:2; Isa. 46:4; Jer. 1:8; Dan. 3:17; Rom. 4:21; 2 Cor. 1:10; Eph. 3:20; Phil. 3:21; Heb. 7:25; Jude 1:24.

[50] Psa. 50:15; 91:14–15; 2 Tim. 4:18.

[51] Mat. 10:30; Luke 12:7.

[52] Deut. 7:9; 1 Kings 8:56; Psa. 78:8, 89:1; 1 Cor. 1:9; 1 Pet. 4:19.

[53] 1 Chron. 29:12; 2 Chron. 25:8; Psa. 62:11; Matt. 19:26; Luke 1:37; Eph. 6:10.

[54] Wesley often spoke about those who had the form of religion without the power of religion. In his Sermon #16, "The Means of Grace," He said, "It is a melancholy truth, that a large proportion of those who are called Christians, do to this day abuse the means of grace to the destruction of their souls. This is doubtless the case with all those who rest content in the form of godliness, without the power. Either they fondly presume they are Christians already, because they do thus and thus,— although Christ was never yet revealed in their hearts, nor the love of God shed abroad therein."

[55] Here, Wesley uses the word *imitable*. This word is now obsolete, and it meant *worthy of imitation*.

[56] 2 Jn. 1:3.

[57] For example, God has not instructed us to remain single, nor has he forbidden us to marry. Some impose celibacy as a higher state than a married state. The Genesis account of creation states, "The LORD God said, 'It is not good that the man should be alone; I will make him a helper as his partner'" (Gen. 2:18). The notion that an unmarried state is higher and holier than a married state has no foundation in Scripture. Other examples are the prohibition of eating meat on a certain day, clerical celibacy, the veneration of Mary, prayers to angles, and dispensations that require payments of money.

[58] 1 Cor. 16:13; Gal. 5:1; Phil. 1:27; 4:1; 1 Thess. 3:8; 2 Thess. 2:15.

our Lord Jesus Christ.[59] He has loved you, and given himself for you.[60] Ascribe to Christ all the good you find in yourself. That includes all of your peace, joy, love, and strength to do and suffer his will through the Spirit of the living God.[61] In the meantime, carefully avoid fanaticism.[62] Do not attribute all of your dreams to the all-wise God.[63] Do not expect either light or power from God, other than through the serious use of all the means he has ordained.[64]

23. Also, be true to your principles pertaining to the opinions and the externals of religion. Use every ordinance[65] you believe is from God. Yet, beware of a narrow spirit toward those who do not use them as you do.[66] Practice those modes of worship that you prefer, yet love as brothers and sisters those who cannot conform to your manner of worship. Emphasize your opinions so that, if possible, others may agree with their truth and reasonableness. Yet, carefully avoid anger, antipathy, or contempt towards those whose opinions differ from yours. Daily, some accuse you of such bigotry (indeed, what is it of which you are *not* accused?). Be careful not to give any grounds for such accusations of intolerance.

---

[59] Rom. 15:6; 2 Cor. 1:3, 11:31; Eph. 1:3, 17, 5:20; Col. 1:3; 2 Thess. 1:1; 1 Pet. 1:3.

[60] Gal. 1:4, 2:20; 1 Tim. 2:6; Tit. 2:14.

[61] Phil. 2:13.

[62] Biblical examples of fanaticism are found in 1 Kings 18:28; Dan. 3:19; John 10:31; Acts 7:59; 9:1; 21:36; 22:23.

[63] On 22 June 1739, Wesley wrote in his journal, "I told them, they were not to judge of the spirit whereby anyone spoke, either by *appearances*, or by *common report*, or by their own *inward feelings*: No, nor by any dreams, visions, or revelations, supposed to be made to their souls; any more by their tears, or any involuntary effects wrought upon their bodies. I warned them, all these were, in themselves, of a doubtful, disputable, nature; they *might* be from God, and they *might not*; and were therefore not simply to be relied on . . . but to be tried by a farther rule, to be brought to the only certain test, 'the law and the testimony' [Scriptures].

[64] Wesley's Sermon #16 is titled, The Means of Grace," in which he explained, "By 'means of grace' I understand outward signs, words, or actions, ordained of God, and appointed for this end–to be the *ordinary* channels whereby he might convey to [us], preventing, justifying, or sanctifying grace. I use this expression, means of grace, because I know none better; and because it has been generally used in the Christian Church for many ages: in particular by our own church, which directs us to bless God both for 'the means of grace and hope of glory'; and teaches us, that a sacrament is 'an outward sign of inward grace, and a means whereby we receive the same.' The chief of these means are prayer, whether in secret or with the great congregation; searching the Scriptures; (which implies reading, hearing, and meditating thereon;) and receiving the Lord's supper, eating bread and drinking wine in remembrance of him; and these we believe to be ordained of God, as the ordinary channels of conveying his grace to the souls of men." (*The Works of John Wesley*, Bicentennial ed., 1:381).

[65] Again, *ordinances* refer to the means of grace found in Methodism's General Rules— "Do no harm; Do good, Use the ordinances of God [means of grace]."

[66] Matt. 7:1; Rom. 14:4, 13; 1 Cor. 4:5; 1 Tim. 6:4; James 4:12.

Do not condemn anyone for not thinking as you think. Let others enjoy the full and free liberty of thinking for themselves. Let others use their own judgment, since each of us must give an account to God.⁶⁷ Abhor the spirit of persecution of any sort or measure. If you cannot reason or persuade others into the truth, never try to force them into it. If love will not compel them to come in, leave them to God, the Judge of all.⁶⁸

24. Yet, do not expect that others will deal with you this way. Indeed, some will attempt to frighten you out of your principles, and some will try to shame you into a more popular religion.⁶⁹ Some will try to laugh at you and draw you from your singular purpose. However, none of these will put you in such great danger as those who assault you with quite different weapons. They use smoothness, good-natured charm, and strong intentions of goodwill (perhaps real intentions). Here, you are to be equally concerned to avoid even the appearance of anger, contempt, or unkindness. In principle and practice, you must hold fast to the whole truth of God.⁷⁰

25. Some people may interpret your fortitude as unkindness. Your former acquaintances will view your refusal to sin or continue in fellowship with them as clear proof of your coldness toward them. You must be willing to bear this burden. Work to avoid all unkindness, discourteous words, cruel speech, timidity, or bizarre behavior. Speak to former friends with complete tenderness and love, and behave with all the pleasantness and courtesy you can. Take care not to give any needless offence to a neighbor, stranger, friend, or enemy.

26. Perhaps for this very reason, I might offer a *fifth* word of advice to the Methodists. *Do not say much about what you suffer, the persecution you endure at different times, or the wickedness of your persecutors.* Nothing tends more to exasperate them than such talk. Although there is a time when with a safe conscience you may need mention these things, it may be a general rule to do so as seldom as you can. As well as its tendency to anger them, complaining has the appearance of evil, pretention, or self-exaltation.⁷¹ It also tends to fill you with pride and to make you think of yourself as someone great. In your heart, such talk certainly enlivens

---

⁶⁷ Deut. 23:16; Jer. 31:30; Ezek. 18:20; Matt, 12:36; 18:23; Luke 12:20; 19:15; Rom. 14:2; 1 Pet. 4:5.

⁶⁸ Gen. 18:25; Psa. 58:11; Eccl. 3:17; Matt. 25:32; Acts 17:31; Rom. 2:16; 14:10; 2 Tim. 4:1; Heb. 12:23.

⁶⁹ Wesley's *Complete English Dictionary, Explaining Most of Those Hard Words, Which are Found in The Best English Writers*, defines *popular* as "belonging to, beloved by the people."

⁷⁰ 1 Thess. 5:21; 2 Thess. 2:16; 2 Tim. 1:13; Heb. 4:14; 10:23; Rev. 2:25; 3:3,11.

⁷¹ 1 Thess. 5:22; 1 Pet. 2:11.

or increases bitterness, anger, and unkind attitudes. At best, it is a waste of time. Instead of talking about the wickedness of others, you could be talking about the goodness of God.

Indeed, to denigrate others is an open, willful sin. It is gossip, backbiting, and evil-speaking.[72] This is a sin you can never enough guard against, and it steals upon you in a thousand forms. Would it not be far more profitable for your soul to pray for others, instead of speaking against them? Confirm your love towards those unhappy people that you believe are fighting against God. Cry out mightily to the Lord in their behalf. Ask God to open their eyes and change their hearts.[73]

27. It now remains only to commend you to the care of him who has all power in heaven and in earth.[74] I implore God that in every circumstance of life you may stand as "firm as the beaten anvil to the stroke."[75] Passionately desire nothing on earth; accounting all things but rubbish, in order to win Christ.[76] Always remember, "It is the part of a good champion, to be flayed alive, and to conquer!"[77]

October 10, 1745.

---

[72] Eph. 4:31; Tit. 3:2; James 3:6; 1 Pet. 2:1.
[73] Matt. 5:44; Luke 23:34; Acts 7:60.
[74] Job 42:2; Psa. 115:3; Isa. 43:13; Matt. 19:26; Luke 1:37; Rev. 19:6.
[75] This phrase comes from a hymn by Samuel Wesley, Jr. (brother of John and Charles Wesley). That hymn appears in *Poems on Several Occasions*, published in London in 1749. These words originally appeared in a letter of St. Ignatius to Polycarp. Ignatius (c. 35–c. 107). Ignatius, Bishop of Antioch, wrote, "Stand firm, as does an anvil which is beaten. It is the part of a noble athlete to be wounded, and yet to conquer. And especially, we ought to bear all things for the sake of God, that he also may bear with us. Be ever becoming more zealous than what you are. Weigh carefully the times. Look for him who is above all time, eternal and invisible, yet who became visible for our sakes; impalpable and impassible, yet who became passible on our account; and who in every kind of way suffered for our sakes."
[76] Phil. 3:8.
[77] A reference to the sufferings and martyrdoms of early Christians.

Selection 5

*The Nature, Design, and
General Rules of the United Societies*

Editor's Introduction

The Nature, Design, and General Rules of the United Societies

In keeping with the methodical nature of Methodism, John Wesley often composed lists of rules for various purposes and circumstances. By no means did John and Charles Wesley prepare Methodism's General Rules as a means of attaining merit through obedience to a set of directives. Nor do Methodism's General Rules constitute the sort of legalism so characteristic of the first-century Pharisees. Each of Wesley's General Rules has a clear foundation in the Scriptures.

Negatively, John and Charles Wesley promulgated these guidelines as a way to weed out "disorderly walkers"—that is, unrepentant members who fell into sinful practices. Positively, the General Rules for Methodists exist to help them grow in grace and to promote better social conditions. For example, when times for elections of members of parliament drew near, Wesley wrote the Methodists at Bristol, "Give, not sell your vote. Touch not the accursed thing [a bribe], lest it bring a blast upon you and your household." If that counsel sounds like a rule, it is clearly in line with Scripture.

In 1743 Wesley visited a Methodist Society at Newcastle-on-Tyne, where he found lax discipline. To his surprise, he found that some of the Methodists cursed, abused alcohol, and disregarded the Lord's Day. Others lied, gossiped, fought, and one Methodist was guilty of beating his wife. To mend the morals and manners of the Newcastle Society, Wesley "put away [expelled] above fifty persons" because they did not "walk according to the gospel."[1]

As Methodism expanded across England and Ireland, the Wesleys concluded that it was necessary to develop clear standards and effective policies for membership in the Methodist societies. Also, many Methodists asked for guidance in their Christian walk. To help these converts grow spiritually, John and Charles Wesley drafted Methodism's "General Rules." To acquaint the New Castle Society with these rules, John Wesley read them to the assembled society on Sunday 6 March 1743. He wrote in his journal,

> I read over in the society, the Rules which all our members are to observe; and desired everyone seriously to consider, whether he was willing to conform thereto or no. That this would shake many of them I knew well; and therefore, on Monday, 7, I began visiting the classes again, lest 'that which is lame should be turned out of the way.'[2]

Some complained that it was improper to formulate rules for the Methodists *after* they had joined the society. Wesley answered that it was true that the only requirements for joining a Methodist society had been "a desire to flee from the wrath to come." He went on to say that *continuance* as a member of a Methodist society depended on observing the General Rules. He clarified that keeping these rules would help keep people from falling into sin and lapsing into a backslidden condition. He contended that wherever a desire to flee from the wrath to come is truly fixed in the soul, this desire will also corroborate itself in its fruits. He concluded, "It is therefore expected of all who continue therein [in a Methodist society] should continue to evidence their desire for salvation."

When first published in 1743, these General Rules sold for one pence (penny) a copy. During John Wesley's lifetime, thirty-nine editions of Methodism's General Rules were printed. Wesley stated that the General Rules were for "a company

---

[1] Wesley's *Journal*, 20 February 1743.
[2] Journal, 6 March 1743, Curnock edition, 3:68. A reference to Heb. 12:13.

of [people] having the form and seeking the power of godliness, united in order to pray together, to receive the word of exhortation, and to watch over one another in love, that they may help each other to work out their salvation."[3]

In 1784, when the American Methodists founded the Methodist Episcopal Church, they included the General Rules in the church's first *Doctrines and Discipline of the Methodist Episcopal Church* Book of Discipline. In 1787, Bishops Thomas Coke and Francis Asbury prepared a slightly revised edition. In 1808 the church's General Conference adopted a number of Restrictive Rules to help stabilize the fast-growing church. Among other principles of American Methodism, its Restrictive Rules forbid the revocation or change of the church's General Rules. In 1878, Bishop Matthew Simpson wrote,

> These rules continue to be respected and observed by all the branches of the Methodist family. . . . The [Book of] Discipline requires that the rules should be read in the churches . . . and that a copy should be given to persons desiring admission in their first meeting in class.[4]

Today, the General Rules continue as a part of United Methodism's Book of Discipline. These General Rules are also among the standards of the African Methodist Episcopal Church, The African Methodist Episcopal Church Zion, the Christian Methodist Episcopal Church, the Wesleyan Church, the Free Methodist Church, the Evangelical Methodist Church, and other Methodist bodies worldwide.

Methodism's General Rules fall under three headings: (1) Doing no harm, (2) Doing good, and (3) Attending upon the ordinances of God. John Wesley said, "These are the General Rules of our societies; all which we are taught of God to observe, even in his written word, the only rule, and the sufficient rule, both of our faith and practice. And all these, we know, his Spirit writes on every truly awakened heart."

---

[3] Phil. 2:12.

[4] "General Rules," *Cyclopædia of Methodism*, ed. Matthew Simpson (Philadelphia: Everts & Stewart, 1878) 400.

The Nature, Design, and General Rules of the United Societies

Originally Published at Newcastle Upon Tyne in 1743

[Price One Penny]

1. In the latter part of 1739, eight or ten people came to me in London, appearing to be deeply convinced of sin, and earnestly grieving[1] for redemption. They asked (as did two or three more the next day) that I would spend some time with them in prayer and advise them how to flee from the wrath to come.[2] They realized that God's judgment continually hung over their heads.[3] So that we could have more time for this great work, I appointed a day when all of them might meet together. Thereafter, they met with me weekly on Thursday evenings. From time to time, meeting with these and as many more as wanted to join with them (their number increased daily), I offered them advice. I spoke about what I judged they needed most. We always concluded our meeting with prayer suited to their different needs.

2. These meetings gave rise to the United Society, first in London, and then in other places. Such a society is simply "a company of people having the form and seeking the power of godliness.[4] They unite to pray together, receive the word of exhortation, watch over one another in love,[5] and help each other work out their salvation."[6]

---

[1] Here, Wesley used the word *groaning*.
[2] Matt. 3:7; Luke 3:7; John 3:36; Rom. 1:8, 2:8; Eph. 3:5.
[3] Psa. 1:5; 9:6–8; 37:30, Jer. 5:4; Ezek. 39:21; Mic. 3:1; Hab. 1:12; Rom. 2:2–3; 1 Pet. 4:17.
[4] 2 Tim. 3:5
[5] 1 Cor. 16:13.
[6] Phil. 2:12.

3. More clearly to discern that they are indeed working out their own salvation, we divided each society into smaller companies, called classes. We formed the classes according to the members' places of abode. There are about twelve people in each class; one of whom we called the Class Leader. These are a leader's responsibilities:

> (i) To meet at least weekly with each person in the class. The leader is to ask how their souls prosper, to advise, reprove, comfort, or encourage. As occasion may require, the leader receives what they are willing to give toward the relief of the poor.
>
> (ii) To meet the minister and the stewards of the society once a week. The class leader informs the minister of those who are sick or who walk disorderly, refusing correction. These leaders give the stewards the money the classes gave during the preceding week, and the leader reports what each member has contributed.

4. There is one only stipulation required of those who desire admission into these societies. This prerequisite is a desire to flee from the wrath to come[7] and to be saved from their sins.[8] Wherever this desire genuinely grips the soul, it will show itself by its fruits.[9] We expect all who remain in our societies to continue to evidence their desire of salvation in the following three ways.

1.
Do No Harm

First, doing no harm, by avoiding evil of every kind—especially that which is most generally practiced.

I refer to such evils as,

- Making wrongful use of the name of the LORD your God.[10]
- Profaning the day of the Lord, either by doing ordinary work or by buying or selling.[11]

---

[7] Matt. 3:7; Luke 3:7.
[8] Psa. 78:38; 85:2; Matt. 1:21; 26:28; Mark 2:4; Luke 3:3; 24:47; Acts 2:38; Col. 2:13.
[9] Matt. 3:8, 7:16, 20; Luke 13:7; John 15:8.
[10] Ex. 20:7; Lev. 19:12, 22:2; Deut. 28:58; Matt. 5:34, 6:9; James 5:12.
[11] Ex. 20:8; 31:14; 34:21; Neh. 13:15; 19:31; Isa. 56:2; 58:13–14; Ezek. 20:13, 22:8.

- Becoming drunk, buying or selling spirituous liquors,[12] or drinking them, unless in cases of extreme necessity.[13]
- Fighting, quarreling, or brawling.[14]
- Going to law, brother against brother.[15]
- Repaying evil for evil,[16] or abuse for abuse.[17]
- Using many words in buying or selling.[18]
- Buying or selling smuggled goods.[19]

---

[12] Prov. 23:20, 21; 23:31; 26:9; Eccl. 10:17; Isa. 5:11; 28:1; Hos. 4:11; Hab. 2:15; Luke 21:34; Rom. 13:13; 1 Cor. 6:10; Eph. 5:18; 1 Thess. 5:7.

[13] Writing about the eighteenth century, novelist William Makepeace Thackeray said, "All the fuddling [drinking to intoxication] and punch-drinking, that club and coffee-house boozing, shortened the lives and enlarged the waistcoats of the men of that age."

[14] Lev. 19:18; Prov. 17:14; 20:3; 22; 24:29; 25:8, 26:17; Matt. 5:39; Rom. 12:17; 1 Cor. 3:3; 6:6; 2 Cor. 12:20; Eph. 4:2; Phil. 2:3; 4:2; Col. 3:3, 13; 1 Tim. 3:3; 2 Tim. 2:14, 24; Tit. 3:2; James 3:17; 1 Pet. 3:9.

[15] Prov. 25:8; Matt. 5:25, 40; 1 Cor. 6:1.

[16] Lev. 19:18; Prov. 20:22, 24:29; Matt. 5:39; Rom. 12:17.

[17] The original word, λοιδορίαν, means *abuse*; *reviling*; *railing* (1 Pet. 3:9). The word is used in John 9:28, where religious leaders scorned Jesus and in 1 Cor. 4:12–13, where St. Paul said, "When reviled, we bless; when persecuted, we endure; when being reviled (λοιδορούμενοι), we speak kindly." The word βλασφημία, which means *blasphemy, slander; railing; reproach*. A slanderer is one who finds fault with the demeanor and conduct of others, expressed by spreading innuendos and criticisms. Jude 1:9 says, "Moses did not dare to bring the devil's condemnation of slander (βλασφημίας) against him, but said, The Lord rebuke you!"

[18] In Wesley's Sermon on the Mount, Discourse 5, he emphasized the importance of honesty in buying and selling: "Are you not an extortioner? Do you not make a gain of any one's ignorance, or necessity; neither in buying nor selling? Suppose you were engaged in trade: Do you demand, do you receive, no more than the real value of what you sell? Do you demand, do you receive, no more of the ignorant than of the knowing, — of a little child, than of an experienced trader? If you do, why does not your heart condemn you? You are a barefaced extortioner! Do you demand no more than the usual price of goods of any who is in pressing want, — who must have, and that without delay, the things which you only can furnish him with? If you do, this also is flat extortion. Indeed you do not come up to the righteousness of a Pharisee."

[19] Wesley is speaking about goods smuggled into the country without paying the government tax. He wrote a tract titled, *A Word to a Smuggler*, in which he said, "Open smuggling . . . is robbing on the highway; and as much harm as there is in this, just so much there is in smuggling. A smuggler of this kind is no honester than an highwayman. They may shake hands together. Private smuggling is just the same with picking of pockets. There is full as much harm in this as in that. A smuggler of this kind is no honester than a pickpocket. These may shake hands together. But open smugglers are worse than common highwaymen, and private smugglers are worse than common pickpockets. . . . You say you believe the Bible. Then I say to you, in the name of God and in the name of Christ, 'Thou shalt not steal.' Thou shalt not take what is not thine own, what is the right of another man. . . . 'Render unto Cæsar the things that are Cæsar's, and unto God the things that are God's.'"

- Giving or taking things on usury; that is, unlawful interest.[20]
- Uncharitable or unprofitable conversation, particularly speaking evil of judges or ministers.[21]
- Doing to others what we would not want them to do to us.[22]
- Doing what we know is not for the glory of God, such as the putting on of gold or costly apparel.[23]

---

[20] Ex. 22:25; Lev. 25:36; Prov. 28:8.

[21] Lev. 19:16; Psa. 5:9; 10:7; 15:1–3; 34:13; 36:3; 50:20; 101:3–5; Prov. 11:13; 12:18, 13:3; 20:19, 21:23; 24:2; 26:20; Matt. 12:34; Rom. 1:28–30; 2 Cor. 12:20; Eph. 4:31; Tit. 3:1–2; James 1:26, 3:6; 4:1;, 1 Pet. 2:1; 3:10.

[22] Matt. 7:12; Luke 6:31. Wesley said in his *Notes upon the New Testament* (on Luke 6:38), "With the same measure that ye mete with, it shall be measured to you again—Amazing goodness. So we are permitted even to carve for ourselves! We ourselves are, as it were, to tell God how much mercy he shall show us! And can we be content with less than the very largest measure? Give then to man, what thou designest to receive of God."

[23] 1 Tim. 2:9–10. Apparel and one's manner of dress was much in the forefront in eighteenth-century England (as it is in some circles yet today). John Wesley's father, Samuel Wesley, wrote *An Epistle to a Friend* (1700). In that work Samuel Wesley penned this couplet in iambic pentameter:

Style is the dress of thought; a modest dress,
Neat, but not gaudy, will true critics please.

In providing guidelines for Methodists, John Wesley could hardly avoid the subject of dress. If his eighteenth-century prescriptions seem peculiar to twenty-first-century readers, an understanding of context is useful. First, the new orientation of life experienced by the "new" Methodists called for reflection on their values and their witness in the way they attired themselves. This was especially important in that culture, which was quite class conscious, and one's social status usually dictated the way they dressed. Alongside the poor, some of the Methodist converts were people of elevated social standing. It was a noteworthy event at town's market cross or village green to see and hear Methodist preachers expostulating to crowds consisting of a mix of ordinary people (the poor) and "people of quality" (the well-to-do). While attired in fashionable extremes, those of higher social standing felt uncomfortable among their impoverished spiritual sisters and brothers. These well-off hearers expressed their spiritual kinship with the poor by not "putting on of gold or costly apparel." The Scots Methodist Lady d'Arcy Maxwell's biographer said, "Her dress which was a much dictated by conscience as formed by taste, was very plain, being without ornament, or anything which could serve only for show. . . . She found that she could relieve many a suffering creature, and give education to many an orphan child, with what numbers [of others] expend in useless decorations."

Another important consideration for the Methodists was the right use of time and money. When Mary Bosanquet—later the wife of John Fletcher, an important first-generation Methodist theologian—became a Christian she asked God what changes she should make in her life. She concluded that she should adjust her manner of living. Regarding apparel, she decided no longer "to be conformed to the customs, fashions and maxims of this world." Many other privileged Methodist converts reached the same conclusion. Wesley sought to steer the Methodists somewhere between the "formal costume" of the Quakers and the ostentatious "fripperies of fashion." Wesley's *Arminian Magazine* for 1778 said, "Let everyone, when he appears in public, be decently clothed, according to his age, and the custom of the place where he lives." Some objected that this standard of dress was

- Participating in entertainments in which we cannot engage in the name of the Lord Jesus.[24]
- Singing those songs, or reading those books, which do not tend to the knowledge or love of God.[25]
- Pampering in softness and needless self-indulgence.[26]
- Storing up for yourselves treasures on earth.[27]
- Borrowing without a probability of paying.[28]

---

too lenient. The complaints prompted a reply from Wesley: "There is no fault in this. It is exactly right. Accordingly, when I appear in public, I am decently appareled [clothed], according to my age and the custom of England. . . . He that does otherwise seems to affect singularity."

[24] Entertainment in eighteenth-century England was often degraded. Bull-baiting and bear-baiting (torturing tethered animals) was popular, and not outlawed until 1835. Cock-throwing, cock-fighting, and dog fights were popular entertainments throughout the eighteenth century. Boxers beat each other senseless. Cricket matches were brutal. Opera performers sometimes danced nude. Many theater productions were vulgar and indecent. Sidney Smith wrote in 1802, "Although Garrick and others had worked hard to eliminate the coarse, obscene, and scandalous from the stage, its state is still very far from satisfactory."

Wesley said in his Sermon #89, "The More Excellent Way," "I could not [see a play] with a clear conscience; at least not in an English theatre, the sink of all profaneness and debauchery. . . Of playing at cards [gambling] I say the same as of seeing plays. I could not do it with a clear conscience. But I am not obliged to pass any sentence on those that are otherwise minded. I leave them to their own Master: To Him let them stand or fall. . . . Are there not more excellent ways of diverting themselves for those that love or fear God?"

[25] Psa. 19:3; 24:3–4; Matt. 5:8; Eph. 5:27; 1 Pet. 1:22; 2 Pet. 3:14. St. Paul wrote in Philippians 4:8, "Whatever is true, whatever is honorable, whatever is just, whatever is pure, whatever is pleasing, whatever is commendable, if there is any excellence and if there is anything worthy of our of praise, think about these things."

[26] Prov. 21:17; 23:1–2; 26:16; Matt. 5:29; 16:24; Luke 14:27; Acts 24:25; Rom. 6:6, 12, 8:13–14; 1 Cor. 9:27; Gal. 5:16, 24; Phil. 3:8; Col. 3:5; Tit. 2:2; James 3:2; 2 Pet. 1:6, 2:11, 4:2.

At the root of this rule for Methodists is Christ's call to self-denial. On 14 August 1744, Wesley wrote a letter to clarify his views on self-indulgence: "I was surprised on Sunday, when you was pleased to tell me, I carried things to extremes, in denying the lawful pleasures in eating. I denied only self-indulgence in eating: All which, I advance, is that he who will be Christ's disciple, must absolutely deny himself. . . . I plainly see every hour produces occasions of self-pleasing: And this I apprehend is a sufficient call for, and rule of, self-denial. For instance: In the morning, it is a great self-denial to rise out of a warm bed; but if I do not, I am immediately condemned as a slothful servant: If I do, I find a great inward blessing. . . . If I deny myself, I often find even a present reward."

[27] Job 27:16–17; Psa. 39:6; Eccl. 2:26; Matt. 6:19; James 5:3. Commenting on Christ's words in Matt. 6:19, "Do not store up for yourselves treasures on earth, where moth and rust consume and where thieves break in and steal," Wesley wrote in his *Notes upon the New Testament*, "He may likewise have a farther view in these words, even to guard against making any thing on earth our treasure. For then a thing properly becomes our treasure, when we set our affections upon it."

[28] Psa. 37:21; Prov. 6:1; 11:15; 17:18; 22:7; 22:26.

- Acquiring merchandise without the prospect of paying for it.²⁹

2.
Do Good

5. Second, it is expected of all those who continue in these societies to continue to evidence their desire of salvation by being merciful in every way as God enables, and as they have opportunity to do good of every possible kind to all people.

- Do good to their bodies, as God gives the ability, by giving food to the hungry,³⁰ clothing the naked,³¹ and by visiting or helping whose that are sick or in prison.³²
- Do good to their souls, by instructing,³³ reproving,³⁴ or exhorting³⁵ all with which they interact. Trample under foot that fanatical doctrine of demons—that we need not to do good unless our hearts feel like it.³⁶

---

²⁹ Rom. 13:8 states, "Owe no one anything, except to love one another; for the one who loves another has fulfilled the law." In Wesley's *Notes upon the New Testament*, he commented on the phrase, "Owe no one anything . . . except to love one another." He said that our obligation to love others is "an eternal debt which can never be discharged, But yet if this [debt] be rightly performed, it discharges all the rest. For he that loved another as he ought hath fulfilled the whole law toward his neighbor." He added, "The same love which restrains from all evil, incites us to all good."

³⁰ Psa. 146:7; Matt. 25:35, 45.

³¹ Isa. 58:7; Matt. 25:36, 43–44; James 2:14–16.

³² Matt. 25:36; James 5:14.

³³ Lev. 10:11; Deut. 6:7; Psa. 78:6; Ezek. 44:23; Col. 3:16; 1 Tim. 4:11; 2 Tim. 2:24.

³⁴ Psa. 141: 5; Prov. 10:17; 12:1; 15:5; 25:12; Luke 17:3; Eph. 5:11; 1 Tim. 5:20; 2 Tim. 4:2; Tit. 2:15.

³⁵ The New Testament verb for *exhort* is παρακαλέω, which means to encourage, beseech, admonish, or to urge one to a course of conduct as in Phil. 4:2, where St. Paul says, "I entreat (παρακαλέω [encourage]) Euodia and I entreat (παρακαλέω [encourage]) Syntyche to agree in the Lord." Another instance is in 1 Thess. 4:10, where the apostle urges, "Indeed you do love all the brothers and sisters throughout Macedonia. But we urge (παρακαλοῦμεν) [encourage] you, beloved, to do so more and more. Other instances of exhortation, for example, are found in 2 Cor. 8:6, 12:18; 1 Tim. 1:3; Heb. 13:19, 22.

³⁶ Wesley was distressed with the tendency of some of the Moravian Christians who depended on feelings, to the neglect of clear biblical commands. In August of 1740, Wesley wrote Count Zinzendorf in Herrnhut, Germany the following exhortation: "You undervalue good works . . . never publicly insisting on the necessity of them, nor declaring their weight and excellency. Hence, when some of your brethren have spoken of them, they [certain Moravian leaders] put them on a wrong foot; viz., 'If you find yourself moved, if your heart is free to it, then reprove, exhort, relieve.' By this means you wholly avoid the taking up your cross, in order to do good; and also substitute an uncertain, precarious inward motion, in the place of the plain written word. Nay, one of your members has said of good works in general, (whether works of piety or of charity,) 'A believer is no more obliged to do these works of the Law, than a subject of the King of England is obliged to obey the laws of the King of France.'" Methodism's General Rules do not rest on one's notions, inner impressions, or feelings. Rather, the General Rules restate clear biblical instructions.

- Do good especially for those of the family of faith, or wanting so to be,[37] by employing them preferably to others, buying from one another, and helping each other in business. Do so even more because the world will love its own, and them only.[38]
- Do good with all possible diligence[39] and living without waste,[40] so that others find no fault with your ministry.[41]
- Do good by running with perseverance the race that is set before you.[42] Deny yourselves and daily take up your cross.[43] Submit to abuse suffered for Christ,[44] and for others to count you as the rubbish of the world.[45] Expect that people will revile you, persecute you, and utter all kinds of evil against you falsely on my account.[46]

3.
USE THE ORDINANCES OF GOD

6. Third, we expect all who desire to continue in these societies to continue to evidence their desire of salvation by using the means of grace.[47] These ordinances include the following:

---

[37] Gal. 6:10.

[38] John 15:19; Acts 2:40; Eph. 5:11.

[39] John 4:35; Rom. 11:14; 1 Cor. 9:22; 2 Pet. 3:14.

[40] In his sermon, "The Use of Money," Wesley cautioned against unnecessary consumption: "Do not waste any part of so precious a talent [money], merely in gratifying the desires of the flesh; in procuring the pleasures of sense, of whatever kind; particularly, in enlarging the pleasure of tasting. I do not mean that we should avoid gluttony and drunkenness only: An honest Heathen would condemn these habits. But there is a regular, reputable kind of sensuality, an elegant epicurism, which does not immediately disorder the stomach, nor (sensibly at least) impair the understanding; and yet (to mention no other effects of it now) it cannot be maintained without considerable expense. Cut off all this expense! Despise delicacy and variety, and be content with what plain nature requires." Wesley would oppose any Christian organization spending money unnecessarily to "pamper the flesh."

[41] 2 Cor. 6:3.

[42] Gal. 6:7; Heb. 12:1; 1 Pet. 1:13; Rev. 3:11.

[43] Matt. 16:24; Mark 8:34; Luke 9:23.

[44] Heb. 11:26.

[45] 1 Cor. 4:13.

[46] Matt. 5:11.

[47] The means of grace are the signs, words, or deeds that serve as channels by which God conveys prevenient, convicting, converting, sanctifying, and enabling grace to us. John Wesley, in his sermon "The Means of Grace" (II, §1–2), declared, "I use this expression, means of grace, because I know none better; and because it has been generally used in the Christian Church for many ages—in particular by our own Church, which directs us to bless God both for the means of grace, and hope of glory; and teaches us, that a sacrament is 'an outward sign of inward grace, and a means whereby we receive the same. . . .' And these [means] we believe to be ordained of God, as the ordinary channels of conveying his

- Attending the public worship of God.[48]
- Listening to the proclamation of the word of God, whether read or expounded.[49]
- Partaking of the Lord's Supper.[50]
- Holding family and private prayer.[51]
- Searching the Scriptures.[52]
- Fasting or abstinence.[53]

7. These are the General Rules of our societies; all which God teaches us to observe. He does so in his written word, the Bible. Scripture is the only sufficient rule of our faith and practice. God's Spirit writes these truths upon every truly awakened heart. If there are any among us that do not observe these biblical rules, and habitually break any of them, let the leader or leaders know. They are to watch over these souls and give an account to God. We will admonish the stumbling ones of their errors, and we will bear with them for a season. However, if they do

---

grace to the souls of men. But we allow, that the whole value of the means depends on their actual subserviency to the end of religion; that, consequently, all these means, when separate from the end, are less than nothing and vanity; that if they do not actually conduce to the knowledge and love of God."

The United Methodist Articles of Religion (XVI) speak of the sacraments as "signs of grace . . . by which [God] doth work invisibly in us" that "quicken" and "strengthen and confirm our faith" in God. United Methodism's Confession of Faith (VI) refers to the sacraments as "means of grace by which God works invisibly in us, quickening, strengthening and confirming our faith in [God]."

[48] Deut. 12:5; Isa. 39:1; Mic. 4:2; Luke 2:36–37, 4:16, 24:53; John 7:14; Acts 2:46.10:25.

[49] On 26 June 1740, Wesley recorded in his journal the outline of a sermon he preached on the means of grace: "I showed, concerning the Holy Scriptures, 1. That to search, (that is, read and hear them,) is a command of God. 2. That this command is given to all, believers or unbelievers. 3. That this is commanded or ordained as a means of grace, a means of conveying the grace of God to all, whether unbelievers . . . or believers, who by experience know, that 'all Scripture is profitable,' or a means to this end, 'that the man of God may be perfect, thoroughly furnished to all good works.'"

[50] Matt. 26:26; Mark 14:22; Luke 22:19; 1 Cor. 10: 16, 11:23. On 25 June 1740, Wesley wrote in his journal, "Although this expression of our Church, 'means of grace,' be not found in Scripture; yet, if the sense of it undeniably is, to cavil at the term is a mere strife of words. But the sense of it is undeniably found in Scripture. For God hath in Scripture ordained prayer, reading or hearing, and the receiving the Lord's Supper, as the ordinary means of conveying his grace to man."

[51] 1 Chron. 16:11; Matt. 7:7, 26:41; Luke 18:1; John 16:24; Eph. 6:18; 1 Thess. 5:17; James 5:13.

[52] Deut. 4:10; 8:3; 11:19; 17:19; Job 23:12; Psa. 19:8; 119:89, 103 105, 130; Isa. 40:8; Jer. 15:16; Matt. 5:18, 22:29; Luke 21:33; 24:32; John 5:39; Acts 1:16; Rom. 15:4, 16:26; Heb. 4:12; James 2:8; 1 Pet.1:25, 2:2; 2 Pet. 1:19.

[53] Psa. 35:13, 69:10; Isa. 58:3; Jer. 14:12; Joel 1:14, 2:12; Zech. 7:5; Matt. 6:17–18, 9:15.

not repent, they have no more place among the Methodists. We have delivered our own souls.

John Wesley
Charles Wesley

"A Prayer for Those Convinced of Sin" (1743)

[Editor's Comment]. At the end of the first edition of the General Rules, John Wesley appended the following Charles Wesley hymn, titled "A Prayer For Those Who are Convinced of Sin." In the thirty-nine editions of the General Rules published during John Wesley's lifetime, all of them but one (#4, 1744) contained the following prayer hymn. "A Prayer for Those Convinced of Sin" was also published in Wesley's *Hymns and Sacred* Poems, 1749, II, 89–91. This composition can be sung or read privately or corporately.[54]

A Prayer for Those who are Convinced of Sin.

1. O most compassionate high priest,[55]
    Full of all grace we know thou art,[56]
    Faith puts its hand upon your breast,
    And feels beneath your panting heart.[57]
2. Your panting heart for sinners bleeds;
    Your mercies and compassions move;[58]
    Your groaning Spirit intercedes,[59]
    And yearn the bowels of your love.[60]
3. Hear then the pleading Spirit's prayer,[61]
    (The Spirit's will to you is known)
    For all who now your sufferings share,
    And still for full redemption groan.[62]

---

[54] The following document was produced by the Duke Center for Studies in the Wesleyan Tradition under the editorial direction of Randy L. Maddox, with the assistance of Aileen F. Maddox. This version is in modernized text.

[55] Heb. 2:17; 4:4; 6:20; 7:26; 8:1.

[56] John 1:14.

[57] John 13:25; 21:20.

[58] Matt. 9:36; 14:14; 15:32; 20:34; 23:37; Mark 1:41; Luke 17:13; John 11:35.

[59] Isa. 53:12; Luke 22:32; 23:34; John 14:16; 17:9; Rom. 8:34; Heb. 7:25.

[60] Although the use of *bowels* in this sense is now archaic, the term was once used to designate the seat of tender and sympathetic emotions. For instance, in the fourteenth century the Wycliffe translation of Phil. 1:7–8 reads, "It is iust to me to feele this thing for alle you, for that Y haue you in herte, and in my boondis, and in defending and confermyng of the gospel, that alle ye be felowis of my ioye. For God is a witnesse to me, hou Y coueyte alle you in the bowelis of Jhesu Crist." As late as 1611, the KJV reads, "For God is my record, how greatly I long after you all in the bowels of Jesus Christ."

[61] Rom. 8:26.

[62] Isa. 39:9; 73:25; Isa. 26:9; Luke 6:21; 1 Pet. 2:2.

4. Poor tempted souls, with tempests tossed,[63]
    And strangers to a moment's peace;[64]
    Disconsolate, afflicted, lost,[65]
    Lost in a howling wilderness.[66]
5. Torn with an endless war within,
    Vexed with the flesh and Spirit's strife,[67]
    And struggling in the toils of sin,
    And agonizing into life.[68]
6. O let the pris'ners mournful cries,
    As incense in your sight appear;[69]
    Their humble wailings pierce the skies,[70]
    If haply[71] they may feel you near!
7. The captive exiles make their moans,[72]
    From sin impatient to be free;
    Call home, call home your banished ones!
    Lead captive their captivity![73]
8. Show them the blood that bought their peace,[74]
    The anchor of their steadfast hope;[75]
    And bid their guilty terrors cease,[76]
    And bring the ransomed pris'ners up.[77]
9. Out of the deep regard their cries,[78]
    The fallen raise, the mourners cheer;[79]

---

[63] Psa. 55:8; Isa. 32:2.
[64] Isa. 48:22.
[65] Isa. 59:8.
[66] Deut 32:10.
[67] Matt. 26:41.
[68] Deut. 28:67; Psa. 107:17; Prov. 3:15; Rom. 2:9; 3:16.
[69] Rev. 8:3.
[70] Jer. 9:18.
[71] The OED deems *haply* to be archaic or poetic. Charles Wesley seems to have used *haply* in a poetic sense, as the word means *perchance* or *perhaps*.
[72] A reference to Israel's and Judah's captivity in Babylon in the six and seventh centuries B.C.
[73] 2 Chron. 6:38; Eph 4:8
[74] Matt. 26:18; Acts 20:28; Rom. 5:9; Heb. 9:24; 1 Pet. 1:18–19; 1 Jn. 1:7; Rev. 1:5.
[75] Heb. 6:19.
[76] Psa. 55:4; 79:19.
[77] This is an analogy drawn from the Hebrews' deliverance from Egypt and the Hebrews' return from Babylonian captivity. See Isa. 35:10; Isa. 51:10; Jer. 31:11.
[78] Psa. 69:14.
[79] Psa. 34:18; Joel 2:13; Mic. 7:18–19; Acts 2:38; 3:19.

        Sun of Righteousness arise,[80]
        And scatter all their doubt and fear![81]
10. Pity the day of feeble things;
        gather every halting soul,
        And drop salvation from your wings,[82]
        And make the contrite sinner whole.[83]
11. Stand by them in the fiery hour,[84]
        Their feebleness of mind defend;[85]
        And in their weakness show your power,[86]
        And make them patient to the end.[87]
12. O satisfy their soul in drought;[88]
        Give them your saving health to see,[89]
        And let your mercy find them out;
        And let your mercy reach to me.[90]
13. Hast thou the work of grace begun,
        And brought them to the birth in vain?[91]
        let your children see the sun![92]
        Let all their souls be born again.[93]
14. Relieve the souls whose cross we bear,
        For whom your suff'ring members mourn;[94]

---

[80] Mal. 4:2.

[81] 1 Jn. 4:18.

[82] Exod. 19:4; Psa. 17:8; 37:6; 57:1; 61:4; 63:7; 91:4; Mal. 4:2; Matt. 23:37; Luke 13:34.

[83] Ezek. 33:11; Luke 5:32; 2 Cor. 5:20; Rev. 3:20.

[84] 2 Cor. 4:16; Heb. 12:5; Rev. 2:3.

[85] Heb. 12:12.

[86] 2 Cor. 12; Psa. 55:4; 79:19. This is an analogy drawn from the Hebrews' deliverance from Egypt and the Hebrews' return from Babylonian captivity. See Isa. 35:10; Isa. 51:10; Jer. 31:11; Psa. 69:14; Psa. 34:18; Joel 2:13; Mic. 7:18–19; Acts 2:38; 3:19; Mal. 4:2; 1 Jn. 4:18; Exod. 19:4; Psa. 17:8; 37:6; 57:1; 61:4; 63:7; 91:4; Mal. 4:2; Matt. 23:37; Luke 13:34; Ezek. 33:11; Luke 5:32: 2 Cor. 5:20; Rev. 3:20; 2 Cor 4:16; Heb. 12:5; Rev. 2:3; Heb. 12:12.

[87] Matt. 10:22; 1 Cor. 13:7; James 1:12.

[88] Isa. 58:11.

[89] 1 Jn. 1:2.

[90] Exod. 34:7; 2 Sam. 22:6; Psa. 103:8; Isa. 55:7; Jer. 3:12; Matt. 9:13; Luke 1:50, 54, 58, 72, 78; Rom. 9:15–16; 9:23; 15:9; Gal. 6:16; Eph. 2:4; Tit. 3:5; Heb. 4:16; James 5:11; 1 Pet. 2:10; 2 Jn. 1:3; Jude 1:2, 21.

[91] Jer. 17:8; Ezek. 36:26; John 1:15; 2 Cor. 5:17; Tit. 3:5; 1 Pet. 1:23.

[92] Eccl. 7:11.

[93] John 3:3, 7; 1 Pet. 1:23.

[94] Rom. 10:1; 11:14; 1 Cor. 9:22.

Answer our faith's effectual prayer:[95]
Bid every struggling child be born.

15. Hark how your turtle dove complains,[96]
And see us weep for Sion's woe![97]
Pity your suff'ring people's pains;
Avenge us of our inbred foe.[98]

16. Whom thou has bound, O Lord, expel,
And take his armour all away;
The man of sin, the child of hell,
The devil in our nature slay.[99]

17. Him and his works at once destroy,
The *being* of all sin erase,[100]
And turn our mourning into joy,[101]
And clothe us with the robes of praise.[102]

18. Then, when our suff'rings all are past,
let us pure and perfect be,[103]
And gain our calling's prize at last,[104]
Forever sanctified in you.[105]

---

[95] James 5:16.
[96] Psa. 74:19.
[97] Isa. 30:19.
[98] Gen. 6:5; 1 Kings 8:46; Psa. 53:3; Prov. 20:9; Isa. 64:6; Rom. 3:23; 1 Jn. 1:8.
[99] John 12:31; Heb. 2:14; 1 Jn. 3:8.
[100] 1 Cor. 15:3; Gal. 1:4; 1 Pet. 2:24; 1 Jn. 2:2; Rev. 1:5.
[101] Isa. 51:11; 61:3; Jer. 31:13.
[102] Psa. 150:1–6.
[103] Heb. 10:22; 1 Pet. 1:22; 1 Jn. 3:3;
[104] Phil. 3:14.
[105] John 17:17; 1 Cor. 1:30; Eph. 5:26; 1 Thess. 4:3; 5:23; Heb. 13:12; 1 Pet. 1:2.

Selection 6

An Estimate of the Manners of the Present Times

Editor's Introduction

An Estimate of the Manners of the Present Times

When John Wesley was seventy-two years old he wrote a sermon titled, "National Sins and Miseries." In that message He stated,

> That vice is the parent of misery, few will deny. It is confirmed by the general suffrage [consent] of all ages. However, we seldom bring this home to ourselves; when we speak of sin as the cause of misery, we usually mean, the sin of other people, and suppose we suffer, because they sin. But need we go so far? Are not our own vices sufficient to account for all our sufferings? Let us fairly and impartially consider this; let us examine our own hearts and lives. We all suffer; and we have all sinned. But will it not be most profitable for us, to consider everyone his own sins, as bringing sufferings on both himself and others.[1]

---

[1] *The Works of John Wesley*, Bicentennial ed., 4 vols. (Nashville: Abingdon Press, 1984–87), 3:568.

Wesley's eighteenth-century tract, "Estimate of the Manners of the Present Times," was an assessment of the people of England, at another time, and in another culture. Nonetheless, in many respects this tract is important in any era and for any culture. Furthermore, the destructive nature of sin and the blessings of authentic Christian commitment are timeless and unchangeable.

Of the twelve of Wesley's treatises in this book, only in this treatise have I have taken the liberty to alter some of Wesley's specifics. For example for the term *England*, I have used *the nation*. For *London*, I substituted *our large cities*. I believe these adjustments help make the following tract as pertinent to our day as it was in 1782 when Wesley addressed it to the people of England. Wesley wrote, "A total ignorance of God is almost universal among us. The exceptions are exceeding few, whether among the learned or unlearned."

Luke Tyerman (1820–89), perhaps John Wesley's most thorough biographer, said that in eighteenth-century England, "people were engulfed in voluptuousness and business; and . . . zeal for godliness looked as odd upon a man as would the antiquated dress of his great grandfather."[2] In 1732, London's *Weekly Miscellany* stated that freethinkers "formed into clubs, to propagate their tenets and to make the nation a race of profligates," and that atheism was "scattered broadcast throughout the kingdom. . . . [and] polygamy, concubinage, and even sodomy were not sinful."

In John Wesley's time, fornication and adultery were common, and the upper classes did not attempt to hide their extramarital affairs. Prostitution flourished, and in some instances wealthy people paid their maids a low income and permitted them by night to become women of the streets to earn extra money. John Cleland's obscene *Memoirs of a Woman of Pleasure* (1749), later renamed *Fanny Hill*, was one of the most popular books of the eighteenth century. Homosexual clubs dotted London. Drinking clubs abounded. A great number of London's population lived in illicit cohabitation without marriage.[3] Gambling left countless people in poverty. For instance, the Duke of Devonshire lost his entire estate in a game of cards. Gambling debts led servants to rob their masters, and clerks embezzled from their employers.[4]

William Hogarth's engravings of eighteenth-century English life contain a scene titled *Rake's Progress*. This drawing shows adult men and women gambling while they paid no attention to a crier announcing that a building was in flames.

---

[2] Luke Tyerman, *The Life and Times of the Rev. John Wesley, M.A., Founder of the Methodists*, 3 vols. (London: Hodder and Stoughton, 1870) 1:217.

[3] Walter Besant, *London in the Eighteenth Century* (London: A. & C. Black, 1902) 384.

[4] William E. Lecky, *History of England in the Eighteenth Century*, 8 vols., (London: Longmans, Green, 1883–90), 1:522.

(Today, gamblers in the United States squander more than $100 billion year, and gambling statistics continue to rise.)

In Wesley's day, some bakers adulterated their bread with chalk and aluminum sulfate; certain merchants used unsafe chemicals to "freshen" rotting meat. When authorities called them to task, these business people demanded their right to "live their own lives without restraint."[5] France, once the leading European nation, was mired in a national sinkhole of godlessness and immorality. This state of affairs led the French people to accept the rise of Napoleon, an arrogant dictator and misogynist who fomented the Napoleonic wars of aggression.

In eighteenth-century England, the Wesleyan revival helped elevate the morals and manners of the nation, and that nation experienced a religious awakening. Cambridge historian J. H. Plumb concluded,

> There can be no doubt of Methodism's appeal; it contained so much that was capable of satisfying the deepest needs of human nature. . . . Methodism gave far more than emotional release; it brought a sense of purpose and a field for the exercise of both will and power. [Methodism strengthened] those moral virtues which were to transform English society.[6]

Along with other faithful servants of God, John Wesley was a man for all seasons. Later, Queen Victoria famously said, "England has become great and happy by the knowledge of the true God and Jesus Christ."

A survey of history reveals that national decadence, disgrace, decline, and defeat come to any nation that ignores or rejects God. On the other hand, national renewal, regeneration, and righteousness always come to any people who turn to God and accept his ways. The Old Testament tells us, "Righteousness exalts a nation, but sin is a reproach to any people."[7] John Wesley's "Estimate of the Manners of the Present Times" can sober us and help spiritually renew us to the favor of God and the benefits that only he can give.

An Estimate of the Manners of the Present Times

---

[5] Besant, *London in the Eighteenth Century*, 301–2.

[6] J. H. Plumb, *England in the Eighteenth Century* (Harmondsworth, Middlesex: Penguin Books, 1950), 95, 97.

[7] Prov. 13:34.

Printed in 1782

1. Some years ago, an ingenious man published a treatise with the title, *Estimate of the Manners and Principles of the Times*.[1] According to that writer, presently the characteristics of the people are sloth and luxury. And this much we may allow: neither sloth nor luxury ever abounded in the land as they do today. With regard to sloth, it was the constant custom of our ancestors to rise at four in the morning. Summer and winter, this was the stated hour, for all that were healthy. According to the rules of the two Houses of Congress, they met at five o'clock a.m.[2] How is it with people of fashion now? They can hardly nestle into their clothes before eight or nine o'clock in the morning. Perhaps some of them do not arise before twelve. And after they have arisen, what do they do?

> *They waste away*
> *In gentle inactivity the day.*[3]

---

[1] Wesley is referring to a treatise written by John Brown (1715–66), an English cleric and author. The Rev. Mr. Brown wrote *Estimate of the Manners and Principles of the Times* (2 vols., 1757–1758). The author said, "There are general Causes, natural or moral, which operate in every State; which raise, support, or overturn it. Among all these various Causes, none perhaps so much contributes to raise or sink a Nation, as the Manners and Principles of its People."

[2] The Journal of both houses of Parliament stated that the sessions were to begin *horâ quintâ ante-meridianâ* [the hour of five before mid-day].

[3] These lines come from the Latin poet Horace [Quintus Horatius Flaccus] (65 B.C.–8 B.C.), *Satires*, II, vi, §61–62:
Somno et inertibus horis
Ducere sollicitae jucunda oblivia vitae.

How many are so far from working with their hands, that they can scarcely set their foot on the ground. How many young, healthy men are too lazy to walk or ride [a horse]? They must ride in carriages that can hardly be made comfortable enough for them. And must not even poorest of the gentry have their own private means of transportation? See this far-reaching cause (together with intemperance) of our innumerable nervous complaints! How imperfectly medicines or baths take the place of exercise. To continue in health, our bodies need exercise as much as we need sleep and food.[4]

2. Equally, we have allowed an abundant increase of luxury, food, beverages, dress, and furniture. What an amazing profusion of food we now see, not only at a wealthy person's table, but also at the tables of ordinary people and workers. What a variety of wines have replaced the common beverages of our ancestors! What luxury of apparel, fashions changing like the moon, in the city and country, as well as in high places! What excess of expensive furniture dazzles in all our wealthy people' houses! Furthermore, luxury naturally increases sloth, keeping us from exercise of body or mind. Sloth also leads to inactivity and more luxuries. And luxuries lead countless numbers of people into gluttony, drunkenness, and even into every kind of vulgarity, which we can hardly separate from gluttony and [alcohol] addiction.

3. Given the reality of all these conditions, they still are not a true estimate of the current manners of the nation. First, whatever may be the characteristics of a nation, they are found in the individuals who comprise it. Or at least these characteristics appear in a great majority of the people, so that the exceptions are not significant. Second, these characteristics are persistent, and they are present not only now and then, but also continually and without pause. Third, these characteristics are distinctively and specific in that nation. Nevertheless, luxury and sloth are neither universal nor constant and unique to the land.

4. Whatever may be the case of many of those with privilege and power (who comprise less than five percent of the nation), it is by no means true that all of the nation's people are slothful. Some of the five percent hold traditional values, and they are patterns of conscientiousness in their relationships with others. It is undeniable that a vast majority of the middle and lower ranks of the people are diligently employed from morning to night, and throughout the year. Indeed, those

---

[4] Wesley advised exercise as a means to good health. He wrote, "I am never tired (such is the goodness of God!), either with writing, preaching, or travelling. One natural cause undoubtedly is my continual exercise and change of air. How the latter contributes to health I know not, but certainly it does." (Journal, Curnock ed., 28 June 1786, 7:175).

who are best acquainted with other nations will not hesitate to say that most of our people are as diligent as any people in the world.

5. So, it is not true that sloth is the defining or universal character of the nation. On many occasions even those that are most infected with slothful tendencies arise and shake the dust off of themselves. Witness the behavior of those of the highest rank when they were engaged in war. Did anyone charge certain prominent people with sloth in war? Witness the behavior of many eminent men in the military who set an example to their troops! Yea, some of them were neither afraid nor ashamed to march on foot at the head of their men!

6. Least of all is sloth *unique* to our nation. Is there no sloth in Holland? Is there none in Germany? Certainly, in every part of France there is plenty of idleness to spare. There is a more abundant harvest of lethargy in Italy, Spain, and Portugal. It is far from the truth to assert that laziness is the present characteristic of our nation!

7. Neither is luxury a defining characteristic of our country. It is neither universal nor common. The food consumed by nine-tenths of our nation is (as it has always been) plain and simple. A vast majority of the nation are strangers to gluttony and drunkenness. Neither are they accustomed to fussiness with regard to food or drink. They are not given to excess in quantity or quality. They consume no more than what nature requires.

8. And as luxury in food is not universal in the land, neither is luxury in apparel. Thousands in every part of the kingdom are utterly innocent of opulence. Whether by choice or necessity, their dress is as plain as their food; and so is their furniture. We may further affirm that even lewdness is not yet universal in the land, although we are making swift advances toward it. Consider our theaters, parties, and arenas.

9. And even where luxury in food and dress is most prevalent, it is not constant. At particular times, the powerful and rich lay aside these luxuries. In time of war, how many of these people disregard luxurious food and clothing. Indeed, what contempt of these did our "high-born heroes"[5] show during times of war, when they fought in the trenches.

10. Thus, luxury is not especially characteristic of our nation. What is our luxury in dress to that of the French? And the French and Germans carry luxury in food to greater levels. In this matter, the French refuse to stand on the same level as the "dull Germans." In the northern kingdoms of Europe, there are as many

---

[5] Those from wealthy and upper class families.

gluttons as in our country, and at least as many drunkards. If we may refer to eyewitnesses, in particular I cite Dr. Johnson[6] and Lady Mary Wortley Montague.[7] What is all the vulgarity of our major cities, to that of Vienna, Paris, Rome, and all the large cities of Italy? Our women are not yet accompanied by their cicisbys [male lovers], nor would any of our husbands tolerate it. Thus, as bad as we are, we are sober and temperate, even moderate when compared to other nations.

11. But if indolence and luxury do not uniquely define us, what *is* the present characteristic of our nation? *It is ungodliness.* At present, ungodliness is the chief characteristic of our nation. Ungodliness is our collective, constant, and particular characteristic. I do not mean Deism, the theory that God does not reveal himself to us.[8] No, a Deist is a respectable person, compared to an ungodly one. By ungodliness I mean, first, a total ignorance of God; and, second, by a total contempt of him.

12. First, a total ignorance of God is almost universal among us. The exceptions are exceeding few, whether among the learned or unlearned. High and low, those who work with their hands, those in serving professions, male and female servants, soldiers, sailors, business people, lawyers, physicians, aristocrats, and wealthy people are as ignorant of the Creator of the world as are Islamists or idolaters. They look up to that "brave o'er-hanged firmament, fretted with golden fires [the sun]."[9] They see the moon coursing in brightness, the sun on its meridian throne [at its zenith]. They look around on the various furnishings of the

---

[6] Samuel Johnson made indelible contributions to the English language as a literary critic, biographer, essayist, and moralist. As a lexicographer he is famous for his 1755 *Dictionary of the English Language*. From his travels, he reported on the customs of places he visited.

[7] Lady Mary Wortley Montagu (1689–1762) was an upper class English woman married to the British ambassador to Turkey. She wrote her travel observations in "Turkish Letters," which had wide circulation among later travelers.

[8] There are several basic views about the existence of God. 1. **Atheism** holds that there is no God. (2) **Polytheism** is the view that there a plurality of gods influence nature and human life. (3) **Theism**, shapes the view of the Hebrew and Christian traditions. This world view posits a personal God who created the world, preserves it, involves himself it the world, and sovereignly governs the world. (4) **Deism**, which Wesley references here, denies that God has communicated with humankind, or that God has given us any revelation of himself. Deism allows that God exists, but he not personally involved in individual lives or in human affairs. Deism insists that we can posit God's existence only by inference as we study nature and natural law. In contrast to Christianity that is rooted in God's divine revelation to humankind, called "revealed religion," deism holds to "natural religion" based on reason, experience, science, and philosophy.

[9] In Shakespeare's *Hamlet, Prince of Denmark* (Act II, Scene 2), Prince Hamlet declares to Rosencrantz and Guildenstern, "I have of late—but wherefore I know not—lost all my mirth, forgone all custom of exercises, and indeed it goes so heavily with my disposition

earth, herbs, flowers, trees, in all their beauty; and coolly ascribe everything to "nature." They have no idea what nature is. Seriously ask them, "What is nature?" They do not know how to answer. Perhaps they will say, "Why, it is the order of what always was and always will be." Always was! To say that the present course of things is from eternity is to say that the world is eternal.[10] If this claim is so, either there are two eternals—nature *and* God—or there is no God at all!

13. That is as much as many of the good people of the land, in general, know about God their Creator! High and low, from the poorest person to the merriest butterfly[11] know only that much about God their Governor. They do not know or even suspect that God governs the world he has made and that God is the supreme and absolute sovereign over everything in heaven and on earth.[12] A poor pagan (even if an ambassador or the leader of the nation) should know *Deorum providentiâ cuncta geri*—that is, "The providence of God directs all things."

I ask, "What is providence? Do you know anything about it?" One might answer, "Yes, I do; I have never denied a general providence." I will respond, "A general Providence! What do you mean by that term? What is a general providence that does not include particulars? What is a whole that does not contain any parts?" To speak of a general providence without allowing particular providence is a self-contradiction. It is outright nonsense. Either, therefore, allow a particular providence, or do not pretend to believe any providence at all. Do you deny that the Governor of the world governs everything in it, small and great? Do you deny that fire, hail, snow, mist, wind and storm, fulfill God's word?[13] Do you not believe that God rules kingdoms and cities, fleets and armies, and all the individuals that compose them, yet without forcing or compelling their actions?[14] Do you deny that God governs anything or has anything to do in the world? Be consistent with yourself: Say that as nature has produced, so chance governs all

---

that this goodly frame, the earth, seems to me a sterile promontory; this most excellent canopy, the air—look you, this brave o'erhanging firmament, this majestical roof fretted with golden fire—why, it appears no other thing to me than a foul and pestilent congregation of vapors."

[10] The Bible opens with the declaration, "In the beginning God created the heavens and the earth" (Gen 1:1).

[11] By the word *butterfly* Wesley means one who lives an idle, carefree life; one concerned mostly with trifles. The OED designates one meaning of the word as "a vain gaudily attired person; a giddy trifler."

[12] Deut. 4:39; Psa. 83:18; 135:6; Dan. 2:20; 4:35; Matt. 6:13.

[13] Ezek. 13:13; Amos 4:13; Jonah 4:8.

[14] Deut. 3:21; 1 Sam 10:18; 2 Kings 19:15; 2 Chron. 20:6; Ezra 1:2; Isa. 37:16; Dan. 2:44.

things. At least, for the sake of honesty, acknowledge God and maintain (as the Deists do) that,

> *Since he gave things their beginning,*
> *He set this whirligig a-spinning.*[15]

They think God left the world and everything in it to continue to spin in its own way.

14. Whether this is correct or not, this Deistic notion is almost the universal sentiment of our nation. And if people high and low are so totally ignorant of God their Governor, are they likely to know any more of God their Redeemer, or of God their Judge, who soon will recompense all people according to their works?[16] Indeed, God is not in all their thoughts;[17] they do not think of him from morning to night.[18] Whether they are forming particular or national schemes, God has no place in their thinking, and they do not consider him. They conduct all their business without him. They do not consider whether God is in the world, or whether he has any part in managing it.

15. And whatever the nature of their activities, whether they have good or bad results, they do not consider that God has any part in the one or the other. They take it for granted, that the race is to the swift, and the battle to the strong.[19] Therefore, if things succeed well, they give no praise to God, but they praise the conduct of their leader and the courage of the people. And if they fail to succeed, they do not see the hand of God, but attribute everything to natural causes.

16. The nation in general, whether high, low, rich or poor, does not speak of God. From day to day, week to week, and year to year, they do not say anything about him. They talk of anything other than of God. They are not as squeamish as the old poet, who would not spend his breath in

> *De villis domibusve alienis;*

---

[15] This couplet expresses the philosophy of Deism, which posits the notion that God started the world, even as a clockmaker who has nothing more to do with the timepiece just assembled. Deism holds that God created the world and left it to run its course, with no further involvement in the world. This rationalistic view of God rejected the Christian belief in divine revelation, and substituted a trust in human reason and human ability to form a good society apart from divine intervention.

[16] Matt. 16:27.

[17] Psa. 10:4.

[18] Psa. 92:2.

[19] In Eccl. 9:11, Solomon summarized a life of vanity: "The race is not to the swift, nor the battle to the strong, nor bread to the wise, nor riches to the intelligent, nor favor to the skillful; but time and chance happen to them all."

Nec male necne Lepos saltet [sed, quod].[20]

The people of our land talk indifferently about everything that comes along—about everything, but God. If, with any degree of seriousness, anyone were to speak of God in good company, suppose at an élite dinner table, would not the others stand aghast? Would not a profound silence follow, until someone introduced a more acceptable subject?

17. Once again, most people in the nation live in the constant neglect of reverence for God. To evaluate my statement, consider a sample from a large city. How few of the inhabitants worship God in public, even once in a week! Do not even fewer of them have any reverence for God in their families? Perhaps there are still smaller numbers that daily worship God in private prayer. If we acknowledge the truth, this consistent ungodliness characterizes the nation!

18. Negative ungodliness (that is, ignoring God) is the least reprehensible part of our national character. Let is turn to the positive ungodliness that washes over every part of our land. The first aspect of this positive ungodliness, which reveals an utter contempt of God—is dishonesty. Lying on the part of the general population is an especially strong temptation in our public Courts of Justice. Consider the appalling manner, contrary to all sense and decency, in which officials administer pledges to tell the truth. Forty years ago, (and perhaps it may be so still,) when an oath was administered in a court, the judge with all on the bench rose up, took off their hats, and no one moved even a foot, or uttered a word, until they sat down again. Do not all judges today have the authority to introduce the same solemnity into every court where they preside? Of course they do. And if a judge does not exert that authority, he or she is inexcusable before God and humankind.

19. Until respect for truth-telling is evident, our shameless manner of administering oaths will increase the constant perjuries in the nation. The telling of falsehoods further increases by our multiplying oaths to such an amazing degree, and that on the slightest occasions. Consequently, perjury infects the whole nation. From month to month and year to year, lying continues. It is a trait that no nation shares to the degree that it is particular to us. There is nothing like it in any other (Christian or Heathen) nation under heaven.

---

[20] This quotation is from the Roman poet Horace [Quintus Horatius Flaccus] (65 B.C.–8 B.C.):
How fine this house, or that estate;
How great a favorite dancer's skill,
Whether he caper well or ill.

20. To get into particulars would be tedious: Suffice it to note in general that there are very few justices of the peace, heads of corporations, officers of the law, church trustees, customs or tax officers, or any politician, who are not constantly perjured. They take oaths they never intend to keep. And to these, add thousands, yes, myriads of the voters at political elections.[21] Add thousands of university students, who swear to a code of honor that they have never read, or plan to read, or to observe. Judge whether there is any nation on earth that rivals us in perjury!

21. There is another kind of ungodliness that, if possible, is still more common among us. It is constant and heard in every street every day in the year; and which is quite particular to our nation and its dependencies. I speak of the stupid, senseless, shameless ungodliness of taking the name of God in vain. Where in the habitable world do the people so continually ask the great God to "damn their souls?" Where else do they so blaspheme the Majesty of Heaven and so casually swear by the name of God? Some shameful "gentlemen" set the example, which the common people follow readily. Without any provocation and without restraint, they pour out these curses and oaths. They do so hastily and without any remorse. Let those who are acquainted with ancient and modern history say whether there is or ever was any heathen nation in which such a total contempt of God and horrid ungodliness so generally and constantly prevailed.

22. See then, what is the undoubted characteristic of the nation—it is ungodliness. To be sure, it was not always so. For many generations we had as much of the fear of God as other nations. However in a recent generation many people who were strangers to godliness made such a great profession of godliness that the nation reacted against it.[22] But at the time of the Restoration the people ran headlong from one extreme to the other. Ungodliness broke in upon us as a flood. When shall its appalling waves be stopped?

23. Is ungodliness an honor to the nation?[23] Let people of reason judge. Is this affront to God, the greatest and best of beings, an admirable condition? Surely, you cannot think so. Does it gain us any honor in the eyes of other nations? No,

---

[21] Dishonesty at election polls manifests itself in such practices as buying and selling votes, election officials who deliberately miscount votes, and cheaters who vote more than one time for the same candidate.

[22] Here, Wesley is referring to Oliver Cromwell (1599–1658) who combined a fervent spirituality with a hatred of the English monarchy. Cromwell formed an army, stirred up a civil war, and took control of England as "Lord Protector." Under a form of religion, Cromwell and his followers executed King Charles I. When Cromwell died, Charles II returned from exile, became king, and the Restoration Period ensued.

[23] Prov. 14:34 states, "Righteousness exalts a nation, but sin is a reproach to any people."

170 John Wesley on Methodism

it is just the contrary. Some of the ungodly people abhor our very Methodist name. They despise us because we are Methodists. They look upon us as monsters, hardly worthy to be ranked among human creatures.

24. You people of candor, judge for yourselves. Does this ungodliness bring any real advantage to our nation? We enjoy innumerable advantages. Yet, might we still have them without abandoning the fear of God? Might we not prosper just as well, by both sea and land, if we did not openly defy God? Would we not continue to prosper if we did not so continually disrespect God to his face, and dare him to do his worst?[24] If God has not left the governance of the world to chance, and if he is really stronger than we are, would not our affairs go on better if God were our friend, than if he were our enemy? Is God an adversary we should despise? Rather, is there not wisdom in those words of the old warrior, Virgil:

> *Non me tua fervida terrent*
> *Dicta, ferox; Dii me terrent et Jupiter hostis!*[25]

We have had excellent, well-appointed navies and many veteran armies. And what have they done? Have we not more and more reason to make that melancholy exclamation,

> *Heu, nihil invitis fas quenquam fidere Divis!*[26]

25. Can you believe that our total ignorance of God and our general contempt of him can be well pleasing to him? Whether we will acknowledge it or not, God still has all power in heaven and in earth[27] We need not care about all the *fervida dicta* [Latin, *firey sayings*], all the *rodomontades* [French, *swaggers, blusters*], of

---

[24] Wesley possibly referring to the common oaths of that day: "God damn you," and "I'll be damned."

[25] Publius Vergilius Maro (70 B.C.–19 B.C.), a Roman poet, is customarily called Virgil or Vergil. This Latin verse translates,
   Not those insulting empty vaunts I dread;
   No. But the gods with fear my bosom move,
   And he, my greatest foe, almighty Jupiter.
   Not those insulting empty vaunts I dread,
   Reply'd the mournful chief (and shook his head);
   No—but the gods with fear my bosom move,
   And he, my greatest foe, almighty Jove.
   (Virgil's *Æneid*, Book 12, lines 1264–67.)

[26] Also from Virgil. The line translates, *But, Heaven, against us, all attempts [must] fail.*

[27] Matt. 28:18; Rev. 5:13.

France and Spain.[28] If the Lord of the universe is against us, ought we not to care? That is, unless we are sure that our armies and navies can prevail against God! Otherwise, would it be any shame to humble ourselves, not to people, but to God? Should we not use every means to secure God for our friend, now that our other friends have failed us? Then, by admitting "there is none other that fights for us, but only you, O God."[29] Then, nothing is able to harm us, and peace and every other blessing shall return both to us and to our land.

---

[28] France and Spain were military powers that, off and on, threatened England.
[29] This line is from the Book of Common Prayer:
O Lord, save your people.
And bless thine inheritance.
Give peace in our time, O Lord.
Because there is none other that fighteth for us, but only thou, O God.
O God, make clean our hearts within us.
And take not your Holy Spirit from us.
See also, 2 Sam. 2:22; Psa. 5:11; 18:2; 31:2; 91:2; 144:2; Isa. 31:5; 37:35; Nahum. 1:7; Zech. 9:15.

Selection 7

Four Serious Admonitions

Editor's Introduction

Four Serious Admonitions

John Wesley intended the following four short open letters to cast the searching light of Scripture on the serious nature of humankind's relationship with their Creator and with their fellow beings. These four letters respectively address (1) profaning the Lord's Day, (2) cursing and misusing God's name, (3) drunkenness and addiction, and (4) sexual sins. In these tracts, Wesley writes with compassion, yet without compromise. He shows the personal effects of these sins and their devastating consequences for society.

In a 1763 sermon titled "The Reformation of Manners," Wesley declared,

> Is it not true that sin brings down the curse of God upon nations? For that reason, to the extent that any kind of righteousness is promoted, the national interest is advanced. So far as sin (especially open sin) is restricted, its curse and condemnation are removed from us. Therefore, those who labor to restrain sin are general benefactors of the nation. They are the truest friends of their government and country. To the degree that their plans succeed, God will doubtless grant national prosperity in fulfillment

of his reliable word, "Those who honor me I will honor" (1 Sam. 2:30).[1]

Using clear language, plain truth, and masterful logic, Wesley wields a double-edge sword both to wound and to heal. In the following four open letters, he guides his readers into health for the body, happiness for the soul, and holiness for the spirit.

---

[1] Kenneth Cain Kinghorn, *John Wesley on Christian Practice, The Standard Sermons in Modern English* (Nashville: Abingdon Press, 2001, 2002, 2003), III, 365.

Editor's Introduction

A Word to a Sabbath Breaker

The Book of Genesis states simply that the Creator created creation. The first thing that God hallowed (sanctified) as holy was a special day called the Sabbath. "Of the many "holy days" that Jews and Christians have designated throughout church history, the chief holy day mandated in Scripture is the Sabbath.[1] The Jewish Torah contains two requirements concerning the Sabbath—to remember it and to keep it. The Jewish *Kiddush* (blessing that ushers in the Sabbath) contains these words:

> Blessed are You, Lord our God, King of the Universe, Who sanctified us with His commandments, and hoped for us, and with love and intent invested us with His sacred Sabbath, as a memorial to the deed of Creation. It is the first amongst the holy festivals, commemorating the exodus from Egypt. For You chose us,

---

[1] Exod 20:9–11; Deut. 5:12, 14–15.

and sanctified us, out of all nations, and with love and intent You invested us with Your Holy Sabbath.

The Old Testament prophets point out that blessings will come to those who properly observe the Sabbath. Said the Prophet Isaiah:

> If you refrain from trampling the Sabbath, from pursuing your own interests on my holy day; if you call the Sabbath a delight and the holy day of the LORD honorable; if you honor it, not going your own ways, serving your own interests, or pursuing your own affairs; then you shall take delight in the LORD, and I will make you ride upon the heights of the earth; I will feed you with the heritage of your ancestor Jacob, for the mouth of the LORD has spoken.[2]

Isaiah also delivered this promise:

> If you keep your feet from breaking the Sabbath and from doing as you please on my holy day, if you call the Sabbath a delight and the LORD's holy day honorable, and if you honor it by not going your own way and not doing as you please or speaking idle words, then you will find your joy in the LORD, and I will cause you to ride on the heights of the land and to feast on the inheritance of your father Jacob."[3]

The Hebrew word for Sabbath can mean *cease*, *desist*, and *rest*.[4] The Christian practice of wearing one's best clothes to church comes from the Hebrew practice of observing the Sabbath by wearing one's best garments, worshipping, receiving religious instruction, and demonstrating love for others. Ordinary work, shopping, and regular activities were set aside in order to honor God's sanctified day.

The New Testament Christian community, which consisted of both Jews and Gentiles, was no longer under the Old Testament ceremonial laws. Nonetheless, the followers of Jesus observed the Sabbath. After the resurrection of Jesus on the first day of the week, the New Testament Christians began to observe the Sabbath on Sunday. St. Paul and the church of Troas met to worship on the first day of the week to worship (Acts 20:7), and that apostle asked his converts to bring their

---

[2] Isa. 58:13–14.
[3] Isa. 58:13–14.
[4] Exod. 34:21; 35:3; Isa. 56:2; 58:13; Neh. 10:31;

gifts on this day (1 Cor. 16:2). St. John called Sunday "the day of the Lord" (Rev. 1:10).[5]

As the church moved into the second century, Sunday continued as the Christian Sabbath. St. Ignatius (c. 35–c. 107) confirmed Sunday observance, and he urged his readers "no longer to live for the [Jewish] Sabbath but for the Lord's day, on which day our life arose."[6] An early second century Christian work, *The Didache*[7] directed Christians to assemble for worship on the Lord's Day.[8] God has never abrogated his command regarding one day in seven as a day of rest, worship, and renewal for body and spirit.

The renowned English jurist William Blackstone (1723–80) declared, "The keeping of one day in seven holy, as a time of relaxation and refreshment as well as public worship is of inestimable benefit to a state, considered merely as a civil institution.... A corruption of morals usually follows a profanation of the Sabbath." Abraham Lincoln observed, "As we keep or break the Sabbath, we nobly save or meanly lose the last best hope by which man rises." In a poetic flourish, Henry Wadsworth Longfellow mused, "Sunday is the golden clasp that binds together the volume of the weeks."

In John Wesley's time, as in ours, some did not observe Sunday as a day that God has hallowed. These people rationalized, "All days are equally holy. Therefore I do not need to observe Sunday as a special day." William Law (1686–1761) veered into that error. Wesley wrote him a letter:

> Christ," you say, "is the Church or temple of God within thee....When thou art well-grounded in this inward worship, thou wilt have learned to live unto God; above time and place. For every day will be Sunday to thee; and wherever thou goest, thou wilt have a Priest, a church, and an altar along with thee." The plain inference is, Thou wilt not need to make any difference between Sunday and other days. Thou wilt need no other church

---

[5] See also Matt. 28:1; Mark 16:9; John 20:1, 19.

[6] *Epistle to the Magnesians* (c. 115), 9:1.

[7] *The Didache* was compiled in the late first century or the early second century as *The Teaching [Didache] of the Lord to the Gentiles by the Twelve Apostles*. This work was compiled from several sources as a manual of ecclesiastical instructions on morals and church order. This work also contains tests to discern false prophets, as well as a final chapter on the second coming of Christ. During the Middle Ages, *The Didache* served to instruct neophytes and Christian believers.

[8] *Didache*, 14:1.

than that which thou hast always along with thee; no other supper, worship, Priest, or altar.

This is right pleasing to flesh and blood; and I could most easily believe it, if I did not believe the Bible. But it teaches me inwardly to worship God, as at all times and in all places, so particularly on his own day, in the congregation of his people, at his altar, and by the ministry of those his servants whom he hath given for this very thing, "for the perfecting of the saints," and with whom he will be to the end of the world.[9]

In the tract that follows, John Wesley says, "The Lord not only hallowed the Sabbath-day, but he hath also blessed it. So that you are an enemy to yourself you throw away your own blessing, if you neglect to 'keep this day holy.' It is a day of special grace. The King of heaven now sits upon his mercy seat, in a more gracious manner than on other days, to bestow blessings on those who observe it. If you love your own soul, can you then forbear laying hold on so happy an opportunity? Awake, arise, and let God give you his blessing! Receive a token of his love!"

---

[9] John Wesley, "An Extract of A Letter to the Reverend Mr. Law, Occasioned by Some of his Late Writings," *The Works of John Wesley*, Jackson ed., 9:505.

Word to a Sabbath Breaker

Remember the Sabbath day, and keep it holy.

Exodus 20:8

Have you forgotten who spoke these words? Do you defy him? Do you call on him to do his worst? Give thought to what you do. You are not stronger than God. Woe to you who contend against your Maker. Earthen vessels do not contend with the potter![1] God sits above the circle of the earth, and its inhabitants are like grasshoppers.[2]

Six days you shall labor and do all your work. However, the seventh day is a Sabbath to the LORD your God; you shall not do any work.[3] The Sabbath is not your day; it is God's day. He claims it for himself. From the very beginning of the world, he has always declared it for his own. By the seventh day, God had finished the work that he had done, and he rested from all he had done.[4] God hallowed the Sabbath—that is, he made it holy. He reserved it for his own purpose. God decreed that as long as the sun, moon, heavens, and earth shall endure, all people should spend this day worshipping him who gives all people their life, breath, and everything.[5]

Therefore, shall we rob God? Are you one who does so? Ponder and think about what you are doing! God gives you all that you have. Is not every day you live his gift to you? Will you return no gift to him? Indeed, will you keep from

---

[1] Isa. 45:9; 2 Cor. 4:7.
[2] Isa. 40:22.
[3] Exod. 20:9–10.
[4] Gen. 2:2–3.
[5] Gen. 2:7; Acts 17:25.

him what already belongs to him? God will not, and cannot resign his claim to the Sabbath. The Sabbath belongs to God. It was so from the beginning, and it will remain so to the end of the age. He cannot give this day to another. Render unto God the things that belong to God.[6] Do so now, while it is yet today.[7]

For whose sake does God claim the Sabbath? For his sake, or yours? Undoubtedly, God did not make the Sabbath for himself.[8] He does not need you or any other person. Look at the heavens; observe the clouds, which are higher than you.[9] If you sin, how does that affect God? If you multiply your transgressions, how do you harm God? If you are righteous, what have you added to God? What of value has he received from your hand?

God ordained the Sabbath for your sake! God your creator did this for *you*. It is for your benefit that he calls you to serve him. For your sake, he asks for a part of your time to be returned to him who gave you everything you have.[10] Acknowledge God's love. As long as you are on the earth, learn to praise the King of Heaven.[11] Spend the Lord's Day as you hope to spend that day which shall never have an end.

The Lord has blessed the Sabbath day, and he has consecrated it for you.[12] Therefore, if you neglect to hallow this holy day, you are an enemy to yourself and you squander your own blessing. The Sabbath is a day of special grace. The King of heaven now sits upon his mercy seat, in a more gracious manner than on other days. He wants to bestow blessings on those who observe his holy day. If you love your own soul, can you then refrain from laying hold of such a blessed opportunity? Wake up. Arise. Allow God to give you his blessing! Receive a token of his love! Call out to him so that you may find the riches of his grace and mercy in Christ Jesus![13] You do not know how many more of these days of salvation you

---

[6] Matt. 22:21; Mark 12:17; Luke 20:25.
[7] Heb. 3:13, 15.
[8] Mark 2:27 states, "The Sabbath was made for humankind, and not humankind for the Sabbath." Adam Clarke, a first generation Methodist commentator and colleague of John Wesley, commented on this verse: "That [we] might have the seventh part of [our] whole time to devote to the purposes of bodily rest and spiritual exercises. And in these respects it is of infinite use to mankind. Where no Sabbath is observed, there disease, poverty, and profligacy, generally prevail. Had we no Sabbath, we should soon have no religion."
[9] Job 35:5.
[10] James 1:17.
[11] Dan. 4:37.
[12] Exod. 20:11.
[13] Heb. 4:16; 2 Jn. 1:3.

may have. How dreadful it would be to leave this world while abusing God's mercy so freely offered![14]

O what mercy God has prepared for you, if you do not trample it under your feet! What mercy he has planned for those who reverence him above all else! Awaiting you is a peace that the world cannot give.[15] God offers joy that no one can take from you,[16] so rest from doubt[17] and fear.[18] God offers us love, which is the beginning of heaven. Are these gifts not for you? Does he who loved you, and gave himself for you, a sinner and rebel against God, not purchase them all for you?[19] He did this for you, who have so long crucified him afresh?[20] Now, "look to Him whom you have pierced!"[21] Even now, say, "Lord, it is enough that I have fought against you so long? I yield. I yield. Jesus, Master, have mercy upon me!"[22]

Today, above everything else, shout aloud and do not hold back.[23] Cry out to the God who hears our prayers.[24] Today is the day he has marked out for the good of your soul—both in this world and in the world that is to come.[25] Never again thwart the purpose of God's love, neither by worldly concerns nor by idle amusements. Does the smallest matter at any time of the day keep you from the house of God? Spend as much as you can of the rest of the Lord's Day, either in thinking about what you have heard, or reading Scripture, or in private prayer, or talking

---

[14] Thomas N. Ralston (1806–91) was a respected Methodist theologian in the nineteenth century. His book, *Elements of Divinity*, was for many years used in the Course of Study for American Methodism's ministers. In that book (p. 813), Ralston said, "Since men are so prone to forget God and neglect religion, under circumstances the most favorable, how greatly would this irreligious proclivity be enhanced by a withdrawal of the influences of the Sabbath! There is a sacred stillness which marks this consecrated day—a solemnity connected with the "sound of the church-going bell and its peacefully-assembling multitudes—that all must feel and acknowledge. Under these influences thousands of the thoughtless and the [frivolous] are led to the house of God, and in this way each returning Sabbath numbers its multitudes reclaimed from vice, and washed and sanctified by redeeming grace, to swell the numbers of the saints on earth, and prepare them for the mansions on high. Blot from existence the holy Sabbath, with all its sacred associations and influences, and how appalling the consequences that would ensue!"

[15] Psa. 119:165; Isa. 26:3; John 14:27; 16:33; Phil. 4:7; Eph. 2:14; Col. 3:15.
[16] Psa. 16:11; Isa. 12:3; 51:11; John 16:24; Rom. 14:17; 1 Pet. 1:8.
[17] Eph. 6:16; Heb. 11:1; 1 Jn. 5:4.
[18] Psa. 27:3; 46:2; 56:4; 118:6; Isa. 35:4; 41:10, 13; 43:1; 44:2; 54:4, 14; Matt. 10:31; Luke 2:10; Rom. 8:15; 2 Tim. 1:7; Heb. 13:6; 1 Jn. 4:18.
[19] John 3:16; Gal. 1:4; 2:20; Eph. 5:25; 1 Tim. 2:6; Tit. 2:14.
[20] Heb. 6:6.
[21] Psa. 22:16; Zech. 12:10; John 19:37.
[22] Psa. 4:1; Matt. 15:22; Mark 10:47; Luke 18:38–39; 1 Tim. 1:16.
[23] Isa. 58:1 in the NRS reads, "Shout out, do not hold back! Lift up your voice like a trumpet! Announce to my people their rebellion, to the house of Jacob their sins."
[24] Psa. 34:15; 94:9; Isa. 59:1; 65:24; James 5:4; 1 Pet. 3:12.
[25] Heb. 3:7, 13, 15; 4:7.

about the things of God.[26] Let his love be ever before your eyes. Let the praise of God always be in your mouth.[27] You have lived many years in folly and sin. Now, give the Sabbath to the Lord.

Do not anymore ask, "What is the harm if after Church I spend the rest of the day working in the fields, or in a tavern, or in taking a little amusement?" You know what the harm is. Your own heart tells you so plainly that you cannot help hearing it. Profaning the Lord's Day is a sordid misuse of your talent. It shows brazen contempt for God and his authority. Even upon the earth, you have heard of God's judgments against those who profane this day.[28] Yet these warnings are just sprinkles of that storm of fiery indignation that in the end will consume God's adversaries.[29]

Glory to God who has now made you aware of the importance of the Lord's Day. Now, you know that God planned this day as a day of blessing. Never again, allow your idleness or irreverence to turn that blessing into a curse. What folly and madness that would be! It would end in much sorrow and anguish. After a short time, death will end the day of God's grace and mercy.[30] Those who spurn grace and mercy now will forever more have no more Sabbaths, sacraments, or prayers. In that day, how they will wish they could recover what they now so idly cast away! However, all such wishes will be in vain. After death, they will find no place for repentance, though they should seek it painstakingly with tears.[31]

O my friend, know the privilege you enjoy. Even now, remember the Sabbath day, to keep it holy. Your time of life and of grace is far spent. The night of death is close. Hasten to use the time you have to recover the last hours of your time on earth. At once, pursue that which brings peace,[32] so that you may stand before the face of God forever.[33]

---

[26] Psa. 104:34.
[27] Psa. 66:8; Luke 19:37; Rev. 19:5.
[28] Exod. 16:27–28; 31:14; Num. 15:32–35; Neh. 13:15; Jer. 17:27; Ezek. 20:13; 22:8, 15.
[29] Ezek. 20:13 reads, "But the house of Israel rebelled against me in the wilderness; they did not observe my statutes but rejected my ordinances, by whose observance everyone shall live; and my Sabbaths they greatly profaned. Then I thought I would pour out my wrath upon them in the wilderness, to make an end of them.
[30] Psa. 90:12; Eph. 5:15; Col. 4:5.
[31] Heb. 12:15–17.
[32] Rom. 14:19.
[33] Num. 6:25;

Editor's Introduction

A Word to a Swearer

Jesus taught, "The things that come out of the mouth come from the heart."[1] The Apostle James declared, "Out of the same mouth come praise and cursing. My brothers, this should not be."[2] Indeed, Scripture forbids profanity, especially misusing the name of God. Indeed, one of the Ten Commandments forbids the wrong use of God's name: "You shall not make wrongful use of the name of the LORD your God, for the LORD will not acquit anyone who misuses his name."[3] Jesus added, "Do not swear at all: either by heaven, for it is God's throne."[4]

Some ancient Jews were so careful to avoid misusing God's name that they went so far as never even to speak his name. They used attributive descriptions of

---

[1] Matt. 15:18.
[2] James 3:10.
[3] Exod. 20:7.
[4] Matt. 5:34.

God, such as *creator, rock, strong one, shelter, mighty one, shepherd,* or *highest*. However, Scripture does not prohibit using God's name. Truly, Scripture admonishes to "call upon the name of the Lord."[5] When Thomas, an apostle, saw Jesus after his resurrection, Thomas declared, "My Lord and my God!" St. Paul taught that, "Everyone who calls on the name of the Lord shall be saved."[6] The New Testament apostles freely and frequently spoke the name of God. The only biblical prohibition against using God's name is using it wrongly.

In Scripture, pronouncing either a blessing upon or a curse is considered more than a wish that prosperity or misfortune fortune will come to a person. Blessing and cursing in the Bible are deemed to possess an inherent power of carrying themselves into effect. Whether or not we know it, blessing and cursing alike invoke the involvement of God, upon whose name we call.

In ancient times, people wrote curses on parchments and threw them into the air. They believed that the winds would carry the curse to its intended destination. People also spoke their curses. Goliath, for example, cursed David by the Canaanite gods (1 Sam. 17:43). Balak believed that Balaam's curse would bring about the defeat of Israel (Num. 22:5–40). Blessings and curses are strengthened due to their association with the deity invoked. Scripture teaches that idols of wood and stone are no gods at all—there is only one God. Consequently, whenever we bless or curse, we call upon the name of God.

Again, Scripture forbids using God's name wrongfully. Common examples of which are such expletives as "I'll be damned" and "Damn you." The careless use of "Damn-it" and "Ohhh, my God" are examples of violating God's command not misuse his name. The famed Bible commentator Matthew Henry (1662–1714) wrote,

> We must not swear lightly and irreverently, in common discourse: it is a very great sin to make a ludicrous appeal to the glorious Majesty of heaven, which, being a sacred thing, ought always to be very serious: it is a gross profanation of God's holy name . . . it is a sin that has no cloak, no excuse for it, and therefore a sign of a graceless heart, in which enmity to God reigns.

The Bible also teaches that one can profane God's name by insincere, deceitful, or careless statements, such as, "I swear, that's the truth;" "By Jove, I will;" "In the name of heaven, stop that loud noise;" For Christ's sake, that referee must be blind." Jesus said, "Let your words be 'Yes' or 'No.' Anything more than this comes

---

[5] 1 Chron. 16:8; Psa. 105:1; 116:13, 17; Isa. 12:4; Zeph. 3:9;1 Cor. 1:2.
[6] Rom. 10:13.

from the evil one" (Matt. 5:37). The Apostle James wrote, "Above all, my beloved, do not swear, either by heaven or by earth or by any other oath, but let your 'Yes' be yes and your 'No' be no, so that you may not fall under condemnation" (James 5:12).

Swearing and profanity were common in the eighteenth-century world of John Wesley. A historian of eighteenth-century England states,

> One feature of the eighteenth-century vocabulary common to all classes was the marked use of very coarse language. Oaths, adjectives bristling with objectionable virility, and nouns now considered as obscene were then heard on every hand. From the youngest to the oldest they could twang off obscenities. . . . Mothers addressed their children in the language of a drunken bully, and gentlemen were in the habit of rapping out a dozen of interjectural oaths every time they spoke.[7]

Judges cursed in court, and some chaplains cursed sailors to make them listen to sermons. The story is told that the Duchess of Marlborough called on a lawyer without leaving her name. The clerk later reported, "I could not make out who she was, but she swore do dreadfully she must be a lady of quality."[8]

In May 1742, Wesley recorded in his journal,

> We came to Newcastle about six; and, after a short refreshment, walked into the town. I was surprised: So much drunkenness, cursing, and swearing, (even from the mouths of little children,) do I never remember to have seen and heard before, in so small a compass of time. Surely this place is ripe for Him who 'came not to call the righteous, but sinners to repentance.'

It is evident that in many spheres of twenty-first century society language is degraded. In public, how common is foul language and invectives that dishonor God's name?

In a failed effort at humor, Mark Twain said, "Let us swear while we may, for in heaven it will not be allowed." Such reckless notions lack both wit and good judgment. President George Washington spoke more wisely: "The foolish and wicked practice of profane cursing and swearing is a vice so mean and low, that

---

[7] J. H. Whiteley, *Wesley's England: A Survey of XVIIIth-Century Social and Cultural Conditions* (London: The Epworth Press, 1954), 223.

[8] W. H. Fitchett, *Wesley and His Century: A Study in Spiritual Forces* (New York: Eaton & Mains, 1908), 139.

every person of sense and character detests and despises it." The renowned English poet and hymn writer, William Cowper, said, "It chills my blood to hear the blest Supreme rudely appealed to on each trifling theme.

Maintain your rank, vulgarity despise.
To swear is neither brave, polite, nor wise."

The Methodist Bible commentator Adam Clarke, a colleague of John Wesley, said, "An oath will not bind a knave nor a liar; and an honest man needs none, for his character and conduct swear for him." In this tract, John Wesley begins abruptly, and ends quickly by telling us that it is never too late to allow God to tame our tongues.

A Word to a Swearer

Swear not at all.

Matthew 5:34

"You shall not make wrongful use of the name of the LORD your God."[1] Are you without God in the world?[2] Have you no knowledge of God, no concern about him? Is God not in all your thoughts?[3] Do you believe there is a God? Where is God? Is he only in heaven? Truly, he fills everything![4] God has said, "Who can hide in secret places so that I cannot see them? Do I not fill heaven and earth?[5]

Where can you go from God's spirit? Where can you flee from his presence? If you ascend to heaven, he is there; if you make your bed in the grave, he is there. If you take the wings of the morning and settle at the farthest limits of the sea, even there his hand shall touch you and his right hand shall hold you fast.[6] God sees you now; his eyes are upon you; he observes all your thoughts; he spans your path; he counts all your steps. God is familiar with all your ways, contemplates your actions, and there is no word on your tongue that he does know completely.[7]

Is it not true that power belongs to God—indeed, all power in heaven and in earth?[8] Is God not able, even while you read or hear these words, to crush you into

---

[1] Exod. 20:7; Lev. 19:2; Matt. 5:34; James 5:12.
[2] Eph. 2:12.
[3] Psa. 10:4.
[4] Deut. 4:39; Psa. 139:8; Prov. 15:3; Isa. 66:1; Jer. 23:24; Acts. 17:27.
[5] Jer. 23:24; 49:10.
[6] Psa. 139:7–10.
[7] 1 Sam. 2:3; Isa. 40:28; Dan. 2:22; Matt. 6:8.
[8] Matt. 28:18; Rev. 5:13.

nothing?[9] Can he not this moment mash you into dust or tell the earth to open and swallow you up?[10] Oh, do not dismiss God as though he were nothing. Do not provoke him by disrespecting his name! Do not brush him aside! Can he not, suddenly, sent forth his lightning and tear you apart, or shoot his arrows and destroy you? What hinders him from cutting you off this instant, immediately sending you into hell? If God did, would he do you any wrong? Think about it! He would be giving you the request of your own lips.[11] What were the words you spoke just now? Did God not hear them? Why, did you pray to God to send you to hell! You asked him to damn your soul! How is it that you are in love with damnation? Are you in a hurry to live in eternal fire, day and night to suffer torment in that flame without a drop of water to cool your tongue?[12] Do you ask God for this? I pray to God that this state may never be either my lot or yours. What a pity, my brother. What if God takes you at your word? What if he were to say, "Be it to you just as you asked!" What if God grants you your wish, and allows you drop into everlasting fire that he has prepared for the devil and his angels![13]

I would rather that you would go to the paradise of God.[14] Would you not also want to go there? Is not going to heaven better than going to hell? Are you not convinced of this in your own conscience? Then, change your prayer. Cry out to God, "Save my soul, for I have sinned against you![15] Save me from all my sins. Save me from all my evil words and evil works, from my evil attitudes and desires! Make me holy, as you are holy![16] Let me know you, love you, and serve you—now and forever!"

Is not God willing to make you holy, so you can serve him? Surely he is willing, because he loves you. He gave his only Son, so that you will not perish, but have everlasting life. Christ died for you; and he that believes on him has everlasting life.[17] Mark that word. Those who receive the life of God know the beginnings of heaven, even now on the earth.[18] God fills these souls with his love, and the love

---

[9] Psa. 115:3; Matt. 19:26; Mark 14:36; Luke 1:37.
[10] Num. 16:32; 26:10; Psa. 106:17; Rev. 12:16.
[11] A common form of swearing in the eighteenth century was the phrase, "Well, I'll be damned." The term *zounds* was a contraction of *God's wounds*, and it had the same force as today's offensive word *damn*. Brewer's Dictionary of Phrase and Table, 16th ed. (London: Cassell, Ltd., 1999), 1298.
[12] Luke 16:24.
[13] Matt. 25:41.
[14] Luke 23:43.
[15] Luke 15:18.
[16] Lev. 19:2; Num. 15:40; 1 Pet. 1:15–16.
[17] John 3:16; 1 Tim. 1:16.
[18] Matt. 3:2; Luke 21:31.

of God is heaven itself. Those who truly believe in Jesus Christ have a peace which this world cannot give.[19] Their minds are forever calm.[20] They have learned to be satisfied, whatever the circumstances.[21] They are always tranquil, peaceful, content, and happy in life and in death. Believers in Christ are not afraid to die.[22] They desire to pass on and to be with him.[23] They want to leave this house of clay, and for angels to carry them to be with Abraham.[24] They wish to hear the archangel's call and with the sound of Gods trumpet,[25] and to see the Son of Man coming in the clouds of heaven.[26] They want to stand at God's right hand, and hear that word (which I earnestly beg of God you and I may hear), "Come, you that are blessed by my Father, inherit the kingdom prepared for you from the foundation of the world."[27]

---

[19] Psa. 29:11; 119:165; Isa. 26:3; 48:18; John 14:27; 16:33; Phil. 4:7.
[20] Rom. 5:1.
[21] Phil. 4:11.
[22] Isa. 25:8; 1 Cor. 15:26, 54; 2 Tim. 1:10.
[23] Phil. 1:21.
[24] Luke 16:22. To be with Abraham was a figure of speech meaning to be with him in paradise.
[25] 1 Thess. 4:16.
[26] Matt. 24:30; 26:64; Mark 14:62.
[27] Matt. 25:34;

Editor's Introduction

A Word to a Drunkard

In uncompromising terms, Scripture speaks of the personal and social evils of drunkenness.[1] The Prophet Isaiah wrote,

> Ah, you who rise early in the morning in pursuit of strong drink, who linger in the evening to be inflamed by wine, whose feasts consist of lyre and harp, tambourine and flute and wine, but who do not regard the deeds of the LORD, or see the work of his hands! Therefore my people go into exile without knowledge; their nobles are dying of hunger, and their multitude is parched with thirst. Therefore Sheol has enlarged its appetite and opened its mouth beyond measure; the nobility of Jerusalem and her multitude go down, her throng and all who exult in her.[2]

The Book of Proverbs sternly warns against the abuse of alcohol:

> Who has woe? Who has sorrow? Who has strife? Who has complaining? Who has wounds without cause? Who has redness of

---

[1] Deut. 21:20–21; 1 Sam. 1:14; Prov. 20:1; 21:17; 23:20–21, 29–35; 31:4–7; Isa. 5:11–12; 19:14; 24:9, 11; 28:1, 3; Jer. 25:27; Joel 1:5; Hab. 2:15–16; Luke 21:34; Rom. 13:13; Gal. 5:19–21; Eph. 5:18; 1 Cor. 6:9–10.

[2] Isa. 5:11–14.

eyes? Those who linger late over wine, those who keep trying mixed wines. Do not look at wine when it is red, when it sparkles in the cup and goes down smoothly. At the last it bites like a serpent, and stings like an adder. Your eyes will see strange things, and your mind utter perverse things. You will be like one who lies down in the midst of the sea, like one who lies on the top of a mast. "They struck me," you will say, "but I was not hurt; they beat me, but I did not feel it. When shall I awake? I will seek another drink.[3]

The New Testament treats such intemperance as a serious sin. Christ himself explicitly said, "Be on guard so that your hearts are not weighed down with dissipation and drunkenness . . . and that day catch you unexpectedly."[4] St. Paul likewise warns against drunkenness:

> Now the works of the flesh are obvious: fornication, impurity, licentiousness, idolatry, sorcery, enmities, strife, jealousy, anger, quarrels, dissensions, factions, envy, drunkenness, carousing, and things like these. I am warning you, as I warned you before: those who do such things will not inherit the kingdom of God.[5]

> So do not be foolish, but understand what the will of the Lord is. Do not get drunk with wine, for that is debauchery; but be filled with the Spirit.[6]

In John Wesley's eighteenth-century England, the abuse of alcohol was common among all segments of society. Many of the upper class boasted about their consumption of distilled liquor, bragging that they were "three-bottle men." William Lecky's extended history of eighteenth-century assesses Britain's gin-drinking addiction as "the master curse of English life."[7] The British government officially encouraged the production of gin because its consumption increased tax revenues. Following the implementation of that government policy, within twelve years, every sixth house in London had become a grog shop for the distribution of gin and rum. Gin halls posted signs promising poor people that they could become drunk for a penny, dead drunk for two pence, with the added offer of

---

[3] Prov. 23:29–33. See also Prov. 20:1; 21:17.
[4] Luke 21:34.
[5] Gal. 5:19–21.
[6] Eph. 5:17–18. See also 1 Pet. 4:3; 2 Pet. 2:13.
[7] William E. Lecky, History of England in the Eighteenth Century, 8 vols., (London: Longmans, Green, 1883–90) 1:476.

straw in the cellar on which to lie free of charge. Drunkenness was a common and uncensored condition in all segments of English society.

Alcohol consumption led to smuggling, poverty, thievery, cursing, adultery, prostitution, graft, and cruel sports. After dark, the drunken brawlers made the streets unsafe. Samuel Johnson wrote about the Strand, a three-quarter-mile London avenue in the central Westminster district:

> Prepare for death if here at night you roam,
> And sign your will before you sup from home.

Doctors voiced complaints against the curse of drunkenness as the cause of incurable physical conditions. Anglican priest, James Townley lamented,

> Gin, cursed Fiend, with Fury fraught,
> Makes human Race a Prey,
> It enters by a deadly Drought,
> And steals our Life away.

John Wesley asserted that addiction to alcohol was one of the greatest evils of the day, only exceeded by the slave trade. Aside from increasing the moral and health problems of the nation, the large consumption of distilled liquors led to a dramatic increase in the cost of bread. Wesley wrote, "Why does bread-corn [grain] bear so high a price? . . . . The grand cause is, because such immense quantities of [grain] are continually consumed by distilling. . . . Add the distillers throughout England, and have we not reason to believe, that (not a thirtieth or a twentieth part only, but) little less than half the wheat produced in the kingdom is every year consumed, not by so harmless a way as throwing it into the sea, but by converting it into deadly poison; poison that naturally destroys not only the strength and life, but also the morals, of our countrymen."[8] Wesley's further admonition remains pertinent:

> Neither may we gain by hurting our neighbour in his body. Therefore we may not sell anything that tends to impair health. Such is, eminently, all that liquid fire, commonly called drams, or spirituous liquors. . . . All who sell them in the common way, to

---

[8] "Thoughts on the Present Scarcity of Provisions," I, §3.

any that will buy, are poisoners general. They murder His Majesty's subjects by wholesale, neither does their eye pity or spare. They drive them to hell like sheep.[9]

John Wesley's ensuing tract, "A Word to a Drunkard," proclaims the gospel message that all people can know deliverance and freedom from addictions though the divine power of Jesus Christ, who died to free those who turn to him.

---

[9] Sermon, "The Use of Money," I, §4. Wesley also spoke of other addictions, such as gluttony and gambling. Today, the use of illegal drugs is a major cause of substance addition, a determent to a civil society, a noteworthy cause of crime, and a threat to life itself. In a sermon, "Spiritual Worship," Wesley said, "A glutton, a drunkard, a gamester [gambler], may be merry; but [they] cannot be happy."

A Word to a Drunkard

1. Are you a man? God made you a man; but you make yourself a beast. In what ways do human beings differ from beasts? Is it not chiefly in reason and understanding? However, you throw away what reason you have. You strip yourself of understanding. You do all you can to make yourself a mere beast. You not only make yourself a fool and a lunatic, but a swine, a poor filthy animal. Go and wallow with the pigs in the mire! Go on, continue to drink until your nakedness is uncovered, and people spit on your dignity.

2. O how honorable is an animal of God's making, compared to one who makes himself an animal! However, there is more. You make yourself a demon. You stir up all the demonic compulsions in you. You also gain other impulses that perhaps were not in you. At least, you intensify and increase the number of your evil impulses. You cause the fires of anger, hatred, or lust to burn seven times hotter than before you became a drunkard. At the same time, you grieve God's Holy Spirit, until you drive him completely from you.[1] You quench and drown whatever spark of good remained in your soul.

3. Now you have discarded everything that is good or virtuous, and you have filled your heart with everything that is base, worldly, sensual, and demonic. Doing so, you have forced the Spirit of God to depart from you because you would

---

[1] Eph. 4:30.

receive none of his reproof.[2] You have given yourself into the hands of the devil to be led blindfold by him at his will.[3]

4. Now, what would hinder the same thing from happening to you that happened to a man to whom a question was posed, "Which is the greatest sin? Is it adultery, drunkenness, or murder?" And which of these sins would you prefer to commit?" The man said that the lesser sin was drunkenness. Soon afterward, he got drunk. Then, he met with another man's wife and raped her. The husband came to help her, and the drunken man murdered the husband. Thus, drunkenness, adultery, and murder went together.

5. I have heard a story of a poor and wild American Indian, far wiser than either the drunken man or you. English merchants gave the Indian a cask of strong alcoholic liquor. The next morning he called his friends together, sat the container of alcohol before them, and said, "These white men have given us poison. This man (calling him by his name) was a wise man, and would harm no one except his enemies. However, as soon as he had drunk of this liquor, he became deranged, and he would have killed his own brother. We will not be poisoned this way." He then broke open the cask, and poured the liquor on the sand.

6. For what reason do you poison yourself by alcohol? For pleasure, you might say. Really? Will you make yourself a beast—or rather, a demon? Will you run the hazard of committing all manner of wickedness, only for the meager pleasure of a few moments while the poison runs down your throat? Never call yourself a Christian! Never call yourself a man! You have fallen beneath most of the animals that that perish.

7. More accurately, do you not drink for the sake of company? Do you not imbibe alcohol to please your friends? "For company," you may say. How is this? Will you take a dose of ratsbane[4] for the sake of the company of others? If twenty men in your presence were to take this poison, would you not want to excuse yourself? How much more should you want exemption from going to hell for the sake of someone's company? Would you drink alcohol just to accommodate your friends? What sort of friends are those you would oblige by destroying yourself? What kind of people would allow you and even entice you to destroy yourself?[5]

---

[2] Psa. 9:5.

[3] 2 Cor. 4:3–4 states, "And even if our gospel is veiled, it is veiled to those who are perishing. In their case the god of this world has blinded the minds of the unbelievers, to keep them from seeing the light of the gospel of the glory of Christ, who is the image of God."

[4] *Ratsbane* is a poison for rats, consisting of trioxide of arsenic.

[5] Prov. 20:1; 23:20; Isa. 5:11; Hab. 2:15; Luke 21:34; Rom. 13:13; Eph. 5:18.

They are villains, your worst enemies. They are the kind of friends who would smile to your face, and stab you in the heart.

8. O, do not search for any excuse! Many people say, "I am no one's enemy but my own." If they do say this, you should not repeat that notion. If it were so, what a poor saying is this one: "I give no soul but mine to give to the devil." Stop! Is that not too much to forfeit? Why should you give your own soul to the devil? Do not do it! Instead, give your soul to God.

However, you are not doing so. You are an enemy to your king, whom you are robbing of a useful subject. You are an enemy to your country, which you defraud of the service you might give as a man or as a Christian. You are an enemy to everyone who sees you in your sin, because your example may prompt others to do the same. A drunkard is a public enemy. I would not at all wonder if you, like Cain of old, were afraid that "anyone who meets you may kill you."[6]

9. Above all, you are an enemy to God, the great God of heaven and earth. You are an enemy of God who surrounds you on every side, and can send you into hell immediately.[7] You continually affront God to his face. You are openly defying him. Oh do not provoke God like this any longer! Have reverence for the great God!

10. If you are a drunkard, you are an enemy of Christ, the Lord who bought you. You openly challenge his authority. You count God's sovereign power and tender love as nothing. You crucify Christ afresh.[8] If you call him your Savior, what is it other than to betray him with a kiss?[9]

11. Oh, repent! Understand and realize what a poor thing you are. Ask God to convince you in your innermost soul.[10] How often have you crucified the Son of God afresh, and put him to an open shame![11] Pray that inwardly and outwardly you may know yourself to be just sin, guilt, and helplessness. Cry out, "Thou Son of David, have mercy on me!"[12] Thou Lamb of God, take away my sins![13] Grant me your peace.[14] Pardon the ungodly.[15] Pray, "O bring me to the sprinkled blood

---

[6] Gen. 4:13–14.
[7] James 4:4.
[8] Heb. 6:6.
[9] Luke 22:47–48.
[10] Psa. 139:23.
[11] Heb. 6:6.
[12] Matt. 15:22; 20:30–31; Mark 10:47–48; Luke 18:38–39.
[13] John 1:29.
[14] John 14:27; 2 Thess. 3:16.
[15] Rom. 4:5; 5:6.

of Christ, [16]that I may go and sin no more,[17] that I may love much, having had so much forgiven![18]

---

[16] Heb. 12:24; 1 Pet. 1:2.
[17] John 5:14; 8:11.
[18] Luke 7:47.

Editor's Introduction

A Word to an Unhappy Woman

In the eighteenth century, the word *unhappy* was a stronger term than being merely dissatisfied. The term connoted near disaster or complete disaster, something lethal. In 1652, James Howell wrote, "An unhappy Bullet came and killed one of the principal of the Blackcoats that was in arms." Samuel Johnson's 1755 *Dictionary of the English Language* defined the *unhappy* as "wretched; miserable; unfortunate; calamitous; distressed." The Oxford English Dictionary defines *unhappy* as "miserable in lot or circumstances." The context of the following tract discloses that Wesley was writing about prostitutes who suffered the tragedy ("unhappiness") of their way of life.

The biblical prohibition of sexual intimacy outside marriage is rooted in the seventh commandment that God communicated through Moses (Exod. 20:14). The New Testament noun for sexual sins is *porneia* (πορνεία), which may refer to *fornication, whoredom, concubinage, adultery, sodomy, lewdness, uncleanness,* and even *idolatry*.[1] Scripture condemns all forms of sexual sin—including incest,[2] prostitution,[3] fornication,[4] adultery,[5] homosexual practice,[6] and sexual relations with

---

[1] Joseph Henry Thayer, *A Greek-English Lexicon of the New Testament*, 532.
[2] Lev. 18:6–18; 20:17; 20:11–23; 1 Cor. 5:1.
[3] Prov. 2:16–18; 5:3–5; 6:23–27; 29:3; Luke 15:30; 1 Cor. 6:16.
[4] Matt. 5:32; Acts 15:29; 1 Cor. 6:18; 7:2; 10:8; Eph. 5:3; Col. 3:5; 1 Thess. 4:3.
[5] Exod. 20:14; Lev. 20:10; 2 Chron. 21:11; Job 24:15; 31:9–11; Isa. 23:17; Ezek. 16:26; Matt. 5:27–28; Acts 15:29; 1 Cor. 6:9, 18; 7:2; 10:8; Eph. 5:3; Col. 3:5; 1 Thess. 4:3; 2 Pet. 2:14.
[6] Lev. 18:22, 29; 20:13; Deut. 23:17–18; Rom. 1:26–28; 1 Cor. 6:9–10; 1 Tim. 1:10. St. Paul says nothing about homosexual orientation, but he condemns homosexual practice.

animals.⁷ The Old Testament prophets often spoke about Israel's national religious apostasy and the sexual immorality that often accompanied the worship of "other gods."⁸ The Old and New Testaments denounce all sexual immorality in clear terms.⁹

On the other hand, the Bible elevates marriage to a new height. The New Testament compares matrimony with the union of Christ and his church.¹⁰ Within Christianity, the standards of moral purity include premarital chastity, monogamous marriage, and marital fidelity. To be sure, there are church leaders in the United States and Europe who argue in favor of accepting homosexual practice, homosexual marriage, and the practice of couples living together apart from marriage. In doing so, they violate Scripture and undermine family structure. The Book of Hebrews states, "Let marriage be held in honor by all, and let the marriage bed be kept undefiled; for God will judge fornicators and adulterers."¹¹ Commenting on this passage, John Wesley wrote in his *Notes upon the New Testament*, "Marriage is honourable [for] all . . . clergy as well as laity. . . but whoremongers and adulterers God will judge—Though they frequently escape the sentence of men."

John Wesley's sermons contain encouragements to repent of immoral sexual behavior, and to trust God for the power to lead a pure and pious life. Of course, Wesley recognized that "there is in the will of [all people] a natural proneness to evil." "Leave the un-renewed will to itself," he said, and "it will choose sin and reject holiness; and that as certainly as water poured on the side of a hill will run downward and not upward." Wesley preached that God can forgive and deliver people from the various kinds of sexual sins.

In his tract, "Thoughts upon Necessity," Wesley insisted that God holds us accountable for our decisions:

> The actions of [people] are quite voluntary; the fruit of their own will. They love, they desire, evil things; therefore they commit

---

That apostle denounces the *indulgence* of wrongful "desires of the heart" (ἐπιθυμίαις τῶν καρδιῶν, Rom. 1:24). St. Paul describes sexual intimacy between persons of the same gender as *uncleanness* (ἀκαθαρσίαν) and *passions of dishonor* (πάθη ἀτιμίας). The apostle states that those who give themselves to such "unclean" passions "do not see fit to acknowledge God" (οὐκ ἐδοκίμασαν τον θεον ἔχειν ἐν ἐπιγνώσει).

⁷ Lev. 18:23, 30; 20:15–16.

⁸ Judges 2:17; 1 Chron. 5:25; Psa. 106:39; Isa. 1:21; Jer. 13:27; Ezek. 16:16; 20:30; 23:35; Hosea 1:2; 4:12; 5:4; 9:1.

⁹ Lev. 20:13; Rom. 1:21–28; 1 Cor. 1:23–27; 5:1–3, 11; 6:9; Col 3:5; 1 Pet. 4:3; Rev. 21:8; 22:15.

¹⁰ Matt. 22:2; 25:10; Eph. 5:22– 32; Col. 1:24; Rev. 19:7.

¹¹ Heb. 13:4.

them. Love and hate, desire and aversion, are only several modes of willing. Now, if [people] voluntarily commit theft, adultery, or murder, certainly the actions are evil, and therefore punishable. And if they voluntarily serve God, and help their neighbors, the actions are good, and therefore rewardable.

In the following tract, Wesley encourages a prostitute to repent, trust Christ, and move into a redeemed life of holiness and happiness.

A Word to an Unhappy Woman

1. Where you going? Are you going to heaven or to hell? Do you know? Do you never think about your destiny? If not, why not? Do you think you will never die? Certainly, it is appointed for all mortals to die.[1] What comes after death? The answer is, "Only heaven or hell."[2] Will thinking about death, shove death further into the future? No. Not for a day or an hour. Will rationalizing about hell save you from hell? Not at all. You know better than that.[3] You also know that every moment you draw closer to hell, whether or not you think about it. Nor are you any nearer to heaven by thinking. Necessarily, you must move closer to the one or the other—heaven or hell.

2. I implore you to think about this clear question: Are you going toward heaven or hell? To which of these destinations is your present way of life leading you? Is it possible that you are ignorant of the answer? Have you never heard that neither adulterers nor fornicators will inherit the kingdom of God, and that God will judge fornicators and adulterers?[4] How dreadful will be their sentence of judgment, "You that are accursed, depart from me into the eternal fire prepared for the devil and his angels."[5]

---

[1] 2 Sam. 14:14; Job 30:23; Psa. 49:10; Eccl. 8:8; Rom. 5:12; Heb. 9:27.
[2] Matt. 13:30, 49; 25:32; Luke 16:26; Acts 17:31; Rom. 2:16; 2 Cor. 5:10; Rev. 20:12.
[3] Heb. 9:27.
[4] Exod. 20:14; Lev. 20:10; 2 Chron. 21:11; Job 24:15; 31:9–11; Isa. 23:17; Ezek. 16:26; Matt. 5:27–28; Acts 15:29; 1 Cor. 6:9, 18; 7:2; 10:8; Eph. 5:3; Col. 3:5; 1 Thess. 4:3; 2 Pet. 2:14.
[5] Matt. 25:41.

3. Surely, you do not want to spurn the word of God! You have not yet sunk this low. Consider the astounding truth that our bodies are the temples of God.[6] Were you not created to be God's dwelling place?[7] Were you not devoted to God in baptism?[8] If a person destroys God's temple, God will destroy that person.[9] O, do not any longer provoke God to do this! Tremble before the great and holy God![10]

4. Do you not understand that your body is, or should be, the temple of the Holy Spirit who is in you? Do you not know that you are not your own, because you are bought with a price.[11] O, how great is that price![12] God ransomed you from the futile ways inherited from your ancestors.[13] He did not do so with perishable things like silver or gold, but with the precious blood of Christ, like that of a lamb without defect or blemish.[14] When will you glorify God with your body and your spirit, which belong to the Lord![15]

5. Ah, poor sufferer! How far are you from this? How low you have fallen! Are you not ashamed of what you do? Conscience, speak in the sight of God! At this very hour, does not your own heart condemn you? Do you not shudder at your condition?[16] For once, be so bold to lay your hand upon your heart, and ask yourself, "What am I doing? And what must the end of my present condition?" Your end would be the destruction of your body and your soul.[17]

6. Yes, I speak of the destruction of both body and soul! Can it be otherwise? Are you not plunging into misery in the present world, as well as in the world to come? What have you already brought upon yourself? What disrepute? What disdain? How can you now stand among those relatives and friends that once you loved so much, and who are still so loving toward you? What torments have you given them? How do some of them in secret places of prayer still weep for you? Will you not weep for yourself, when you see nothing before you but poverty, pain, diseases, and death? O, spare yourself! Have pity on your body, if not on your soul! Stop now! Stop before you decay, before you die, before you perish!

---

[6] 1 Cor. 3:16.
[7] Eph. 2:22.
[8] Col. 2:12.
[9] 1 Cor. 3:17.
[10] Dan. 6:26.
[11] 1 Cor. 6:20.
[12] Matt. 13:46.
[13] 1 Pet. 1:18.
[14] 1 Pet. 1:18–19.
[15] 1 Cor. 6:20.
[16] Joel 2:1.
[17] Matt. 10:28.

7. Do you ask what you should do? First, sin no more.[18] This is your first definite step. Now—this instant, escape for your life. Do not linger. Do not look back.[19] Whatever you do, sin no more. Starve or die rather than sin.[20] Be more concerned for your soul than for your body. Take care of your body, but put your poor soul first.

8. You may think you have no friend, at least none that can help you. Indeed, you *do* have such a friend—one who is a present help in time of trouble.[21] You have a friend that has all power in heaven and earth,[22] even Jesus Christ the righteous.[23] In times of old he loved sinners, and he still does.[24] He allowed the publicans and harlots to come to him.[25] One of them washed his feet with her tears, and wiped them with the hairs of her head.[26] Would to God that you were in her place! Say, Amen! Lift up your heart,[27] and it shall be done. Christ will quickly say, "Be of good cheer, your sins, which were many, have been forgiven.[28] Go in peace.[29] Sin no more.[30] Love much, for much has been forgiven.[31]

9. Do you still ask, "What shall I do to have food and clothing?" I answer that in the name of the Lord God (Mark this well, for his promise shall not fail), "Strive first for the kingdom of God and his righteousness, and God will give you all these things as well."[32] Settle this first in your heart: "Whatever I have or do not have, I will not choose everlasting fire. I will not sell my soul and body for bread. I would rather starve on earth than burn in hell." Then, ask God for help. He is not slow to hear.[33] He has never failed those who seek him.[34] He who feeds

---

[18] Gen. 19:15–17, 26; John 8:11. Repentance means confessing sorrow for one's sins and also leaving them.
[19] Luke 17:32.
[20] Prostitutes often complained that they would starve if they left prostitution.
[21] Psa. 46:1; John 15:15.
[22] Matt. 28:18.
[23] 1 Jn. 2:1.
[24] John 15:13; Rom. 8:35.
[25] Matt. 11:19; Luke 7:34.
[26] Luke 7:44.
[27] Lam. 3:41.
[28] Luke 7:47.
[29] Luke 7:50.
[30] John 8:11.
[31] Luke 7:47–48.
[32] Matt. 6:33; Luke 12:31.
[33] 2 Sam. 22:7; Psa. 34:15; 94:9; Isa. 59:1; 65:24; James 5:4;1 Pet. 3:12.
[34] Deut. 7:9; 1 Kings 8:56; Psa. 89:1; 1 Cor. 1:9; Heb. 6:18; 1 Pet. 4:19.

the young ravens that call upon him[35] will not let you perish for lack of sustenance.[36] In ways you do not think, God will provide for you if you seek him earnestly. Oh, let your heart incline toward him; seek him wholeheartedly![37] Fear sin more than hunger or death. Call out mightily to Christ who bore your sins to provide you with bread to eat that the world knows nothing about.[38] God will give you the food of angels, which is the love of God shed abroad in your heart.[39] Call on God until you can say, "I know that my Redeemer lives and that he has loved me and given himself for me.[40] After worms destroy my body, then in my flesh I shall see God.[41]

---

[35] Psa. 147:9.
[36] Matt. 6:2.
[37] Deut. 6:5; Psa. 119:2; Prov. 3:5; Jer. 29:13; Joel 2:12.
[38] John 4:32.
[39] Rom. 5:5.
[40] Gal. 2:20.
[41] Job 19:26.

Selection 8

Prayers for Families

Editor's Introduction

Prayers for Families

In January of 1767, John Wesley recorded two instances of preaching sermons on the family:

> *Sun.* 16.—I strongly inculcated family religion, the grand desideratum [something needed and desired as essential] among Methodists. Many were ashamed before God, and at length adopted Joshua's resolution, "As for me and my house, we will serve the Lord."[1]

> *Sun.* 30—I preached on the Education of Children, wherein we are so shamefully wanting. Many were now deeply convicted of this. I hope they will not stifle that conviction.[2]

In several ways, John Wesley was ahead of his eighteenth-century contemporaries in recognizing the importance and potential of children. It is true that he

---

[1] Josh. 24:15.
[2] Wesley's sermons, "On Family Religion" and "On the Education of Children" contain timeless principles for perpetuating Christianity in the family and passing Christianity on to succeeding generations. (Sermons 94 and 95, *The Works of John Wesley*, Bicentennial ed., 3:333–60.)

did not understand the developmental stages of children, and he may be charged with the error of forbidding children any time to play. Robert Southey, one of Wesley's biographers, jibed,

> Wesley learnt a sour German proverb, saying, "He that plays when he is a child, will play when he is a man;" and he had forgotten an English one, proceeding from good nature and good sense, which tells us by what kind of discipline Jack may be made a dull boy.[3]

Wesley's somewhat unconvincing reply would have been, "Why should the lad learn now what by and by he must unlearn."

Wesley's rule against play must be seen in the light of its eighteenth-century context. In Wesley's day, play in schools almost always included coarse violence, barbarizing, and demoralization. The value of sportsmanship and cooperative games was almost completely unrecognized.[4] Arthur Wellington (Duke of Wellington) once quipped that the Battle of Waterloo was won earlier on the playing fields of Eton, insinuating that fierce rough-and-tumble play at school had prepared the boys to become fighters.

Even at the University of Oxford "the teaching was singularly unimaginative, the statues out of date, and the general life of the students undisciplined."[5] When Wesley was at the University of Oxford, he and the members of the Holy Club drew up a statement: "Whether we may not contribute what little we are able toward having . . . children clothed and taught to read? Whether we may not take care that they be taught their catechism and short prayers for morning and evening?"[6] Although the study of children made little perceptible advances in eighteenth-century England, Wesley's kindness toward, and love for, children attracted them to him. They liked to be near him.

Wesley was at odds with those Anglican clergymen who believed that children were too young to understand the truths of Scripture and the love of God. n 1768,

---

[3] Robert Southey, *The Life of Wesley and the Rise and Progress of Methodism*, 2 vols. (London: Printed By Strahan and Spottiswoode for Longman, Hurst, Rees, Orme, and Brown, Paternoster-Row, 1820), 2:159

[4] Thomas E. Brigden, "John Wesley," *A New History of Methodism*, 2 vols., ed. by W. J. Townsend, H. B. Workman, and George Eayrs (London: Hodder and Staughton, 1909), I, 220.

[5] John R. H. Moorman, *A History of the Church in England* (New York: Morehouse-Barlow Company, 1959), 327.

[6] *The Works of John Wesley*, Journal and Diaries ed. by W. Reginald Ward and Richard P. Heitzenrater (Nashville: Abingdon Press, 1988), 18:128.

he wrote in his journal, "I met with the children, a work which will exercise the talents of the most able preachers in England."[7] Some years later, he wrote, "I preached both morning and evening, on the education of children. I now spoke chiefly to the parents, informing them that I designed to speak to the children at five the next morning. At five not only the . . . chapel was well filled, but many stood. . . . I trust they did not come in vain.[8]

When Wesley preached in Ireland, he reported from Dublin,

> The number of children that are clearly converted to God is particularly remarkable. Thirteen or fourteen little maidens, in one class, are rejoicing in God their Saviour; and are as serious and stayed in their whole behavior as if they were thirty or forty years old. I have much hopes that [they] will be steadfast in the grace of God which they now enjoy.[9]

Wesley often urged his preachers to spend time with the children in their congregations. In 1748, the English Methodist conference of preachers agreed to meet separately with the children in their congregations and gave them "suitable exhortations."

In 1766, Wesley drew up a yearly examination for the Methodist preachers. One of the questions was, "Will you diligently and earnestly instruct the children, and visit from house to house?" Sometimes a Methodist preachers would neglect to meet with children, offering the excuse that they "lacked a gift for working with them." Wesley replied, "Gift or no gift, you are to do it; else you are not called to be a Methodist Preacher. Do it as you can, till you can do it as you would. Pray earnestly for the gift, and use the means for it. Particularly, study the Instructions and Lessons for Children."[10] Wesley instructed the Methodist preachers to conduct Saturday afternoon classes for children, and for many years this was the common practice in the Methodist societies. Until receiving instruction, many children did not know that there was a God or that they had eternal souls, or that God loved them and wanted them to know him.

Wesley exclaimed that children are "fair blossoms . . . and if they be duly attended, there may be good fruit!"[11] In Wesley's preface to *Hymns for Children*, he offered the following advice:

---

[7] *Journal*, 31 August, 1768.
[8] *Journal*, 17, 18 July, 1785.
[9] *Journal*, 6 April, 1785.
[10] *The Works of John Wesley*, "Minutes of Several Conversations, from 1744–89" (Jackson edition, London: The Wesleyan Conference Office, 1882), VIII, 316.
[11] Journal, 30 June 1772.

> There are two ways of writing or speaking to children: the one is, to let ourselves down to them; the other, to lift them up to us. Dr. [Isaac] Watts has [written] on the former way, and has succeeded admirably well, speak to children as children, and leaving them as he found them. The following Hymns are written on the other plan: they contain strong and manly sense, yet expressed in such plain and easy language as even children may understand. But when they do understand them, they will be children no longer, only in years and stature.[12]

One of Wesley's biographers, Thomas Jackson, wrote,

> For nothing was [Wesley] so remarkable than his love to children. Often did he lay his hands upon them and bless them in the name of his great Master. He was in the habit of selecting small silver coins of peculiar freshness, and of presenting them to the children . . . as memories of his affection.

Children often came to him so he could lay his hand upon their heads and bless them. Customarily, Wesley ordered his chaise a half an hour before he needed it, and he packed it with children so they could enjoy a ride with him.

Wesley preached a Children's Sermon, in a "simple, plain familiar style," using no words of more than two syllables. He established a Junior Society Class. On an occasion, Wesley paused before two children who came to receive Holy Communion. Laying his hands on Robert, the younger boy, Wesley intoned, "Suffer [allow] the little children to come unto me, for of such is the Kingdom of Heaven." The boys never forgot that moment, and when they were adults they became Methodist lay preachers who served for a half a century. Another time, Wesley laid his hand on a youth who was preparing to enter the army. He said, "Never turn your back on a friend or a foe." That young man later became Sir Edward Nicholls, and he recalled, "I have never forgotten this advice. My wounds prove that I always faced the foe, and my presence here shows that I have not turned my back on my friends."[13] Hundreds of children, when adults, remembered John Wesley long after he died. As late as 1863, seventy-two years after Wesley's death, Nanny Wood reminisced that when she was about twelve she heard Wesley preaching in his gown and bands with the sun shining on his face.

---

[12] Preface to the abridged edition of "Hymns for Children," VI, 369.
[13] Leslie F. Church, *The Early Methodist People* (London: The Epworth Press, 1948), *240*–41.

In the eighteenth century, the rigid English social system did not provide the children of poor families any opportunity for schooling. Consequently, these children had little prospect of rising above the "station" into which they were born. In 1748, Wesley led an educational venture—Kingswood School for poor children. He wanted the school to be such that "would not disgrace the Apostolic age." Wesley also started other schools for poor children in London and Newcastle. Today, Kingswood School is one of the finest of its kind in England. When Wesley was in his eighty-fifth year, he wrote in his journal,

> We went on to Bolton. Here are eight hundred poor children taught in our Sunday-schools, by about eighty masters, who receive no pay but what they are to receive from their Great Master. About a hundred of [the children] are taught to sing; and they sang so true, that, all singing together, there seemed to be but one voice. The House was thoroughly filled, while I explained and applied the first commandment. What is all morality or religion without this? A mere castle in the air. In the evening, many of the children still hovering round the House, I desired forty or fifty to come in and sing *Vital spark of heavenly flame*.[14] Some of them were silent, not being able to sing for tears, yet the harmony was such as I believe could not be equaled in the King's chapel."[15]

Nine months later, Wesley returned to Bolton, and he wrote in his journal,

> We went on to Bolton, where I preached in the evening in one of the most elegant Houses in the kingdom, and to one of the liveliest congregations. And this I must avow, there is not such a set of singers in any of the Methodist congregations in the three kingdoms. There cannot be; for we have near a hundred such trebles, boys and girls, selected out of our Sunday-schools, and accurately taught, as are not found together in any chapel, cathedral,

---

[14] Although this three stanza hymn is about death, the children sang it with reverential devotion. The final stanza:

> *The world recedes—it disappears;*
> *Heav'n opens on my eyes; my ears*
> *With sounds seraphic ring!*
> *Lend, lend your wings! I mount! I fly!*
> *O grave! where is thy victory!*
> *O death! where is thy sting?*

[15] Journal, 27 August 1787.

or music-room within the four seas. Besides, the spirit with which they all sing, and the beauty of many of them, so suits the melody, that I defy any to exceed it; except the singing of angels in our Father's house.[16]

In 1763, Charles Wesley published *Hymns for Children*, and subsequent editions of Methodist hymnals had a section of children's hymns. Charles Wesley's six stanza hymn for children was sung at the opening of Kingswood School. Stanzas five and six contain words that many within the Wesleyan tradition hold dear:

> 5. *Unite the pair so long disjoined,*
> *Knowledge and vital piety:*
> *Learning and holiness combined,*
> *And truth and love, let all men see*
> *In those whom up to thee we give,*
> *Thine, wholly thine, to die and live.*
>
> 6. *Father, accept them through thy Son,*
> *And ever by thy Spirit guide!*
> *Thy wisdom in their live be shown,*
> *His name confessed and glorified;*
> *Thy power and love diffused abroad,*
> *Till all the earth is filled with God.*

In eighteenth-century England, Methodism played an important role in the emerging Sunday School Movement for children. In 1769, eleven years prior to Robert Raikes's Sunday School initiative, a Methodist, Hannah Ball, with John's Wesley's backing, established a Sunday school for children.[17] The Methodists taught children practical skills, reading, writing, arithmetic, geography, and basic Christian doctrine. For many poor children, the Methodist Sunday Schools offered their only formal educational experience. These Sunday Schools also provided soap, food, and clothing for these "children of the gutter."

John Wesley used short words and simple language in the following Prayers for Children. He said, "I continually alter hard words into easy, and long sentences into short." His words for the young contain important truths, yet he expresses

---

[16] Journal, 19 April 1788.
[17] J. Wesley Bready, *England: Before and After Wesley, The Evangelical Revival and Social Reform* (London: Hodder and Stoughton, n.d.), 353.

them clearly. To repeat a quotation, Wesley said that when children grasp Christian truth, they will be children no longer, even though they are young in years and small in stature.

Prayers for Children

John Wesley's Prayers for Children contain morning and evening prayers for each day of the week. Below are Wesley's introduction to these prayers, morning and evening prayers for Sundays, and some additional children's prayers.

My Dear Child,

A lover of your soul has here drawn up a few prayers to help you in the duty of praying. Be sure that you do not neglect coming to God in prayer, at least each morning and evening. You need to pray for mercies and praise God for blessings. Be careful not to pretend before God, speaking with your lips, while your heart is far from him.[18] God sees you and knows your thoughts.[19] Therefore, speak with your lips and pray with your heart. So that you will not pray with empty words, renounce sin and make every effort to do what God has shown you to do. Scripture says, "The prayers of the wicked are disgusting to the Lord."[20] So, ask God for the blessings you want, in the name, and for the sake, of Jesus Christ.[21] God will hear and answer you.[22] He will do more for you than you can either ask or think.[23]

John Wesley

A Prayer for Sunday Morning

Almighty Creator of us all, in you we live, and act, and exist.[24] You make the morning and the evening to rejoice.[25] Allow me now to approach your divine grandeur with complete reverence and godly awe.[26] I want to worship your sacred name,[27] because in your goodness you have brought me safely to see the beginning of a new day and another Sunday. I bless you, who has out of love for my soul and for the glory of your name, set this day apart for holy purposes. You call me to your service, in which I find my nobility and happiness. This is your day. O Lord,

---

[18] Matt. 15:8.
[19] Psa. 139:23; Isa. 66:18.
[20] 1 Pet. 3:12.
[21] Eph. 5:20
[22] Jer. 42:4.
[23] Eph. 3:20.
[24] Acts 17:28.
[25] Psa. 65:8.
[26] Psa. 33:8.
[27] Psa. 29:2; 66:4; 86:9; 138:2; Rev. 15:4.

help me to rejoice and be glad for it.[28] May I always remember to keep this day holy, not doing my own work, seeking my own pleasure, or speaking my own words.[29] May I delight in you, so that you may give me the desires of my heart.[30] Heavenly Father, bless to me your word and the ways to worship you. May I not use them foolishly or to my own harm, but to instruct my mind, reform my life, and so find your salvation.[31] Save me from all stubbornness of heart and disrespect for your word.[32] Increase my love for your word, help me to hear it humbly, to receive it with pure love, and to produce the fruit of good living. Open my mind to love and receive your truth. Imprint your truth so powerfully on my heart, and root it so deeply in my soul, that its fruits will be in my life to your glory and praise. May I always hear, read, keep, learn, and digest your word, so that it may be a taste of life in my soul. O let me never offer empty worship to the Lord, praying with my lips, while my heart is far from you.[33] Enable me to worship you with holy devotion, joy, benefit, and delight. Fill me with a contented sense of your presence. May I may serve you with reverence and godly respect,[34] to the wellbeing of my soul and the glory of your name. O Lord God, clothe your ministers with righteousness, and let your holy people rejoice and sing.[35] Break the bread of life to all our souls, so that we may receive it and live forever. O Lord, hear my prayers, and let them come before you. Do more and better for me than I can desire or deserve. I pray the sake of my blessed Savior and Redeemer, Jesus Christ, to whom, with you and the Holy Spirit, be all the praise and glory, now and forever. Amen.[36]

Our Father in heaven, hallowed be your name, your kingdom come, your will be done on earth as it is in heaven. Give us today our daily bread. Forgive us our debts, as we also have forgiven our debtors. And lead us not into temptation, but deliver us from the evil one. For yours is the kingdom, and the power, and the glory, for ever and ever. Amen.

---

[28] Psa. 118:24; Isa. 25:9.
[29] Exod. 20:8.
[30] Psa. 37:4.
[31] Psa. 25:5.
[32] Rom. 2:5.
[33] Matt. 15:8; Mark 7:6.
[34] Heb. 12:28.
[35] Psa. 7:17; 9:11; 30:12; 89:1; 92:1; 95:1; 96:2; 104:33; 147:1.
[36] This phrase, followed by the LORD's Prayer, appears often at the end of the Collects in the Book of Common Prayer.

A Prayer for Sunday Evening

Merciful God, allow me now to give you my evening offering of praise and thanksgiving for all the blessings and favors you so freely and continually give to my body and soul. O Lord God, you have dealt graciously with me.[37] You have been exceedingly good and kind to me beyond all that I could expect, or I am able to express. I bless you, O Lord, for every aid I enjoy to improve my present and eternal good. I want to give all praise and glory to you alone, to whom praise and glory are due. O Lord, I bless you that your church is open to me, the bread of life is offered me, the word of salvation preached to me, and your Spirit works within me.[38] O let me not receive your grace to no purpose. Do not let your word be lost on me. Apply your word to my heart, and stamp it on my memory, so that it may be a blessing to my soul.[39] In mercy, O Lord, pass by all things which in your pure and holy eyes have been wrong this day; pardon my neglect and wrongdoing. As I have heard how to live and please you, O my God, help me to walk more worthy of the Lord to all please you in everything. May I may grow in true reverence and love.[40] Give me the true knowledge and faith of our Lord Jesus Christ.

With the power of your grace and Holy Spirit, please confirm every word of instruction that I have received. Above all, Oh blessed God, give me a heart filled with your love, a heart lifted up in your praise, and devoted to your honor and glory all the days of my life. Oh Lord God, my Savior, receive me, into your gracious care and protection. Preserve me from all dangers throughout the night. Let me lie down and sleep in your arms. When the trumpet shall sound,[41] and at last call me from the sleep of death, caught up together with them in the clouds to meet the Lord in the air, and so we will be with the Lord forever.[42] All these mercies, O my God, I most humbly ask, alone for the sake of Jesus Christ, my Redeemer. Amen.

Our Father in heaven, hallowed be your name, your kingdom come, your will be done on earth as it is in heaven. Give us today our daily bread. Forgive us our debts, as we also have forgiven our debtors. And lead us not into temptation, but deliver us from the evil one. For yours is the kingdom, and the power, and the glory, for ever and ever. Amen.[43]

---

[37] Gen. 33:11.
[38] Rom. 8:11.
[39] Heb. 4:12.
[40] 2 Pet. 3:18.
[41] 1 Cor. 15:52.
[42] 1 Thess. 4:17.
[43] Matt. 6:9–13.

A Prayer for Relatives, Friends, and Those I Know

O Lord, promise me you will bless my father, my mother, and all my relatives with reverence for your name. Bless them in their souls and bodies, complete them in every good word and work,[44] and be their guide until death. Bless my friends, forgive my enemies; and give to all people the knowledge and love of yourself. Have mercy on all who are distressed in mind, body, or condition of life. Give them patience in their sufferings, and a good result from all their afflictions. Receive them and me at last into your blessed kingdom, for Jesus Christ's sake. Amen.

A Prayer before Meals

O Lord, I pray that you will give your blessing on the meal that your mercy has provided here before me, that whether I eat or drink, or whatever I do, I may do everything to your glory and praise, through Jesus Christ my Lord. Amen.

A Prayer after Meals

O Lord my God, I bless your holy name for this mercy, which I have now received from your bounty and goodness. Now feed my soul with your grace, so I may make this grace my food and drink to do your gracious will, through Jesus Christ my Savior. Amen.[45]

The John Wesley Teapot

In March of 1760, John Wesley preached to the pottery workers at Burslem. He talked with Josiah Wedgwood who was working in his home garden next to his factory. Wedgwood manufactured pottery that was superior in texture and durability to that of every pottery maker on the continent. By 1763, Wedgwood was receiving orders from the highest levels of the British nobility, including Queen Charlotte. Afterward, the queen allowed him to give this line of pottery the name, "Queen's Ware." In honor of John Wesley, Wedgwood made a special teapot that held a full gallon of tea. John Cennick, then a Methodist lay preacher, wrote two

---

[44] Phil. 1:6.
[45] When John Wesley was dying, someone moistened his lips with water, and he instinctively uttered a prayer he had often prayed after meals: "We thank Thee, O Lord, for these and all Thy mercies; bless the Church and King; grant us truth and peace, through Jesus Christ our Lord, forever and ever."

table blessings to be placed on opposite sides of the teapot. Charles Wesley corrected and published several of Cennick's hymns. Cennick's teapot verses, which follow, became known as "Wesley Table Graces."

In 1908, the teapot was reproduced by Anna Onstott (later nicknamed "Teapot Annie"), who engaged Wedgwood Company to manufacture them. She introduced these reproductions, to Methodist churches and women's groups which sold them to raise money for Christian missions. These pieces contain the following prayers.

Blessing before the Meal
Be present at our Table Lord
Be here and everywhere ador'd
These creatures bless and grant that we
May feast in Paradise with thee.

Thanksgiving after the Meal
We thank thee Lord for this our food
But more because of Jesus' love.
Let manna to our Souls be given
The bread of Life sent down from heaven.

Selection 9

Thoughts upon Methodism

Editor's Introduction

Thoughts upon Methodism

Many of John Wesley's eighteenth-century converts worked diligently, exercised frugality, and saved their money. Numerous Methodists rose from the ashes of ignorance and poverty to achieve education and prosperity. If thrift, honesty, sobriety, industry, and hard work were religious virtues, they were also business assets. Factory owners often chose Methodists as supervisors and managers, and some Methodists came to own factories. This upward social and economic climb brought prosperity, and Wesley became concerned about the dangers that riches so often pose, and concerning which Scripture warns.[1] Methodist historian Maldwyn Edwards noted, "The lynx eyes of John Wesley were quick to see the change coming over his Society, and in his later years he preached repeatedly against the danger of riches and the necessity of using money as a trust from God.[2]

Wesley reminded the Methodists of the importance of following Christ's instructions to his disciples: "Do not store up for yourselves treasures on earth . . .

---

[1] Deut. 8:13–14; Psa. 62:10; Prov. 28:28:20; Matt. 4:19; 6:19; 19:24; Luke 16:19–31; 1 Tim. 6:9–10..

[2] Maldwyn Edwards, *Methodism and England: A Study of Methodism in its Political Aspects During the Period 1850–1932* (London: The Epworth Press, 1943), 207.

but store up for yourselves treasures in heaven.... For where your treasure is, there your heart will be also."[3] Christ's point, and Wesley's as well, was that we are not to store up wealth for *ourselves*. Wesley's three-fold advice to the Methodists is well known: "Gain all you can; save all you can; give all you can." Wesley explained his meaning:

(1) We ought to gain all we can gain, without buying gold too expensively or paying more for it than it is worth. But this it is certain we should *not* do; we ought not to gain money at the expense of life or (which is in effect the same thing) at the expense of our health. Therefore, no gain whatever should induce us to enter into, or to continue in, any work that entails such hard or long labor that it impairs our physical wellbeing. Neither should we begin or continue in any business that deprives us of adequate food and sleep that our bodies require.

(2) Save all you can. Do not throw money away in worthless expenses, which is just the same as throwing money into the sea. Expend no part of your money merely to gratify the desire of the flesh, the desire of the eye, or the pride of life.[4] Do not waste any valuable money only to gratify the desires of the flesh; in procuring the pleasures of sense, of whatever kind.... Do not waste any part of your valuable earnings just to to gratify the desire of the eye, by unnecessary or expensive apparel or needless ornaments. Waste no part of money in unusually adorning your houses with superfluous or expensive furniture, costly paintings, embellishment, books, or in elegant but not useful gardens. And why should you throw away money upon your children, any more than upon yourself, on tantalizing food, elegant or costly apparel, or any kind excesses? Why should you purchase for your children any pride, lust, vanity, or foolish and harmful desires? They do not need any more, as they have enough already. Nature has made ample provision for them! Why should you expend money to increase their temptations and snares, and to pierce them through with more sorrows?[5] Do not leave money to

---

[3] Matt. 6:19–21.
[4] 1 Jn. 2:16.
[5] 1 Tim. 6:10.

them to throw away. If you have good reason to believe they would waste what is now money only to gratify and increase, the desire of the flesh, the desire of the eye, or the pride of life. This would imperil your soul and theirs. Do not set such traps for them.

(3) Give all you can, or, in other words, give all you have to God. . . . Render unto God, not a tenth, not a third, not half, but all that belongs to God, whether is more or less. Let all that you spend on yourself, your household, the household of faith,[6] and all humankind so you can give a good account of your stewardship, when you can be stewards no longer. . . . Unless we manage our Lord's goods in this manner, can we be wise or faithful stewards? We cannot. Both the word of God and our own conscience bears witness. Then why should we delay? Why should we consult any longer with flesh and blood, or people of the world?[7] Our kingdom, our wisdom, are not of this world. . . . We follow no men any farther than they are followers of Christ. Hear ye him: Yea, to-day, while it is called to-day, hear and obey his voice! At this hour, and from this hour, do his will: Fulfil his word, in this and in all things! I entreat you, in the name of the Lord Jesus, act up to the dignity of your calling! No more sloth! Whatsoever your hand findeth to do, do it with your might! No more waste! Cut off every expense which fashion, caprice, or flesh and blood demand! No more covetousness! But employ whatever God has entrusted you with, in doing good, all possible good, in every possible kind and degree, to the household of faith, to all men! This is no small part of "the wisdom of the just."[8] Give all ye have, as well as all ye are, a spiritual sacrifice to Him who withheld not from you his Son, his only Son: So laying up in store for yourselves a good foundation against the time to come, that ye may attain eternal life!

---

[6] In Gal. 6:10, οἰκείους τῆς πίστεως can be translated *household of faith*, *family of believers*, or *family of faith*.
[7] Gal. 1:6.
[8] Luke 1:17, KJV.

In 1780, Wesley wrote a sermon titled "The Danger of Riches." His text for that sermon was 1 Tim. 6:9—"They that will be rich fall into temptation and a snare, and into many foolish and hurtful desires, which drown men in destruction and perdition. "Wesley opened that sermon with these words:

> How innumerable are the ill consequences which have followed from men's not knowing, or not considering, this great truth [the danger of riches]! Even in the Christian community, how few are those who either know or duly consider the danger of riches! Indeed, how small is the number of those, even among real Christians, who take this matter into account! Most Christians pass very lightly over this danger, hardly remembering that there is such a text in the Bible. And many put such a construction upon such warnings so as to make them of no effect. They say that they will be rich no matter whether it is right or wrong. They are determined to carry their point to achieve this goal by whatever means to attain it. They fall into temptation, and into all the evils enumerated by Paul the Apostle.[9]

Wesley closed that sermon, saying,

> Thus have I given you, O you wealth-builders and lovers and possessors of riches, one more warning—it may be the last. O that it may not be in vain! May God write it upon all your hearts! Though 'it is easier for a camel to go through the eye of a needle than for a rich man to enter into the kingdom of heaven,'[10] yet the things impossible with us are possible with God.[11] Lord, speak! and even the rich men that hear these words shall enter thy kingdom, shall take the kingdom of heaven by violence,'[12] shall 'sell all for the pearl of great price;'[13] shall be crucified to the world,[14] and count all things as refuse, that they may win Christ!"[15]

---

[9] 1 Tim. 6:9. The NRSB translated this verse, "But those who want to be rich fall into temptation and are trapped by many senseless and harmful desires that plunge people into ruin and destruction.
[10] Matt. 19:24; Mark 10:25; Luke 18:25.
[11] Matt. 19:26; Mark 10:27; Luke 18:27.
[12] Matt. 11:12.
[13] Matt. 13:46.
[14] Gal. 6:14.
[15] Phil. 3:8.

In 1787, just four years before Wesley died, he wrote another sermon, "On God's Vineyard," to warn against the dangers of increased prosperity. This sermon contained "plain talk" about the importance of maintaining faithfulness to God and obedience to biblical guidelines. Wesley said,

> Truly, when I saw what God had done among his people between forty and fifty years ago; when I saw them warm in their first love, magnifying the Lord, and rejoicing in God their Savior; I could expect no less than that all these would have lived like angels here below. I expected that they would have walked as continually seeing Him that is invisible;[16] having constant communion with the Father and the Son;[17] living in eternity, and walking in eternity. . . . But, instead of this, it brought forth wild grapes—fruit of a quite opposite nature.[18]

Wesley proceeded to list certain unchristian attitudes and behaviors that had crept into the lives of some financially comfortable Methodists. He talked about the temptations and dangers that almost always accompany the accumulation of money.

John Wesley wrote the tract below, *Thoughts upon Methodism*, in 1786. He was eighty-three years old, and he apparently wrote this piece in day's time.[19] Wesley published *Thoughts upon Methodism* in the *Arminian Magazine* in 1787.[20] This tract also appears in the Jackson edition of Wesley's works,[21] and in the Bicentennial edition of his works.[22] The year before Wesley died, he wrote another sermon titled "The Danger of Increasing Riches," in which he said, "After having served you between sixty and seventy years; with dim eyes, shaking hands, and tottering feet, I give you one more advice before I sink into the dust. Mark those words of St. Paul: 'Those that desire or endeavour 'to be rich,' that moment 'fall into temptation.'"[23] The aged Wesley said,

---

[16] Heb. 11:27.

[17] 1 Jn. 1:3; 2:24; 2 Jn. 1:9.

[18] Isa. 5:2, 4.

[19] On Friday 4 August he scribbled in his diary the following brief account: "Prayed, Acts xxii, tunes; 8 read narrative, tunes; 12 within; 12:30 letters; 2:30 dinner, conversed, writ Th[ough]ts [u]p[on] Meth[odis]m; 5 tea, conversed, garden; 6:30 prayed, writ narrative; 8 supper, conversed, prayer; 9:30."

[20] *Arminian Magazine* (1787) 100; 155.

[21] *The Works of John Wesley* (Jackson ed.) 9:527—30.

[22] *The Works of John Wesley* (The Methodist Societies: History, Nature, and Design, ed. Rupert E. Davis, Nashville: Abingdon Press, 1989) 13:258—61.

[23] 1 Tim. 6:9.

> From that express declaration of our Lord, "It is easier for a camel to go through the eye of a needle, than for a rich man to enter into the kingdom of heaven," we may easily learn, that none can have riches without being greatly endangered by them. But if the danger of barely having them is so great, how much greater is the danger of increasing them! This danger is great even to those who receive what is transmitted to them by their forefathers; but it is abundantly greater to those who acquire them by their skill and industry. Therefore, nothing can be more prudent than this caution: "If riches increase, set not thine heart upon them."[24]

Wesley scholar Albert Outler said, "It would be his last sermon to be published in the [*Arminian*] *Magazine* that he had founded; his successors would deliberately leave this fact unnoted. There is here an irony: the patriarch's last word turns out to have been his least heeded."[25]

In the tract that follows, Wesley asks "How, then, is it possible that Methodism, that is, the religion of the heart . . . should continue in this state? For the Methodists in every place grow diligent and frugal; consequently, they increase in goods. Hence they . . . increase in pride, in anger, in the desire of the flesh, the desire of the eyes, and the pride of life." Wesley closes this tract with what he believes is the biblical remedy for a "continual declension of pure religion."

---

[24] Psa. 62:10.
[25] Albert Outler, ed., *The Works of John Wesley*, Sermons, 4 vols. (Nashville: Abingdon Press, 1987) 4:177.

Thoughts upon Methodism
1786

1. I am not afraid that the people called Methodists will ever cease to exist, either in Europe or America. However, I am concerned that they might exist only as a dead sect, holding to the outward form of godliness but denying its power.[1] Undoubtedly, this will be the case unless they cling to the doctrine, spirit, and discipline with which they first began.

2. What was their fundamental doctrine? It is that the Bible is the whole and sole rule of Christian faith and practice.[2] From the Scriptures, they learned the following:

    (i) Religion is an inner principle, and it is having the mind that was in Christ.[3] In other words, religion is being clothed with the new self,[4] created according to the likeness of God[5] in true righteousness and holiness.[6]

    (ii) This state cannot be ours, except by the power of the Holy Spirit.[7]

    (iii) We receive this and every other blessing, solely due to Christ.[8]

    (iv) All who have the mind that was in Christ[9] are our brothers, sisters, and mothers.[10]

---

[1] 2 Tim. 3:5.
[2] 2 Tim. 3:16.
[3] Phil. 2:5.
[4] 2 Cor. 5:17; Gal. 6:15.
[5] Col. 3:10.
[6] Luke 1:74–75; 2 Cor. 7:1; Eph. 4:24.
[7] Rom. 15:13.
[8] John 1:4; 11:25; 14:16; Rom. 5:21; 2 Tim. 1:10.
[9] Phil. 2:5.
[10] Matt. 12:50.

3. In 1729 four young students at Oxford agreed to spend their evenings together.[11] They were all zealous members of the Church of England, and they had no abnormal opinions.[12] They were characterized only by their constant attendance at church and holy communion. By 1735, the group had grown to fifteen, at which time their leader[13] embarked for America, intending to preach to the heathen Indians. Methodism at Oxford then seemed to die away. However, Methodism revived again in 1738.[14] Methodism began to grow especially after I began to preach in the fields. (Many ministers did not allow me to preach in their churches.) One after another came to me to ask what they must do to be saved.[15] I asked them to meet together with me. They did so, and their numbers increased continually. In November of 1739, a large building, called the Foundry, became available.[16] So that the people's work would not be impeded, I began preaching in the Foundry on mornings at 5:00 and on evenings at 7:00.

4. From the beginning, the men and women sat in separate sections, as they did in the ancient church.[17] None were allowed to call any seat their own; the early comers sat down first. There were no pews, and the benches for rich and poor were of the same construction.[18] I began the service with a short prayer. Next, we sang a hymn, and I preached, (usually about half an hour). Then we sang a few

---

[11] Here, Wesley includes himself in the Oxford "Holy Club."

[12] The young Oxford Methodists did had no wish to begin a new religion or sect. They wanted only to study, apply, and embody the truths of Christian orthodoxy.

[13] Again, Wesley is speaking of himself.

[14] John Wesley's heartwarming experience took place on 24 May 1738.

[15] Acts 16:30.

[16] This building in London had once been used for casting cannons for the English government, but due to a devastating explosion the ruined building had sat in a dilapidated condition. On 11 November 1739, Wesley paid £115 for this "vast uncouth heap of ruins." Workers repaired the Foundry, and on 23 July 1740 Wesley began worship services there in a "chapel" that seated fifteen-hundred people. This preaching place was necessary because the Anglican Bishop of London and the Archbishop Canterbury would not allow John and Charles Wesley or George Whitefield to preach in the churches. Thousands of unreached people found Christ in the Foundry, and this building became "the cradle of Methodism."

[17] In a book published in 1698 titled *The Protestant Monastery*, George Wheler lamented, "The promiscuous mixture of Men and Women together in our [Anglican] assemblies, is an Abuse crept in, not meant by our first Reformers, as is manifest from the first C[ommon] P[rayer] Book of Edw[ard] VI."

[18] In Wesley's century, some Anglican churches had pews; others had benches. Some churches rented seating places, and others allowed congregants to sit wherever they wished. The Methodist places of worship had only benches, and all seating was unrestricted. *The Spectator* #630, 8 December 1714 said, "Pews [with high backs] are too often a screen to sitting, instead of kneeling, during prayers, and to talk, or sleeping during the sermon."

verses of another hymn, and concluded with prayer. Our constant doctrine was salvation by faith, preceded by repentance, and followed by holiness.[19]

5. When a large number of people joined, our chief difficulty was to keep them together for worship.[20] The people continually scattered here and there, and we knew no way to fix the problem. God, however, provided for this need when we did not know what to do. A year or two later, I met the chief of the Methodist Society in Bristol, and asked, "How shall we pay the debt on the preaching-house?"[21] Captain Foy arose and said, "Let everyone in the society give a penny a week, and it will easily be done." Someone said, "But many of them do not have a penny to give. "True,"said the captain, "then put ten or twelve of them with me. Each week, let each of them give what they can, and I will supply what is lacking." Many others made the same offer. Therefore, I divided the societies among them, assigning a class of about twelve people to each of them, whom we called *leaders*.[22]

6. Not long afterward, one of these leaders informed me that, calling on a member in his house, he found him quarrelling with his wife. Another man was drunk. It immediately came to my mind that class meetings were the very thing we needed. The leaders could both receive the contributions and watch over the souls of their brothers and sisters. Learning about this plan, the society in London readily followed the example at Bristol. From that time, every Methodist society in Europe or America organized class meetings. By this means it was easy to discover that if any member grew weary or faint,[23] we could quickly help them. If any

---

[19] In *The Principles of Methodism Further Explained*, Wesley said, "I have again and again, with all the plainness I could, declared what our constant doctrines are; whereby we are distinguished only from Heathens, or nominal Christians; not from any that worship God in spirit and in truth. Our main doctrines, which include all the rest, are three, — that of repentance, of faith, and of holiness. The first of these we account, as it were, the porch of religion; the next, the door; the third, religion itself." (*The works of John Wesley*, Jackson ed., 14 vols., VI, 472.)

[20] Here, Wesley is talking about Methodism's spread to Bristol. With a population of 30,000, Bristol was the second largest city in England. Wesley initially visited Bristol in 1739. Many Methodist "firsts" took place in Bristol, including the first Methodist chapel, class meetings, the circuit system, watch night services, and the founding of Kingswood School. Wesley often preached in Bristol for the next fifty years. Charles Wesley and his wife lived in Bristol from 1749 to 1771 and wrote many of his hymns there.

[21] In May 1739, the Methodists of Bristol, "with the voice of praise and thanksgiving," began construction on a meeting place for the Methodist society. The building became known as "the New Room in the Horsefair." Later it became known as "Wesley's Chapel, Broadmead." This structure is the oldest standing Methodist building, and a popular tourist site.

[22] Commonly called Class Leaders.

[23] Gal. 6:9.

walked disorderly, we promptly discovered it, and we either amended the problem or dismissed them from the society.

7. For those who knew him in whom they had believed,[24] we provided another means of help. Five or six, either married or single men, met together at a convenient hour.[25] This measure accorded with the direction of the Apostle James, "Confess your sins to one another, and pray for one another, so that you may be healed."[26] Also, five or six of the married or single women met together for the same purpose. Innumerable blessings have attended the institution of the Band Meetings, especially for those who were going on to Christian perfection. When any member seemed to have attained this blessing, they were allowed to meet with a select number,[27] who, as far as humans can judge, appeared to be partakers of the same "great salvation."[28]

8. From this short sketch of Methodism anyone of understanding may easily discern that Methodism is simply a plain, scriptural religion, fortified by a few prudential guidelines. The essence of Methodism is holiness of heart and life.[29] The circumstantial evidences point to this fact. As long as the people are united among those called Methodists, no weapon fashioned against them shall prosper.[30] Basic Methodism will soon be lost if the people scorn even part of its attendant aspects. If these indispensable parts ever would evaporate, what remains of Methodism will be dung and dross.

9. It directly concerns us to understand how the case presently stands with us Methodists.[31] I fear that wherever riches have increased, (there are exceeding few exceptions) the essence of religion (which is having the mind that was in Christ)[32] has decreased in the same degree. Therefore, in the nature of things, when people become rich I do not see how it is possible for any prolonged revival

---

[24] 2 Tim. 1:12.

[25] This initiative marked the beginning of Methodism's Band Meetings.

[26] James 5:16.

[27] This plan was the beginning of Methodism's Select Band, which was to consist of mature Christians who evidenced entire sanctification and the fruits of the Holy Spirit (Gal. 5:22–23). Wesley had intended for this group to provide counsel for him. This Select Society was of short-lived duration.

[28] Heb. 2:3.

[29] Exod. 19:6; Lev. 11:44–45; Lev. 19:2; 20:7; 1 Pet. 1:15–16; 2 Pet. 3:11.

[30] Isa. 54:17.

[31] Wesley wrote *Thoughts upon Methodism* in 1786.

[32] Phil. 2:5.

of true religion to continue. Religion necessarily produces both industry and frugality. These virtues always produce wealth. As wealth increases, so will pride, anger, and the love of the world in all its features.[33]

10. Therefore, how is it possible that Methodism, the religion of the heart, though it now flourishes as a green bay tree,[34] can continue in this state? The Methodists in every place grow diligent and frugal, and accordingly they increase in possessions. Consequently, they proportionately grew in pride, anger, the desire of the flesh, the desire of the eyes, and the pride of life. Although the form of religion remains, the spirit is swiftly vanishing away.[35]

11. Is there no way to prevent this regression, this continual decline of pure religion? We should not forbid people to be diligent and frugal: We must exhort all Christians to gain all they can, and to save all they can—that is, in effect, to grow wealthy! I ask again, "What way can we take so that our money will not sink us into the nethermost hell?" There is one way only, and there is no other under heaven: If those who gain all they can, and save all they can will likewise *give* all they can, then, the more they gain, the more they will grow in grace,[36] and the more treasure they will lay up in heaven.[37]

London

4 August 1786.

---

[33] The Apostle John wrote, "Do not love the world or the things in the world. The love of the Father is not in those who love the world; for all that is in the world—the desire of the flesh, the desire of the eyes, the pride in riches—comes not from the Father but from the world. And the world and its desire are passing away, but those who do the will of God live forever" (1 Jn. 2:15–17).

[34] Psa. 37:5. Bay trees grew to heights of forty to sixty feet. These desirable trees were evergreen, with fragrant leaves, which were used as a spice and for garlands.

[35] 2 Tim. 3:5.

[36] 2 Pet. 3:18.

[37] Matt. 6:19–20.

Editor's Conclusion

This collection of John Wesley's tracts on Methodism book closes with a hymn by Charles Wesley—"Lift Up Your Hearts to Things Above." John Wesley chose this hymn as the final hymn in the 1780 Methodist hymnal, titled *Collection of Hymns for the Use of The People Called Methodists*. This hymnal was the definitive collection of hymns to appear during the lifetime of John Wesley. The brothers Wesley selected 525 hymns from more than fifty hymnbooks published during the preceding half century. John Wesley designed the arrangement of the hymns to be "a little body of experimental and practical divinity."

In the Preface to the 1780 Methodist Hymnal, Wesley wrote,

> The hymns are not carelessly jumbled together, but carefully ranged under proper heads, according to the experience of real Christians. So that this book is in effect a little body of experimental [experiential] and practical divinity. . . . I am persuaded no such hymn-book as this has yet been published in the English language. In what other publication of the kind have you so distinct and full an account of scriptural Christianity. Such a declaration of the heights and depths of religion. . . . And so clear directions for making our calling election sure, for perfecting holiness in the fear of God? . . . . When poetry thus keeps its place,

as the handmaid of piety, it shall attain, not a poor perishable wreath, but a crown that fadeth not away.[1]

"Lift Up Your Hearts to Things Above," is a fitting finish to this collection of tracts on the marrow of Methodism. The final stanza in this hymnal summarizes John Wesley's message to those who follow his train:

Let all who for the promise wait

The Holy Ghost receive,

And raised to our un-sinning state

With God in Eden live!

Our Savior now prepares our home—

Go on! We'll meet you there.

---

[1] Concerning this collection of hymns, hymnologist Bernard Manning said, "You may think my language about the hymns extravagant: therefore I repeat it in stronger terms. This little book ranks in Christian literature with the Psalms, the Book of Common Prayer, and the Canon of the Mass. In its own way, it is perfect, unapproachable, elemental in its perfection. You cannot alter it except to mar it; it is a work of supreme devotional art by a religious genius."

Lift up Your Hearts to Things Above

Lift up your hearts to things above,[1]
Ye followers of the Lamb,[2]
And join with us to praise His love,
    And glorify His name.[3]
To Jesus' name give thanks and sing,[4]
    Whose mercies never end:[5]
Rejoice! rejoice! the Lord is King;[6]
    The King is now our friend![7]

We, for His sake, count all things loss;[8]
    On earthly good look down;
And joyfully sustain the cross,[9]
    Till we receive the crown.[10]
O let us stir each other up,[11]
    Our faith by works to approve,[12]
By holy, purifying hope,[13]
    And the sweet task of love![14]

Love us, though far in flesh disjoined,[15]
    Ye lovers of the Lamb;[16]

---

[1] Col. 3:1–2.
[2] John 1:25, 36; Col. 3:1–21; Pet. 1:19; Rev. 5:8, 12–13; 7:9–10, 14, 17; 13:8; 14:1, 4; 15:3; 19:7, 9; 21:14, 22–23; 22:1, 3.
[3] Psa. 86:9; 102:18; Isa. 24:15; Luke 19:37; Rom. 15:9; 1 Cor. 4:5; Rev. 15:4.
[4] Heb. 13:15.
[5] Psa. 18:49; 30:4; 69:16; 89:1; 119:156; 145:9; Isa. 63:7; Jer. 42:12; Lam. 3:22; Hos. 2:19; Acts 13:34; 2 Cor. 1:3.
[6] Psa. 2:11; 5:11; 9:2, 14; 13:5; 20:5; 31:7; 32:11; 33:1, 21; 35:9; 40:16; 63:7; 68:3–4; 70:4; 71:23; 118:24; Isa. 13:3; John 14:28; 16:22; Rom. 5:2; 15:10; Phil. 4:4; 1 Thess. 5:16; 1 Pet. 1:8; Rev. 19:7.
[7] Matt. 11:19; Luke 19:7; John 15:15; James 2:23.
[8] Phil. 3:8.
[9] Luke 9:23.
[10] 2 Tim. 4:8.
[11] 2 Tim. 1:6; Heb. 10:24; 2 Pet. 1:13; 3:1.
[12] Matt. 5:16; 1 Thess. 1:3; 1 Tim. 6:18; Tit. 2:7; James 2:17–18; 1 Pet. 2:12.
[13] James 4:8.
[14] 1 Cor. 13:7.
[15] 1 Thess. 2:17.
[16] Rev. 5:12.

And ever bear us on your mind,[17]
    Who think and speak the same:[18]
You on our minds we ever bear,[19]
    Whoe'er to Jesus bow;[20]
Stretch out the arms of faith and prayer,[21]
    And lo! we reach you now![22]

The blessings all on you be shed,[23]
    Which God in Christ imparts;[24]
We pray the Spirit of our Head[25]
    Into your faithful hearts.[26]
Mercy and peace your portion be,[27]
    To carnal minds unknown,[28]
The hidden manna,[29] and the tree
    Of life,[30] and the white stone.[31]

Let all who for the promise wait[32]
    The Holy Ghost receive,[33]
And raised to our un-sinning state[34]
    With God in Eden live![35]
Live till the Lord in glory come,[36]
    And wait His Heaven to share:[37]

---

[17] Rom. 1:9; Eph. 1:16; Phil. 1:4; Col. 1:3; 1 Thess. 1:2.
[18] Rom. 12:5; 1 Cor. 10:17; Gal. 3:28.
[19] John 15:12; 1 Thess. 3:12; 1 Pet. 1:22.
[20] Gal 3:28.
[21] James 5:16.
[22] Mark 11:24.
[23] Eph. 1:3.
[24] Exod. 23:25; Eph. 1:3.
[25] Luke 11:13.
[26] Acts 1:8.
[27] Gal. 6:16; 1 Tim. 1:2; 2 Tim. 1:2; 2 Jn. 1:3; Jude 1:2.
[28] Rom. 1:28; 8:7–8; Eph. 4:17; Tit. 1:15.
[29] Rev. 2:17.
[30] Rev. 22:2, 14.
[31] Rev. 2:7.
[32] Acts 1:4.
[33] Luke 24:49; Acts 1:4.
[34] Rom. 6:1–2, 11; Gal. 5:24; Col. 3:3; 1 Pet. 2:24.
[35] Isa. 51:3; Rev. 21:1.
[36] Tit. 2:13.
[37] Matt. 16:27; 24:27; 24:44; 25:31, 64; Mark 8:38; Luke 12:37, 40; 21:27; John 14:3; Acts 1:11; 1 Cor. 1:7; 4:5; Phil. 3:20–21; Col. 3:4; 1Thess. 5:2, 23; 2 Thess. 1:7–8; 2 Tim.

Our Savior now prepares our home—[38]
Go on! we'll meet you there.[39]

4:1. 6:14; Tit. 2:13; Heb. 9:28; 10:37; James 5:8; 1 Pet. 5:4; 1 Jn. 2:28, 3:2; Jude 1:14–15; Rev. 1:7; 3:11; 16:15; 22:20.
[38] John 14:2.
[39] 1 Thess. 4:17.

www.ingramcontent.com/pod-product-compliance
Lightning Source LLC
Chambersburg PA
CBHW030341240426
43661CB00052B/1709